IDENTITY AND MARGINALITY IN NORTHEAST INDIA

IDENTITY AND MARGINALITY IN NORTHEAST INDIA

Challenges for Social Science Research

Edited by

Hoineilhing Sitlhou

With a foreword by

Purendra Prasad

Orient BlackSwan

IDENTITY AND MARGINALITY IN NORTHEAST INDIA:
CHALLENGES FOR SOCIAL SCIENCE RESEARCH

ORIENT BLACKSWAN PRIVATE LIMITED

Registered Office
3-6-752 Himayatnagar, Hyderabad 500 029, Telangana, India
e-mail: centraloffice@orientblackswan.com

Other Offices
Bengaluru, Chennai, Guwahati, Hyderabad, Kolkata,
Mumbai, New Delhi, Noida, Patna

First published by Orient Blackswan Private Limited 2023

ISBN 978-93-5442-387-1

042820

Typeset in
Adobe Garamond Pro 11.5/13.75
by Le Studio Graphique, Gurgaon 122 007

Printed in India at
Kensington Printing & Packaging, Noida 201 301

Published by
Orient Blackswan Private Limited
3-6-752 Himayatnagar, Hyderabad 500 029, Telangana, India
e-mail: info@orientblackswan.com

To
my mother Zakimi Singson
and
my father (L) Lalkholun Sitlhou

CONTENTS

TABLES

ABBREVIATIONS

ASIDE	Assistance to States for Developing Export Infrastructure and other Allied Activities
BCM	Baptist Church of Mizoram
BPO	business process outsourcing
BTA	Border Trade Agreement
CPR	Common Property Resources
ECM	Evangelical Church of Mizoram
FMPCW	Foreign Mission of the Presbyterian Church of Wales
FXB	François-Xavier Bagnoud
ICSSR	Indian Council of Social Science Research
ICSSR-NERC	Indian Council of Social Science Research - North-Eastern Regional Centre
IDP	internally displaced persons
JNU	Jawaharlal Nehru University
KIM	Kuki Inpi Manipur
LGBT	lesbian gay bisexual transgender
LGBTQ	lesbian gay bisexual transgender queer
MCD	Municipal Corporation of Delhi
MHIP	Mizo Hmeichhe Insuihkhawm Pawl
MPC	Mizoram Presbyterian Church
MSM	men who have sex with men
MSU	Mizo Students' Union
MUP	Mizo Upa Pawl
MZP	Mizo Zirlai Pawl

NDMC	New Delhi Municipal Council
NEFA	North-East Frontier Agency
NEHU	North-Eastern Hill University
NEPED	Nagaland Environment Protection and Economic Development through People's Action/Nagaland Empowerment of People through Economic Development
NER	North Eastern Region
NESCH	North East Support Centre and Helpline
NSDP	net state domestic product
NTFP	non-timber forest product
SLORC	State Law and Order Restoration Council
SLRD	State Land Regulations Department
SRS	Supply Reduction Service
UGC	University Grants Commission
UNDP	United Nations Development Program
UNLF	United National Liberation Front
YMA	Young Mizo Association
ZDRB	Zoram Drivers Ramthim Board

FOREWORD

Northeast India is more diverse than any other region in India. However, three broad generalisations are usually made about the region and its communities: one, the region comprises various ethnic communities but is somehow considered homogenous, possessing similar cultural traits and values; second, the region is characterised by widespread conflicts and insurgency and the communities are violent and rebellious; third, the communities are backward, impoverished and confined to their rural spaces. A careful reading of Northeast India would indicate that contrary to these stereotypes, the communities there are vibrantly diverse, heterogeneous and creative in their own ways. While any region refers to a concrete, objectively verifiable empirical reality, at the same time, it is also loaded with non-verifiable social imaginaries which are nonetheless real and influential. Every region is thus both concrete and conceptual.

However, the tendency to conceptualise Northeast India as a single homogenous territory is problematic as this presumes the idea of a shared identity among people from various parts of the region and this has determined the way the region is governed, earlier by the colonial rulers and now by the Indian state. The Northeast, considered a marginal geographical space, is as diverse as India itself in terms of linguistic, cultural and ethnic representation. Thus, the prevailing narratives about the Northeast are quite inadequate as they fail to represent the reality. The present volume edited by Hoineilhing Sitlhou attempts to fill this void by focusing on the issues of identity and marginality in Northeast India.

At the core of the subject of marginality lies the issue of identity. Behind the genesis of movements in the Northeastern region is a thrust for recognition and representation of the diverse identities. Marginalised groups face challenges in defining and enacting their own identities. It is identity that provides the basis of collective oneness among the members of a community. Search for identity is justifiable as it contributes to a sustainable existence. However, one's identity is not based on one single factor. It is an amalgamation of one's ethnicity, region, religion, culture, caste and so on. Hence identities are not single and homogeneous but multiple and heterogeneous. In a pluralistic society like that of India, a peaceful co-existence often becomes difficult as diverse communities clamour for their identity to gain access to sharing of power, a prerequisite to improving their socio-economic status. Precisely this has led to the emergence of identity conflicts in the past few decades in the Northeast. The problem today has assumed such serious proportions that it needs serious attention and requires a closer analysis and better understanding of the democratic process.

It is important to recognise the socio-economic and historical context in which this range of issues have cropped up in Northeast India. The region witnesses on the one hand, state violence, atrocities on women, insurgency, militarisation, army and police abuse and illegal migration, and on the other hand, there are processes of marginalisation within the marginalised groups. For instance, there was strong opposition from tribal bodies of the state contending that 33 per cent reservation for women would infringe on Naga customary laws and tradition protected by the Constitution of India. Similarly, even though popular narratives glorify the status of women in Manipur and the matriarchal structure in Khasi society, in actuality the system is only matrilineal with the power resting with maternal male members, and thus inherently patriarchal like any other society. Several chapters in this volume provide insights into the elements of heterogeneity of different groups and their experiences, contestations and conflicts in the region.

In a sense, the volume explains how the region expresses incompleteness and how contradictions are in-built here, with dormant, unfulfilled aspirations, even when there is no overt conflict. By bringing diverse theoretical frameworks and perspectives, the volume argues that communities in Northeast India have ideas of alternate nationalism and demand equal citizenship. Despite the multiple challenges faced in bringing out an ambitious volume covering themes as diverse as colonialism, race, ethnicity, migration, gender, culture, identity, indigeneity, land, borders, state and the market, the scholars have been successful in generating a meaningful, important and wide-ranging debate, and I commend all of them for their efforts.

Purendra Prasad
Professor,
Department of Sociology,
University of Hyderabad.

PREFACE

This book is an outcome of the proceedings of the national seminar, 'Identity and Marginality in North East India: Challenges for Social Science Research,' organised by the Department of Sociology, University of Hyderabad, sponsored by the University Grants Commission Special Assistance Programme (UGC-SAP) and the Indian Council of Social Science Research (ICSSR) on 16–17 January 2017. The papers presented at this seminar were reworked by the respective authors and these have found their place as chapters in this volume. In addition, I invited my colleagues working in different parts of India and on different social sciences projects to write on areas and themes that were not covered in the seminar. Since the book is largely an offshoot of the discussions and presentations in the seminar, it is necessary to highlight some of the critical ponderings from the mentioned academic symposium, which though relevant, could not be accommodated in the volume for various reasons.

The symposium coincided with the mayhem in Nagaland following the debate over 33 per cent reservation for women in urban local bodies of Nagaland, including the Kohima Municipal Council. There was opposition from tribal bodies of the state including the Naga Hoho, the apex body of all eighteen tribes of the hill state. They contended that granting 33 per cent reservation for women would infringe on Naga customary laws and tradition as protected under Article 371(A) of the Constitution of India (Kashyap 2017). In his keynote address at the seminar, Sanjoy Hazarika, then Director of the Commonwealth Human Rights Initiative, argued that this resistance to women's empowerment coupled with high women and child mortality rates in parts of the Northeast challenge the common assumption of gender equality in the area and forces one to re-examine the nature of equality, both within the Northeast and in comparison to the rest of India. He said, 'It is extremely important that we take a view on issues like this because is it possible that in 2017, you can have a situation in any part of the country where women have the right to vote but not to be represented?' With regard to the nature of military and police abuse in the Northeast, Hazarika condemned the Armed Forces (Special Powers) Act (AFSPA), 1958 and drew attention to the need for its replacement with a more humane law. On the issue of illegal migration, he discussed how migration is a dynamic process—as people enter the Northeast and settle there, Northeasterners also move to different parts of the country for education, work and better lifestyles. In 2012, Northeasterners faced security issues, such as targeted violence, in states like Karnataka and returned home in large numbers (*India Today* 2012). Incidents like this show that people are still discriminated against based on their appearance, which brings us back to the crucial question: What is an Indian supposed to look like? Universities in India ought to include the history of the Northeast in their curricula to allow better engagement with its past and generate interest in its present.

Tiplut Nongbri talked about the three main challenges in research concerning Northeast India: the methodological question, the substantive question and the ethical question. On the ethical question, she raised issues pertaining to the consequences of the research and the ethical challenges that scholars face, such as: Is the research beneficial for the people living in Northeast India or is it harmful? Earlier, Northeasterners had neither the space nor the opportunity to conduct a study or do research on themselves. But fortunately, now the situation has changed. Supported by academic bodies like the UGC and the ICSSR, many scholars from the Northeast are taking up research projects on the region in various Indian universities.

On the methodological challenges, there are no coherent perspectives, frames or models that one can use to study the problems in the Northeast, a region that is culturally heterogenous historically. For instance, looking at tribal societies through the prism of caste is inadequate and problematic. Researchers, thus, cannot rely on the dominant models and universal frameworks. Popular narratives such as the glorified status of women in Manipur and the matrilineal structure of Khasi society are often misleading and need in-depth analyses. In this regard, Soibam Haripriya's paper at the seminar, 'From the Shackles of Tradition: Motherhood and Women's Agitation in Manipur' (now published as Haripriya [2017]) rejected the popular notion that women in the Northeast have a significantly higher status as compared to their counterparts in the rest of the country. She discusses the case of Meira Paibis (the women torchbearers) in Manipur to bring out the dialectical trajectory of the representation of women and the 'real' status and power that women possess in the Meitei society. Nongbri has written extensively on Khasi society; of how it is 'matrilineal' rather than 'matriarchal', meaning that the actual control of property is in the hands of the maternal uncle. The prevalent narratives are inadequate and fail to represent the reality. To understand the Northeast, it is necessary to look at it from various viewpoints as limiting it to one viewpoint would render the research inadequate. Besides ethnographic and anthropological approaches, research from other perspectives are also necessary in order to understand the complex, heterogeneous and multi-layered social problems. It is crucial to combine these disciplines in order to have diverse theoretical frameworks and perspectives.

Sarah Hilaly's paper 'Trajectory of Colonial Intervention in the Arunachal Himalayas,' spoke of the ways in which British presence in the state kept it in a constant state of flux where boundaries kept getting redrawn and colonialism was justified on the basis of the 'barbarity' of the population within these boundaries. Arunachal was used as a buffer zone due to its strategic location on the borders of Tibet, Bhutan and Myanmar. The porous borders that witnessed a flow of population from time to time ended up becoming a major transitional zone. Geraldine Forbes' paper at the symposium, 'Reading Missionary Accounts for Naga Masculinity' discussed the construction of the Naga male in the works of Samuel Alden Perrine. Perrine was a missionary stationed in the Naga Hills, who, in his letters, reports and articles characterised the Naga man as a superior breed compared to men from other regions of India, describing them as 'manly men' and the 'Anglo-Saxons of the Orient.' Similarly, P. Thirumal, Laldinpuii and Lalrozami Chawngthu's paper 'Reading the Acoustic Archive: The Play of Puma Zai (1907–1911)' (now published in Thirumal et al. 2020) examines the way in which music and poetry in the form of Puma Zai became a source of colonial resistance among the Mizo community in the early twentieth century. Puma Zai emerged as an alternative to the Christian hymns as the Mizos wrote and sang their own songs in an attempt to oust the colonisers'culture.

Bauna Panmei's paper 'Webs of Flow: Circulation, Survey and Violence in the Naga Hills, 1840–1880' discussed the geographical surveys and military expeditions done by the colonial officials during the first half of the nineteenth century in the Naga Hills. In the same vein, Ajailiu Niumai's paper 'The Daughter of North East India: Rani Gaidinliu' (now published as Niumai [2018]) attempted a critical enquiry into the role of Rani Gaidinliu in the Heraka cult/practices and the Zeliangrong Naga movement. The paper highlighted how Rani Gaidinliu as a woman contested the colonial Britishers and the structured patriarchs of the Naga National Council, and how the Hindutva ideologues like the Vishwa Hindu Parishad (VHP) and the Rashtriya Swayamsevak Sangh (RSS) positioned her as a political and religious icon/protagonist in the Northeast.

Many of the papers in the symposium dealt with the ramifications of colonial interventions in Northeast India. There were also discussions that focused on the geopolitical aspect of the impact of colonialism. There were extensive debates on identity, the social realities of Northeast India, issues such as migrant Northeasterners' marginalisation in other states of India as well as discrimination faced by outsiders who move to the Northeast. Ilito Achumi's paper 'Nagas Response to Unauthorised Migration: Identity and Destination Impact' (now published as Achumi [2019]), examined the Nagas' response to unauthorised migration, mainly of the illegal immigrants from Bangladesh. Her argument evolved around the 2015 incident in Dimapur where a man (an illegal migrant) was lynched for allegedly raping a Naga girl (*Foreign Policy* 2015). The narratives and past stories of violence inflicted by outsiders on the Nagas were used to justify the collective action. Eviction campaigns, public lynching, and stereotyping continue as the fight for survival go on among various identities in the region.

It is the aim of this book (as was the intent of the seminar) to broaden these existing discourses, encourage more research in this area and build up a new community of multi-disciplinary academic scholars in and of Northeast India.

REFERENCES

Achumi, Illito H. 2019. 'Perceived Illegality of the Body: Reclaiming the Space in Nagaland'. *Sociological Bulletin* 68(2): 204–220. Available at https://doi.org/10.1177/0038022919848263 (accessed April 2023).

Foreign Policy. 2015. 'The Lynching of Syed Sarifuddin Khan', 20 March. Available at https://foreignpolicy.com/2015/03/20/the-lynching-of-syed-sarifuddin-khan/ (accessed April 2023).

Haripriya, Soibam. 2017. 'From the Shackles of Tradition: Motherhood and Women's agitation in Manipur'. In Melanie Vandenhelsken, Meenaxi Barkataki-Ruscheweyh and Bengt G. Karlsson (eds), *Geographies of Difference: Explorations in Northeast Indian Studies*. India: Routledge.

India Today. 2012. 'Karnataka CM Convenes High-level Meet, Says People from North-East Are Safe in Bangalore', 17 August. Available at https://www.indiatoday.in/india/south/story/jagadish-shettar-north-east-people-flee-bangalore-113376-2012-08-16 (accessed April 2023).

Kashyap, Samudra Gupta. 2017. 'Opposed to 33% Reservation for Women, Naga Bodies Call for Boycott of Civic Polls'. *The Indian Express*, 5 January. Available at https://indianexpress.com/article/india/opposed-to-33-reservation-for-women-naga-bodies-call-for-boycott-of-civic-polls-4458791/ (accessed March 2023).

Niumai, Ajailiu. 2018. 'Rani Gaidinliu: The Iconic Woman of Northeast India'. *Indian Journal of Gender Studies* 25(3): 351–367. Available at https://doi.org/10.1177/0971521518785666 (accessed April 2023).

Thirumal, P., Laldinpuii and C. Lalrozami. 2020. *Modern Mizoram: History, Culture, Poetics*. India: Routledge.

PUBLISHERS' ACKNOWLEDGMENTS

For granting permission to reproduce copyrighted material in this volume, the publishers would like to thank the following organisations:

Indian Sociological Society for 'Census and Identity Politics among the Plains Tribes in Colonial Assam' by Suryasikha Pathak, previously published as 'Census as a Site of Contestation: Identity Politics among the Plains Tribes in Colonial Assam' in the ISS e-journal *Explorations* 5(2): 105–124, and 'Northeastern Migrants in Delhi: Racial Discrimination, Violence and State Response' by Hoineilhing Sitlhou and Salah Punathil, a part of which was previously published in 'Racial Discrimination and Violence against North Easterners and Bezbaruah Committee Report' in the ISS e-journal *Explorations* 1(1): 91–102. We thank ISS also for 'Northeast Youth Migration to Cities: The Kuki Case in Delhi' by Thanggoulen Kipgen, a part of which was previously published in 'Migrants and Their Social Networks: A Study of Kuki Migrants in Delhi' by Thanggoulen Kipgen and Biswambhar Panda in *Sociological Bulletin* 68(3): 342–356.

Pachhunga University College for 'Alternative Sexuality and Civil Society in Mizoram' by Lalhmingmawii, a part of which was previously published in 'Transcending Boundaries: Alternative Sexuality and Church Response' in *Senhri Journal of Multidisciplinary Studies* 1(2): 1–13.

North-Eastern Hill University Publications, Shillong for 'Livelihood Interventions and Marginalisation in Land and Forest Rights of Rural Khasi Women' by Rekha M. Shangpliang, previously published as 'Livelihood and Gender: Marginalisation of Khasi Rural Women in Land and Forest Rights' in *The NEHU Journal* 16(2): 86–100.

M. N. Rajesh, Series Editor of *Pasts and Futures: Readings in a Contemporary World* (Cambridge Scholars Publishing, Newcastle, UK) for 'Colonialism and History Writing: The Mizo Experience' by Malsawmdawngliana, a part of which was published in 'Sources of Writing Mizo History and their Limitations' in Rila Mukherjee and M. N. Rajesh (eds), *Locality, History, Memory: The Making of the Citizen in South Asia* (2009) by Cambridge Scholars Publishing, Newcastle, UK.

ACKNOWLEDGMENTS

In writing this book, I am grateful to a lot of people who have contributed in different capacities at different points in time. Thanks to all the contributors of the thirteen chapters of the book and the Orient BlackSwan team: Nilanjana Majumdar, Suchetana Ghosh Dostidar, Moyna Mazumdar and Nagalakshmi. I also thank Kham Khan Suan Hausing for his critical and constructive inputs to the first draft of the introductory chapter.

I want to acknowledge with gratitude the support given by Aparna Rayaprol as the Head of Department of Sociology, Purendra Prasad as the Director of UGC-SAP (Special Assistance Programme) and Sujata Patel as the President of the Indian Sociological Society when the seminar, from which this book evolved, was conducted in 2017. To all my colleagues in the sociology department: N. Annavaram, Anurekha Chari Wagh, Asima Jena, C. Nagalakshmi, C. Raghav Reddy, G. Nagaraju, Lam Khan Piang, Pushpesh Kumar, R. Thirunavukkarasu, Sasheej Hegde, Satya Priya Rout, Tanweer Fazal and V. Janardhan, for all that I have learned from each one of you, I am indebted. May you all continue to inspire!

Then, there is my family: my husband (Chongroilen Sampar), who has always supported me in words and deeds by believing in me and tirelessly correcting the grammatical errors of my writings; my sons (Shomchungvar and Lunsanglen) who may frequently interrupt my work with their antics, but are nevertheless the basic ingredients of my mental wellbeing and happiness.

I am forever indebted to my PhD supervisor Susan Visvanathan. I teach and write today because of her.

Finally, I thank God who has made all of this possible.

Introduction

Identity and Marginality

Hoineilhing Sitlhou

Is Northeast India a marginal region? What social phenomenon in Northeast India qualifies for a discussion on or justifies the relevance of the concept of marginality or marginalisation? This is a question that requires clarification before we embark on a scientific deliberation and make a sociological enquiry on the issues of marginality and identity in the context of Northeast India. In popular discourses, marginality has to do with the process of societal integration, which emphasises the need for everyone to be integrated into the so-called mainstream society. It is therefore a concept referring to those at the edge of a system—cultural, social, political or economic—or to certain domains or phenomena that do not correspond to mainstream philosophy (Pelc 2017).

A pamphlet published by the Center for Development Research, University of Bonn describes marginality as, '…an involuntary position and condition of an individual or group at the margins of social, political, economic, ecological and biophysical systems, preventing them from access to resources, assets, services, restraining freedom of choice, preventing the development of capabilities and eventually causing extreme poverty'.[1] Likewise, according to the International Consultative Forum on Education for All (EFA Forum) (2000), marginalisation occurs '…when people are systematically excluded from meaningful participation in economic, social, political, cultural and other forms of human activity in their communities and thus are denied the opportunity to fully develop themselves as human beings'.

At the core of the subject of marginality lies the issue of identity. We tend to live our lives in and through 'identity shelves': males–females; dominant–non-dominant, etc. Though we all have identity shelves, not all the shelves are tightly attached and there is always room for identity construction in many areas (Dennis 2005: 5). In any complex society there are bound to be layers of identity inclusive of social groupings, religious affiliations, gender and class allegiances and so many others (Ray 2016). Identities are shaped by and help to shape wider social and cultural contexts (Kay 2005). 'Each person's self is formed by a reflexive process, in which our perception of how others see us plays a paramount part…individual self-images and group we-images are not separate things' (Stephen Mennell, as cited in Kay 2005). Among the classical sociological theorists, one finds detailed references to the question of identity in the writings of Charles Horton Cooley and George H. Mead. Cooley introduced the concept of 'the looking-glass self' in his book *Human Nature and the Social Order*. According to him, the idea of 'self' is formed through the process of introspection (Cooley 1922). This idea of self is also determined by how the self is perceived by others (ibid.: 184–185). A social self of this type is called the reflected or looking-glass self (ibid.: 184). The self-idea has three principal elements: 'the imagination of our appearance to the other person; the imagination of his judgement of that appearance, and some sort of self-feeling, such as pride or mortification' (ibid.). For Cooley, self-consciousness and social consciousness are thus inseparable.

The concepts of 'self' and 'I' also take a central place in the works of George H. Mead. In his work *Mind, Self and Society*, Mead refers to the transformation of the biological individual to the minded organism or self. According to Mead, the quality which marks out man from other animals is that they have minds using which they can gain control over others. This takes place through the agency of language, and language in turn presupposes the existence of a certain kind of society (Mead 1972).

> The self has a character, which is different from that of the physiological organism proper. The self is something which has a development; it is not initially there, at birth, but arises in the process of social experience and activity, that is, develops in the given individual as a result of his relations to that process as a whole and to other individuals within that process. (Mead 1972: 135)

The origin and foundations of the self, as in the case of thinking, are social (ibid.). So, identities are also socially constructed and determined by wider social, cultural, political and economic contexts. Sometimes, 'they may be reinterpreted or even imposed upon certain groups or individuals by others, often as a result of inequalities of power and authority. In this case identities may be divisive and repressive or even rebellious and subversive' (Kay 2005).

Representation of the marginalised can challenge the normative values produced by dominant discourses about the Self and the Other. Marginalised people use their identities both individually and collectively as a means of challenging normative assumptions and prescriptive values (Kay 2005). For B. G. Verghese (2004), the genesis of movements in the Northeast is due to the thirst for recognition of identity. When a community's culture, tradition and identity are threatened by any actor, it often evokes a violent response in the name of safeguarding said identity (Haokip 2018: 47). This form of identity politics is often a basis for the development of a very public form of protest against the homogenising tendencies of dominant identities as well as the social and cultural norms which they embody. Marginalised groups face challenges in defining and enacting their own identities. They may feel compelled to assimilate the norms and values of the dominant group or may choose to emphasise a separate identity in contrast to the dominant norms. The latter may invite further isolation for them in society or prompt a repressive backlash from the dominant group if they perceive a threat to their dominance (Kay 2005).

SPATIAL MARGINALITY OF NORTHEAST INDIA

The north-eastern part of India has a unique topographical structure and is characterised by enormous demographic diversity. It comprises of eight states—Arunachal Pradesh, Assam, Manipur, Meghalaya, Mizoram, Nagaland, Sikkim and Tripura. 'Geographically, the region covers an area of approximately 2,63,000 sq. km. (8 per cent of the country), and its population is about 4.56 crores (3.77 per cent of the country) as per 2011 population census' (Singha and Singh 2016: 1). Ninety-nine per cent of the Northeast represents international borders shared with Nepal, Bhutan, China (Tibet), Myanmar and Bangladesh (Verghese 2004: 1–2).

Theorists have a tendency to use concepts such as caste, class, race, ethnicity and gender to establish the workings of societal marginality. Besides the societal aspect, the mechanism and methodology of marginality and its operation can also be studied within the framework of spatial marginality. Spatial marginality is essentially physical or geographical remoteness or positioning away from centres of power, growth and development. The common experience in both types of marginalities is that 'such people are usually discriminated against, ostracised, oppressed and habitually disregarded by the "centre", causing disparity, social inequality and exclusion' (Ray 2016). The positioning of the Northeast within the cultural map of India is evident in the works of B. G. Verghese who has used sociologist Immanuel Wallerstein's concept of core and periphery:

> The locus of the Northeast within the cultural map of India has been portrayed as a relationship between core and periphery. The core is identified with the north-central Hindi-Hindu heartland, with an associated core to the West, South and East of the country which is non-Hindi but Hindu. This then leaves two peripheral zones: one to the northwest consisting of the Sikh, Muslim, Buddhist regions of Punjab, J&K and upper Himachal and the other in the Northeast with its Buddhist, Christian, Muslim and

> tribal communities and indigenous faiths such as *Donyi-Polo* among the *Adis* in Arunachal. (Verghese 2004: 5)

The concept of the 'mainstream' can unintentionally suggest a conceited or dismissive attitude towards 'little' traditions that are variously labelled regional, parochial or peripheral and which are sought to be 'integrated' (ibid.).

The Northeast region is geographically secluded from the rest of the Indian subcontinent. There could be two possible explanations for this. Firstly, it is connected to the rest of the country only by a narrow 20-kilometre-wide chicken's neck corridor at Siliguri town in West Bengal. Secondly, it stands at the crossroads of a great ethno-cultural frontier that separates two of Asia's largest civilisations: the Indo-Gangetic and the Southeast Asian. In many ways, the Northeast of India resembles the highlands of Southeast Asia (Bhaumik 2000: 143). In fact, many of the communities in the region trace their lineage to Southeast Asia with a few centuries of acculturation in between (McDuie-Ra 2012: 27), and the strategic location of the Northeast is at the confluence of South, Southeast and East Asia (Nongbri 2017: 5). Most communities in the Northeast either have their roots outside India or have migrated into the region from the Indian heartland (Verghese 2004). Margins are also often sites of excessive violence and militarisation. The margins of Manipur state along the Indo-Myanmar borderlands have witnessed protracted conflict and guerrilla warfare involving the Kuki armed groups, the valley-based United National Liberation Front (UNLF) armed groups and the Indian Army. In such zones of conflict, resulting from competing claims over land and territory, civilians have to bear the brunt of violence and face manifold challenges to life (Haokip 2018).

The people of the region experience spatial marginality as their physical and geographical positioning has resulted in underdevelopment and obstructed their access to resources and opportunities which are due to them. An article that appeared in *The Hindu* on the Northeast quotes a news agency stating,

'...Isolation and years of neglect by the Indian government have fuelled underdevelopment, occasional tribal unrest and insurgency in the region, thus hampering the overall growth of the Northeastern states....' (Krishnan 2016). Tiplut Nongbri argues that the category 'Northeast' is in fact a construct and not an objective notion. The idea that geography is one of the core factors that unifies the Northeast as a category crumbles if one looks carefully at the nomenclature, its etymological background and the related issues. The region is seen as a frontier, as a hinterland where civilisation ends, which is outside civilisation and inhabited by 'wild tribes'. And these 'wild tribes', if and when they rebelled, could be suppressed through militarisation (Nongbri 2017).

COLONIAL ADMINISTRATIONS, BOUNDARY LINES AND CLASSIFICATIONS

The arrival of the British in Northeast India goes back to 1761 when the East India Company and the Nawab of Bengal (through their combined armed forces) assaulted Tripura (Chaube 1973: 3). The British ousted the Burmese from Assam in 1826 in the First Anglo-Burmese War, which concluded with the Treaty of Yandabo, after which the former steadily consolidated and expanded their presence in the Northeast. The generic term 'Northeast' was first used to collectively refer to the seven different units (Assam, Meghalaya, Manipur, Nagaland, Tripura, Arunachal Pradesh and Mizoram) after the reorganisation of the composite state of Assam and the formation of the North Eastern Council.[2]

Tribal communities, designated as Scheduled Tribes, constitute the bulk of the population in Arunachal Pradesh, Meghalaya, Nagaland and Mizoram, and are the majority in the hill districts of Assam, Manipur and Tripura (McDuie-Ra 2012: 27). Not all tribes live in the hill areas and this is evident in the states of Assam and Manipur. It is during the British and post-British period that 'tribe' became a primary reference point for identity among the residents of the hill regions of the Northeast. As per the 2011 census, the tribal population constitutes 94.44 per cent of the total state population in Mizoram, 86.46 per cent in Nagaland, 86.15 per cent in Meghalaya, 68.79 per cent in Arunachal Pradesh, 35.14 per cent in Manipur, 31.76 per cent in Tripura, 33.72 per cent in Sikkim and 12.45 per cent in Assam.[3] Of the 5633 communities in India, 635 are categorised as tribal, of which more than 200 live in Northeast India. Of the 325 languages listed in the *People of India*, 175 belong to the Tibeto-Burman family of tribes residing in the Northeast (Bhaumik 2000: 143).

'Contradictory British policies in the transformation of the internal social relations within the tribal and non-tribal communities constitute another conditioning factor of the history of the region' (Mackenzie 2007[1979]: 10). Not only did the various British policies label members of some racial or ethnic groups as more dominant than others, these policies designated the habitats of the tribal communities as 'backward areas', or 'excluded' and 'partially excluded' areas under the Government of India Act, 1935. 'Categorising people (and compelling people to define themselves accordingly) is a means of exercising power and control over them' (Caliendo and McIlwain 2011: xxiii). Many ethnic groups in Northeast India were named by the colonisers. For example, take the case of the Kukis, one of the three major ethnic groups of Manipur. Today the generic name 'Kuki' is considered to be contentious as there are critics who insist that it is a foreign term and a baseless colonial construct for administrative convenience. 'Kuki' meaning 'hill people' is allegedly a Bengali word originating in Sylhet of erstwhile East Bengal. It first appeared in Bengal in an essay by John Rawlins entitled 'Cucis or Mountaineers of Tipra' in the journal *Asiatic Researches* in 1790 (cited in Shaw 1929: 11) and later in a paper written by John McCrae in the same journal in 1799 (McCrae 1979). In the postcolonial world, while many ethnic groups have retained their colonial designations, some have changed them for more self-determined or nativised ethnic group titles (Caliendo and McIlwain 2011: xxiii).

After the Treaty of Yandabo in 1826, the British consolidated and expanded their presence in the Northeast. Boundary lines were re-drawn, altering the geographical landscape as well as the folk geographies, for the purpose of administration and in the guise of protecting the local population. Thus began a state of marginalisation that was later reinforced and reproduced in post-independent Northeast India. According to Subir Bhaumik (2000: 310), the term 'Northeast' in India has evolved from the concept of the north-eastern frontier, which is a colonial edifice. Alexander Mackenzie wrote in 1979:

> The north-east frontier of Bengal is a term used sometime to denote a boundary line, and sometimes more generally to describe a tract. In the latter sense it embraces the whole of the hill ranges north, east and south of the Assam valley, as well as the western slopes of the great mountain system lying between Bengal and independent Burma, with its outlying spurs and ridges. (Mackenzie 2007[1979]: 1)

In 1872–73, the power of summary legislation for backward tracts given to the executive government was extended to Assam. It was first used to pass a regulation for the frontier districts. This regulation empowered the Lieutenant-Governor to prescribe a line called 'the inner line', beyond which no British subject of certain classes or foreign residents without a licence were allowed. Rules were laid down in the areas of trade, possession of land beyond the line, and other matters under the effective control of the executive government (Mackenzie 2007[1979]: 55–56). The term 'British subjects' was replaced by 'citizens of India' in 1950. Though the concept of the Inner Line Permit was originally formed by the British to safeguard their commercial interests, the permit system continues in independent India officially in the name of protecting tribal cultures in Northeast India. Therefore, it was colonialism that created the 'centre' and the 'margin'.

Before the 1960s, the term Northeast existed only in the case of the North-East Frontier Agency or NEFA, which was the present-day Arunachal Pradesh. NEFA, though it was a part of the then Assam, was administered by the Ministry of External Affairs until 1965 and then by the Ministry of Home Affairs till 1972 when it was turned into a Union Territory with a new name: Arunachal Pradesh (Singh 2007: 7). The Northeastern region now incorporates not seven but eight states in all. The term 'Northeast' does not signify a permanent idea. The meaning has varied from time to time. Nowadays, the Northeast is seen as an ideal bridge between the Southeast Asian countries and India as in the case of the Look East Policy (Nongbri 2017).

WRITING FROM THE MARGINS AND CONSTRUCTION OF THE 'OTHER'

In the context of Northeast India, the influence of the British administrators remained after they left the region. 'It was conquest which empowered the conquerors to impose on the colonised a past written from the coloniser's point of view and uphold that writing as foundational to the law of the land' (Guha 1998: xiv). The early narratives of British expansion in Northeast India (Mackenzie 2007[1979]: 7) are replete with references to the numerous 'savage' and 'warlike' tribes that frequently raided the plains of Assam for slaves and booty. Many writers have used the term 'rebels' or 'recalcitrant tribes' to describe the different Northeastern tribes and communities. A form of re-colonisation is evident in literatures written by the local inhabitants of Northeast India who continue to reproduce the derogatory descriptions given in colonial ethnographies while narrating their own history (Sitlhou 2017). For Bhabha (2001: 391), the negative labelling of the native population by the coloniser was done in order to justify conquest and to establish systems of administration and instruction. In the discourse of colonialism, the colonised subject is the 'Other' of the Westerner, essentially outside Western culture and civilisation (Bhabha 1994: 66–84).

In the present day, this idea of 'the Other' is still relevant in analysing the 'mainland Indian' perspective of the Northeasterners.

In many metros in India, the Northeasterners are referred to by various derogatory terms because of their physical and cultural attributes. 'As a mode of discourse, the stereotype functions to exaggerate the difference of the "Other", and as a mode of identification, it operates a series of mutually exclusive categories differentiating "Self" and "Other"' (Sitlhou and Punathil 2017: 93). A priest of the Mar Thoma Syrian Church, Rev. Merin Mathew, ministering in the parishes of Northeast India (Guwahati, Assam) wrote in his diary dated 18 January 2013 about his preliminary notions about the region. He wrote:

> When I received the news of my first assignment, I have to be honest that my first reaction was 'why the Northeast?' Like an average Indian, I had stereotypes that simplified the entire NE (Northeast) … Images fed by the media, general perceptions about Northeast are that of insurgency, instability, militancy and general tumult. Some friends opined that since morality is very low among the people of the NE, I must take special care and be cautious. When I was in college, I believed with great conviction that sex and drugs is the only pre-occupation in the NE (Matthew 2013).

The media is also responsible for shaping the mainstream Indian's negative perception of the Northeast. They usually report with some amount of sensationalising with the intention of gaining popularity among patrons and consumers on often-capitalised issues like insurgency, conflicts, drug abuse, weird cultural practices, etc. Attitudes like this are fuelled by ignorance about the history, mores and values of the Northeasterners; deeply internalised ideas about a homogenised India are responsible for this form of racism (Ngaihte 2014: 15). The idea of the 'tribal' in the average Indian imagination has always been that of the impoverished and 'backward' subaltern who belongs to the fringes of society (Misra 2014: 5). The Northeastern tribals are no longer confined to their villages but are moving into broader urban spaces in the mainland with their ideas of alternate nationalism and demand to be treated as equal citizens (ibid.: 5–6).

The cultural history of the various communities of Northeast India is also marginalised through its consistent exclusion from the national curriculum of Indian history.

> Such neglect prompted the historians of North East India to take up research on the area but they failed to communicate them to the rest of India. As a result, North East continues to suffer from historiographical exclusion. But unless the stories of North East are integrated with the history of the rest of the country, a true national history can never be achieved. (Nag 1998: 6)

Writing has always been considered a sign of superior civilisation. Frantz Fanon calls for the indigenous (local) intellectual to create a new literature and to work for the cause of constructing a national culture, exhibiting an ideology different from the dominant narrative (as cited in Smith 2005: 103). In fact, the 82-page report and recommendations given by the Bezbaruah Committee (2014) to address the concerns of the Northeasterners living outside Northeast India includes the following:

> In order to educate the people about the North East, Universities have been advised that history of North East and participation in the freedom movement of the country should be taught at graduation level and post-graduation level, and for this purpose, curriculum be changed.[4]

THE PROCESS OF MARGINALISATION WITHIN MARGINALISED GROUPS

The ideology of the 'Other' also motivates and guides identity politics within the Northeast region (Goswami 2015).

> The atmosphere of mistrust generated by fears of domination and vengeance over one group by another has been heightened in the wake of various ethnic conflicts in the region in the past few years, particularly after the phase of formation of states almost got over in the 1980s. (ibid.: xxii)

The Northeast region is the home of numerous ethnic communities that have migrated from all points of the compass, with the majority of them belonging to the Indo-Chinese Mongoloid racial grouping (Downs 2011: 223). The tendency of conceptualising the region as a singular homogenous territory is problematic as this construction determined how it was governed by the colonial Britishers as well as how it is governed now by the Indian state, that is, by construing the idea of a shared identity among peoples from various parts of the region. The Northeast, considered a marginal geographical space, is as diverse as India itself in terms of linguistic, cultural and ethnic representation. The recurrent theme of this book is that the region cannot be portrayed merely as a homogenous category. There is a need to highlight the elements of heterogeneity of the different groups and their experiences, contestations and conflicts.[5]

The issues of the process of marginalisation do not apply only to the binary categories of the coloniser and the colonised or that of the state and the people. They are not just simple oppositions but consist of several relations, some more clearly oppositional than others. The development of different layers that has occurred within each group and across the two groups is often not taken into account (Smith 2005: 101). There are also processes of marginalisation within marginalised groups: atrocities on women, breach of human security in conflict situations, discrimination against alternative sexualities, discrimination against illegal immigrants. It is necessary to take into account the social realities of the region through a discussion on topics such as indigeneity, polity, economy, migration land rights, insurgency, militarisation, state violence and AFSPA, reservation, and so on. The Northeasterners as migrant citizens experience marginality in other states of India, in cities like Delhi, Hyderabad, Mumbai, and Bengaluru. On the other hand, there is discrimination against outsiders living in Northeast India as well. Violence on migrant labourers and the demands for Inner Line Permit system in many states of Northeast India are examples.

Identities are socially constructed and determined by wider social, cultural, political and economic contexts. They may be reinterpreted or even imposed upon certain groups or individuals by others, often as a result of inequalities of power or circumstances. Inter-ethnic and intra-ethnic conflicts have led to innumerable cases of strife-induced internal displacement in the seventy-two years of the Indian Republic. Bhaumik (2000: 154) listed six such major cases of displacement: of Bengalis from Assam (particularly Bodo areas) and Meghalaya; of Bengalis from Tripura; of 'tea tribes' in western Assam; of Reangs from Mizoram; of Nagas, Kukis and Paites in Manipur; and of Chakmas from Arunachal Pradesh and Mizoram.

The emphasis of the book is thus on understanding the underlying dynamics of power in the Northeast and studying the causes of marginality with the objective of rewriting identity and redefining marginality in Northeast India. With this aim, this book is divided into six main sections: Politics of Difference and the Articulation of Identities; Colonialism and Northeast India; Race, Ethnicity and Migration; Negotiating Gender, Culture and Identity; Indigeneity, Land and Identity; and Borders, States and Markets. These chapters deliberate on the relevance of the concept of marginality in understanding social issues in Northeast India today.

I. Politics of Difference and the Articulation of Identities

Sajal Nag's chapter 'Tribes, Colonialism and Postcolonial Predicament in Northeast India' traces the root cause of the problem of identity crises of the various tribes of Northeast India, triggering their transformation from self-confident and powerful tribes into subdued subjects. Once upon a time, these tribes who dwell mostly in the mountainous region considered themselves more cultured than the plainsmen with whom they had regular transaction. After being defeated and dominated by British colonisers, they were subjected to scrutiny and constant ridicule by both the British administrators and the colonial missionaries who branded the tribes as 'uncivilised'.

Papori Bora's chapter 'Interrogating India's Northeast as an Object of Knowledge Production' critically engages with the question of knowledge production in the constitution of India's Northeast. It specifically examines colonial historical and ethnographic discourse in the constitution of the Northeast, and the postcolonial renderings of the same discourse in the social sciences, especially the category of the 'tribe'. In recent decades there has been a realisation that the dominant frames within which the Northeast has been analysed is problematic and hence an attempt has been made to move beyond what is seen as the most persistent way of seeing the Northeast—i.e., through the national lens. There has been critical evaluation of the frames of anthropology and epistemic nationalism that limit the knowledge produced on the Northeast. This phenomenon becomes the motivation to examine recent frameworks for rethinking the Northeast in the form of new disciplinary formations in Indian universities.

II. Colonialism and Northeast India

Malsawmdawngliana's chapter, 'Colonialism and History Writing: The Mizo Experience', discusses the development of Mizo history from orality to textualisation during the colonial period. It also highlights the varied ramifications of the colonial agency, their influence in historical writing and also the problems and inadequacy of their project. The transition from oral culture to print culture, and the Mizo language, knowledge and culture have often been misrepresented in the academic and popular discourses. The chapter argues that the need of the hour is a re-writing and re-righting of the Mizo people's position in history in which they would tell their own stories, write their own versions, in their own ways and for their own purposes.

Suryasikha Pathak looks at early censuses and the debates they generated within the purview of identity articulation in 'Census and Identity Politics among the Plains Tribes in Colonial Assam'. Early colonial censuses were ethnographic classificatory exercises. The census has been an important historical source as a part of ethnographic inquiry, but it is also necessary to inquire into the relationship between quantitative and qualitative definitions of populations. Though census enumeration and its awareness led to a considerable rigidity in defining collective identities, it also made nationalist, ethnic, communal and other identities more fluid. The situation in terms of enumeration and classification was complex in Assam, where the diversity of communities combined with remarkable fluidity in demographic structure made it challenging to pin down communities. It is within such complexities that identities reified and articulated their politics.

III. Race, Ethnicity and Migration

Hoineilhing Sitlhou and Salah Punathil's chapter, 'Northeastern Migrants in Delhi: Racial Discrimination, Violence and State Response', explores the prejudice and hostility that Northeasterners have experienced in the national capital in the recent past. The chapter critically engages with the state response to the problem of discrimination and violence in the form of the Bezbaruah Committee, 2014, and the receptions and perceptions among migrants in Delhi about its implementation. The chapter also highlights the significance of the internal differences within the category of the Northeast in terms of region, class, gender, physical appearance and culture by mapping the divergent experiences of discrimination and violence. The rich empirical data presented in the chapter contribute towards a new theorisation of race and violence in India today.

Migration of people from Northeast India to Indian metropolises for various reasons has increased rapidly in the last few decades. This social phenomenon amongst the Kukis of

Manipur is problematised by Thanggoulen Kipgen in his chapter, 'Northeast Youth Migration to Cities: The Kuki Case in Delhi'. There has been frequent migration of the Kukis to large Indian metropolises such as Bangalore, Kolkata, Mumbai, Hyderabad and Delhi in recent times. Among these metropolises, Delhi is one of the most favoured. Based on fieldwork and secondary sources, Kipgen argues that opportunities in Delhi, particularly in the service sector, and demands for labour from the Northeast have contributed to the Kukis' out-migration to the capital city in recent years. The chapter also examines how social networks have played a crucial role in making Delhi a popular destination for the Kukis in spite of the marginalisation, discrimination and precarity they have to encounter in the city.

IV. Negotiating Gender, Culture and Identity

Lalhmingmawii's 'Alternative Sexuality and Civil Society in Mizoram' engages with the marginalisation and stigmatisation faced by the LGBT (lesbian, gay, bisexual and transgender) community in Mizo society, which is predominated by Christian ideology and heterosexism. In Mizoram, a state with a population of ten lakhs, there are people of varying sexual orientations and there exist many alternative forms of sexuality. While LGBT movements in other parts of India have prompted courts of law and authorities to legalise alternative forms of sexuality, the emancipation of the LGBT community in Mizoram has been curbed by civil society groups like Young Mizo Association (YMA) and women's organisations like Mizo Hmeichhe Insuihkhawm Pawl (MHIP). This chapter highlights the standpoint of these groups while addressing and contextualising the issue of alternative sexualities in Mizoram.

Ruth Nengneilhing's chapter, 'Women in Conflict Situations: Experiences of Marginalisation of Displaced Kuki Women in Manipur', focuses on women displaced during the Kuki-Naga clash of the 1990s in Manipur. The chapter studies the resettlement colonies in Chavangphai village of Moreh town along with two other affected villages, Gelnel and Vaichong, in the Sadar Hills West sub-division of Senapati district of Manipur, and shows how Kuki women have suffered due to the inequitable system and maldistribution of resources in the resettlement colonies.

V. Sawmveli's chapter, 'Christianity and Gender: A Study of Protestant Mizo Women', discusses how Protestant Christianity has contributed to the continuation of traditional gender relationships and inequality in Mizo society. It studies the cases of the Mizoram Presbyterian Church (Synod), the Baptist Church of Mizoram (BCM) and the Evangelical Church of Mizoram (ECM). The study looks at the nature of gender dynamics within the community, the established norms for both men and women, and how certain belief systems and cultural practices are actively perpetuated by members of the community even after the introduction of western education.

V. Indigeneity, Land and Identity

Venusa Tinyi in 'Megalithic Culture of the Chakhesang Nagas: Reinterpreting the Self' gives an ethnographic account of the Chakhesang Nagas who were formerly known as the Eastern Angamis. The chapter highlights the communities' unique relationship with stones through a discussion of the 'Feast of Merit'. Although the ritual feast is no longer celebrated today, the monoliths remain standing as a reminder of their past—of how the ancestors of the Chakhesang people communicated and lived in harmony with nature and of the values and beliefs that structure and regulate the community. Exploring the nature of this relationship may also shape their perspective as to how a native individual might understand and represent the 'self' in contrast to or as an alternative to the modern discourses on identity and history of the Nagas in general and the Chakhesang tribe in particular.

Rekha M. Shangpliang explores the role of women in natural resource management in 'Livelihood Interventions and Marginalisation in Land and Forest Rights of Rural Khasi Women'. In recent times due to changes in human–nature relationship and increasing pressure on land and other resources, there has been an invisibilisation of women's livelihood strategies and marginalisation of women's rights over NTFPs (non-timber forest products) and other resource bases leading to a 'feminisation of poverty'. Issues such as overpopulation, rapid development, land acquisition and alienation, and legislative policies of the government have further undermined the role of rural Khasi women in resource management, thereby denying them access to and control over livelihoods.

VI. Borders, States and Markets

N. William Singh's chapter, 'Marginalisation: Everyday Life Activities at the Myanmar-Mizoram Borderland', details the collective consciousness of marginalised communities and the politics of marginalisation, which disowns the very people who are the real constituents of a civic order. Their oppressed voices and their stories of insecurities recount the everyday life activities for Chin migrants from Myanmar at the borderlands of Mizoram. The author highlights the role of media, the existing flow of migrant labour and the role of civil society when it is a host. Singh discusses the wide gaps between livelihood, consumption, health, education and insecurities between the migrant community and the host society in the making of marginalised identities at the borderlands.

Lalhmangaihi Chhakchhuak's chapter, 'Global Markets, Local Risks and Social Marginality: A Study of Cancer-Affected People in Mizoram', discusses the changes in the social and economic organisation of Mizo society over the past few decades which has resulted in a new set of relations and networks. By the early 1990s, new market and trade relations between neighbouring states as well as border trade between Myanmar and Bangladesh brought a variety of cheap goods and food, allowing the possibilities of social risk. The socio-political regimes in fact facilitated these transitions and processes of marginalisation. Globalisation and economic growth brought with it a shift in the patterns of consumption and lifestyle. This chapter attempts, by using the political economy perspective, to analyse new hazards and dangers to social life, including diseases such as cancer that has affected a significant number of people in Mizoram because of these shifts.

This book is an academic exercise aimed at developing a sociological enquiry into the various issues affecting Northeast India. It has brought in diverse writings from different social science disciplines, thus encouraging a broad, interdisciplinary and national-level discussion and debate to try and find solutions to the contradictions that beset Northeast India. As already mentioned, this book questions and critiques the tendency to conceptualise the region as a single homogenous territory, and instead emphasises on the heterogeneity of the different groups and their experiences, contestations and conflicts. The Northeast needs to be understood as a distinct entity in terms of its indifference to various shared social values of the Indian social system, like the caste system for instance. This would mean, '… the exercise of the constitutional right of northeastern indigenous communities to be accepted as Indians on equal grounds, without being "integrated"' (Misra 2014: 6). There is, therefore, a need to redefine the idea of nationalism and the concept of ethnicity itself in order to better grasp the complexities of the Northeast of India.

NOTES

1. Pamphlet titled 'Marginality: Addressing the Root Causes of Extreme Poverty', Center for Development Research, University of Bonn. Available at https://www.zef.de/fileadmin/webfiles/downloads/projects/margip/downloads/Poster-marginality-tropentag.pdf (accessed on 28 April 2023).

2. The North Eastern Council is the nodal agency for the economic and social development of the North Eastern Region. The North Eastern Council was constituted in 1971 by an Act of Parliament.

3. See Statewise Total & Tribal Population of India, 2011 Census. Available at https://trti.maharashtra.gov.in/index.php/en/statewise-total-tribal-population (accessed on 20 August 2021).

4. See Bezbaruah Committee (2014). The Ministry of Home Affairs had constituted a committee under the chairmanship of Shri M. P. Bezbaruah, retired IAS and member of the North Eastern Council, to look into the various concerns of the citizens hailing from the Northeastern states who are living in different parts of the country and to suggest suitable remedial measures including legal measures which could be taken up by the government. The 11-member committee headed by M. P. Bezbaruah submitted its report on the discrimination against racial attacks on members of the Northeastern community in metros of India.

5. Another book *Deconstructing Colonial Ethnography: An Analysis of Missionary Writings on North East India* (2017) authored by Sitlhou has a similar objective.

REFERENCES

Bezbaruah Committee. 2014. *Report of the Committee under the Chairmanship of Shri M. P. Bezbaruah to Look into the Concerns of the People of the Northeast Living in Other Parts of the Country.* Ministry of Home Affairs. Available at https://www.mha.gov.in/sites/default/files/filefield_paths/ReportOfMPBezbaruahCommittee.PDF (accessed April 2023).

Bhabha, Homi K. 1994. *The Location of Culture.* London: Routledge.

_____. 2001. 'The Other Question'. In Steven Seidman and Jeffrey C. Alexander (eds), *The New Social Theory Reader: Contemporary Debates.* London and New York: Routledge.

Bhaumik, Subir. 2000. 'Negotiating Access: Northeast India.' *Refugee Survey Quarterly* 19(2): 142–158.

Caliendo, Stephen M., and Charlton D. McIlwain (eds). 2011. *The Routledge Companion to Race and Ethnicity.* London and New York: Routledge.

Chaube, S. K. 1973. *Hill Politics in North East India.* New Delhi: Orient Longman.

Cooley, Charles Horton. 1922. *Human Nature and the Social Order*. New York: Charles Scribner's Sons.

Dennis, Rutledge M. 2005. 'The Age of Marginality'. In Rutledge Dennis (ed.), *Marginality, Power and Social Structure: Issues in Race, Class and Gender*, Research in Race and Ethnic Relation, Vol. 12. UK: Elsevier Ltd.

Downs, Frederick S. 1992. *History of Christianity in India*, Vol. V, Part 5. Bangalore: The Church History Association of India.

_____. 2011. 'Christian Conversion Movements in Northeast India.' In T. K. Oommen (ed.), *Social Movements I: Issues of Identity*. New Delhi: Oxford University Press.

Goswami, Sandhya (ed.). 2015. *Troubled Diversity: The Political Process in Northeast India*. New Delhi: Oxford University Press.

Guha, Ranajit. 1998. *Dominance without Hegemony: History and Power in Colonial India*. Calcutta, Chennai, Mumbai: Oxford University Press.

Haokip, S. 2002. *The Kuki Rising 1917–1919*. Paper presented at a seminar organised by Kuki Student Organisation (Delhi Branch) at Jawaharlal Nehru University.

Haokip, Robert Lunkhopao. 2018. 'State Making and the Geography of Violence at the Margins: A Case Study of the India-Myanmar Borderland'. M.Phil Dissertation submitted to the Special Centre for the Study of North East India, School of Social Sciences, JNU, New Delhi.

International Consultative Forum on Education for All. 2000. *Status and Trends 2000: Assessing Learning Achievement*. Available at https://unesdoc.unesco.org/ark:/48223/pf0000119823 (accessed on 28 April 2023).

Kay, Rebecca. 2005. 'Identity and Marginality'. *eSharp* 1(6.1): 1–6.

Krishnan, Ananth. 2016. 'India's Northeast Most Neglected, Says China'. *The Hindu*, 21 May. Available at https://www.thehindu.com/news/international/world/indias-northeast-most-neglected-says-china/article5883212.ece. (accessed on 8 May 2017).

Mackenzie, Alexander. 2007[1979]. *The North-East Frontier of India*. New Delhi: Mittal Publications.

Mathew, Rev. Merin. 2013. 'Bread of Life: Transforming Crowd into a Eucharistic Community—Reflections Based on the Issue of "Illegal Migrants of Assam"', Blog 'Northeast Diaries: Through My Lens', 18 January. Available at http://northeastdiariesmerinmathew.blogspot.in. (accessed January 2014).

McCrae, John (communicated by J. H. Harington). 1979[1801]. 'Account of the Kookies, or Lunctas'. In *Asiatic Researches*, Vol. VII, 183–198. New Delhi: Cosmo Publications.

McDuie-Ra, Duncan. 2012. *Northeast Migrants in Delhi: Race, Refuge and Retail.* Netherlands: Amsterdam University Press.

Mead, George H. 1972. *Mind, Self and Society: From the Standpoint of a Social Behaviourist.* Chicago and London: The University of Chicago Press.

Misra, Udayon. 2014. *India's North East: Identity Movements, State and Civil Society.* New Delhi: Oxford University Press.

Nag, Sajal. 1998. *India and North-East India: Mind, Politics and the Process of Integration, 1946–1950.* New Delhi: Regency Publication.

Ngaihte, Thangkhanlal. 2014. 'Nido Taniam and the Fraught Question of Racism in India'. *Economic and Political Weekly* XLIX(11): 15–17.

Nongbri, Tiplut. 2017. 'Identity and Marginality in North East India: Challenges for Social Science Research'. Paper presented in the valedictory session of the national seminar organised by the Department of Sociology, Hyderabad Central University on 16–17 January.

Pelc, S. 2017. 'Marginality and Marginalization'. In R. Chand, E. Nel, and S. Pelc (eds), *Societies, Social Inequalities and Marginalization*, Perspectives on Geographical Marginality. Springer, Cham. Available at https://doi.org/10.1007/978-3-319-50998-3_2 (accessed April 2023).

Rawlins, John. 1790. 'On the Manners, Religion, and Laws of the Cucis, or Mountaineers of Tipra'. In *Asiatic Researches*, Vol. II, 187–193.

Ray, Dhriti. 2016. *Interrogating Marginality: The Fiction of J. M. Coetzee.* PhD thesis submitted to the Department of English and Other Modern European Languages, Visva Bharati University. Available at https://shodhganga.inflibnet.ac.in/handle/10603/103339 (accessed May 2023).

Shaw, William. 1929. *Notes on the Thadou Kukis (Journal of the Asiatic Society of Bengal).* Calcutta: Asiatic Society of Bengal (published on behalf of the Government of Assam).

Singh, K. S., and S. Manoharan. 1993. *People of India*, Vol. IX. Delhi: Oxford University Press.

Singh, Kshetrimayum Imokanta. 2007. 'The Social Dynamism of Shumang Lila of Manipur: A Sociological Analysis of Some of its Contemporary Manifestations'. Thesis submitted to the Centre for Study of Social Sciences, School of Social Sciences, Jawaharlal Nehru University, New Delhi.

Singha, Komol, and M. Amarjeet Singh. 2016. *Identity, Contestation and Development in Northeast India*. New Delhi: Routledge.

Sitlhou, Hoineilhing. 2011. 'Land and Identity: A Sociological Study of the Thadou Kuki Tribes of Manipur'. Thesis submitted to the Centre for Study of Social Sciences, School of Social Sciences, Jawaharlal Nehru University, New Delhi.

Sitlhou, Hoineilhing. 2017. *Deconstructing Colonial Ethnography: An Analysis of Missionary Writings on North East India*. New Delhi: Ruby Press & Co.

Sitlhou, Hoineilhing, and Salah Punathil. 2017. 'Racial Discrimination and Violence against Northeasterners and Bezbaruah Committee Report, 2014 (Research in Progress)'. *Explorations* 1(1), April: 91–102.

Smith, Linda Tuhiwai. 2005. 'Imperialism, History, Writing and Theory'. In Gaurav Desai and Supriya Nair (eds), *Postcolonialisms: An Anthology of Cultural Theory and Criticism*. Oxford: Berg Publishers.

Verghese, B. G. 2004. *India's Northeast Resurgent: Ethnicity, Insurgency, Governance, Development*. Delhi: Konark Publishers.

I

Politics of Difference and the Articulation of Identities

1

Tribes, Colonialism and Postcolonial Predicament in Northeast India

Sajal Nag

In 1929 the members of the Indian Statutory Commission visited the Naga Hills to know the views of the people regarding the kind of political reforms they would like to have in the hills. Since the Nagas had not been exposed to any aspect of modernity, be it education or bourgeois politics, they were not in a position to make any representation. Some Nagas who were mostly former tribal chiefs and interpreters for the British and who had once formed an organisation called the Naga Club, submitted a memorandum to the Commission (1930) which stated,[1]

> Before the British Government conquered our country in 1879–1880, we were living in a state of intermittent warfare with the Assamese of the Assam valley in the North West and the Manipuris to the south of our country. They never conquered us, nor were we ever subjugated to their rule. On the other hand, we were always a terror to these people ... we should not be thrust to the mercy of those people who could have never conquered us themselves [...] but to leave us alone to determine for ourselves as in ancient times.

This memorandum was a celebration of the sovereignty that the Nagas had before the coming of the British. They were proud that neither of the mighty medieval states of Manipur or Ahom were ever able to conquer them. The document also mentions that it was only the British who conquered them and hence they had no qualms in being subjects to them. The Nagas worshipped valour and considered any group or people that could subdue them as superior. This is why they could never accept the idea of being ruled over by people who had never conquered or subjugated them. What is most significant in this memorandum, which was barely a page long, is that they do not fail to mention how they were a terror to the people of the plains and how ridiculously helpless the plains people were against the invasions of the tribals.

Indeed, the hill men, both the Nagas and the Mizos, had a relationship of interdependence with the plains people of the Ahom, Bengal and Cachar states, respectively. On one hand, the Nagas and the Mizos were dependent on the plains as an outlet where they bartered their products, and most importantly, it was the area for the perpetration of raids and headhunting. On the other hand, the plainsmen of the Brahmaputra, Barak and Suma Valley too were dependent on the Nagas for salt, herbs and medicines, elephant tusks, rhino horns, rubber and other such forest products. The tribals had an image of the plainsmen as being a friendly lot. Moreover, these people were also easy prey to tribal raids, kidnapping and headhunting, and were terrified of the tribals who would suddenly descend from the hills and carry away their dear ones as slaves or prisoners, destroy the standing crops and hutments, and even behead people to carry their heads as trophies. In general, the tribals did not have a high regard for these plainsmen and viewed themselves as 'superior' and 'mighty'. The tribal chiefs considered the frequently raided area as their sphere of influence and the inhabitants as their subjugated subjects even though the area did not really fall under their suzerainty and they had not formally conquered it; they only raided and perpetrated kidnapping and headhunting in the area frequently. As a matter of fact, the maharajas of Manipur, Tripura and Cachar claimed suzerainty over the Naga and Mizo hills respectively but they had no control over these areas or the tribals who considered themselves sovereign and free. It is interesting to note that while the plainsmen considered these hillmen as savage and barbaric on account of the raids and murders, the Naga and the Mizo in turn looked down on these plainsmen as people who lacked the courage to fight. They found them to be ridiculously weak and inferior, incapable of defending themselves and their women and children from the tribal raids. Their warfare and weaponry were too backward to fight and thwart the warlike hillmen descending upon them suddenly. The fact that the inhabitants of the foothills lived at the mercy of the tribals made the Nagas and the Mizos feel powerful and mighty, and they considered themselves a symbol of terror for the plainsmen of Assam, Cachar and Sylhet. The memorandum submitted to the Indian Statutory Commission (1929) by the Naga delegates had made a reference to this.[2] The tribals therefore, had no occasion to view these 'weaklings' as any kind of threat because in the relationship between the tribals and non-tribals it was the hillmen who were supreme and had arbitrary powers.

But by 1947 when the British were about to withdraw from India, the same Nagas were talking in a different tone. They asserted that the backward Nagas were no political match for the advanced Indians and there was 'every possibility that thrown among forty crores of Indians, the one million Nagas with the unique system of life will be wiped out.'[3] They did not want to be left to the mercy of those Indians after the British left. They appealed to India to leave them to themselves. What then happened in the twenty years that followed? What caused their metamorphosis? To understand this one has to first trace the encounter between the white man and the tribals of Northeast India.

THE UGLY 'SAVAGE'

The early missionary texts pertaining to the tribes are full of pejorative and uncharitable terms as was common in colonial texts that were defined by western parameters. Even before they reached the Lushai hills, they were convinced that,

> the inhabitants were regarded by the few Europeans then residing in Bengal, as the fiercest and most barbarous of all the tribes within the province, notorious for their headhunting expeditions

to neighbouring plains. The object of these raids was to obtain human skulls with the object to adorn the graves of their ancestors, the belief prevailing that the spirits of the slain would become the slaves of their ancestors in the spirit world. (Morris 1930: 77)

Two of the earliest missionaries to enter the Lushai hills were F. W. Savidge (*Sap Upa*[4]) and J. H. Lorrain (*Pu Buanga*[5]) who came to Aizawl in 1884, and stayed for a period of four years. Lorrain left a detailed account of his visit to a Lushai village in his logbook. It reflects the impression he had of the Lushais which were in line with his colonial colleagues:

> Upon entering a Lushai village, you will see children and swine playing together in the mud, and you will wish that there was someone to teach these people to raise their standard of living to a level slightly higher than those of animals. Despite their primitive-like behaviour, with the right teaching, they had the look of a people who could be quite intelligent. There is a huge behavioural difference between those who have interacted with foreigners, and those who haven't. The former group are better dressed, and their faces cleaner. The first time we saw the Lushai people, we had difficulty distinguishing between the men and the women.[6]

This difficulty was because both sexes had long hair. Lorrain did not change his opinion of the Lushais even after a stay of one year and after visiting several villages:

> Their houses are closely spaced, and the lack of hygienic living conditions is similar to all, from the poorest section to the chief's house. We must have the courage of spirit to tell these unfortunate people that only through the Gospel can they be uplifted to become a self-sufficient and a healthy race.[7]

Indeed, what the missionaries abhorred was the lack of cleanliness and hygiene amongst the Lushais:

> One of the best-loved children's game was to wallow in the monsoon-drenched mud along with the pigs. It was hard to distinguish between swine and children. Their hair would be matted with clumps of mud, and instead of taking baths afterwards, they would wash themselves in the rain … One can

> easily access their homes at any time. The first thing that struck us when we first saw their homes was the filth. They were smoke-filled and black cobwebs hung from the beams. Insects scurried about freely, and right in the center, they would have the hearth, where a fire would always be kept going. The ceilings were very low, and if you stand upright, your head would touch the ceiling … During mealtimes, the whole family would sit on the floor, crouched around a common wooden trough … One of the elder women would spoon a huge quantity of rice onto it, and one of the boys would spoon some side-dish in the center. They usually eat near the hearth, and they all used a common spoon to drink the stew … Clean drinking water was not a chief concern of theirs. The village water points were usually unclean, having a coffee-coloured appearance.[8]

Lorrain wrote extensively on the lack of hygiene of the Lushais. He wrote about how unbearable the stench that came off the children's bodies was:

> Mothers let their children wallow in their own filth. It would be impossible to make a European understand how dirty they were. The dirt stuck firmly to their skin, and some mothers would perfunctorily scratch away at these spots of dirt. When the children cried out from the pain, they would comment, 'There! It's pointless to try to clean them, they complain so! They don't want to be cleaned'. Not all European children like taking baths, but if these Lushai mothers had bathed their children with warm water and soap, some would have undoubtedly liked it.[9]

The missionaries not only disapproved of the manner of living of the Lushais, they also had very low opinion of the Lushais' intelligence, their knowledge and education and thus they described the Lushais as primitive and ignorant. It bothered the missionaries greatly to see how the children were brought up by the Lushais as a consequence of their ignorance.

> We need to preach not just the Gospel but also a lot of other things to the Lushais because they are still very ignorant. Sometimes it feels like animals have more intelligence than these people do. For one, they were absolutely comfortable with dirt and they need

> to be made aware of how harmful this is. Secondly, a day after a baby is born, the mother leaves her immediately to work in the fields.[10] The babies are left in the care of other children or some old woman too old to work anymore. When the baby is hungry, they feed him mashed rice which is barely digestible for the infant's stomach. Even animals give more care to their young than the Lushai mothers. The children, if they survive [Lorrain wrote elsewhere that around 50 per cent of Lushai children die in infancy], grow up with congenital stomach problems which causes them a lot of trouble. Another thing is that, these infants are unclothed till the time they reach childhood, as a result of which many die due to various illnesses.[11]

To the missionaries, tribal religion was nothing but 'demon worship'. 'All these hill people are demon worshippers; but each tribe has its own demons and its own ceremonies, preserved in pristine purity or largely modified by their environment' (Moore 1997: 15). As far as the religious faith of the tribes was concerned, it was repeatedly emphasised that their religion 'was a crude form of demonology. Its main principle consists in the endeavour to propitiate evil spirits by the offering of sacrifices. A vague belief exists in a supreme being' (Morris 1910: 54). The religion of the Khasis was frequently described as animism or spirit worship, in which the worship of demons or evil spirits were repeatedly emphasised. These reports also concluded that the Khasis did not have any definite idea about religion as such (ibid.).

Another characteristic which the missionaries associated with tribalism was the flexible concept of marriage. They often frowned upon the sexual openness of the tribals but what they strongly disliked besides polygamy was the ease with which tribal men abandoned their married wives. In other words, the absence of divorce laws and the weak institution of marriage itself were associated with tribal life.

> The worst feature in the manner of the people and one likely to be a serious obstacle to the missionary is the laxity of their marriage … indeed divorce is so frequent that their unions can hardly be honoured with the name of marriage. (Yule 1894: 612)

For the missionaries, the diversity was immense. According to D. E. Jones, a Welsh missionary working amongst the Lushais, 'It is a country well-fitted for a Christian missionary with so many languages, cultures and barbarisms [living] side by side. Some of its people are still in the Stone Age' (Jones 1998).

During her first encounter with the Ao tribes, whom she had come to evangelise, Mary Mead Clark was full of contempt. When offered a goat in sale, she screamed,

> 'I don't want the goat. I don't want it, I will not have it, take it away, take it away'… *Yet these strange, uncivilised men* … still persisted in dragging up the steps of the veranda [of] our bungalow, a large, long and horned hill goat, hoping to receive from us double or quadruple its value. (Clark 1978: 1, emphasis added)

Clark continued,

> I was introduced to these stalwarts, robust warriors, dressed mostly in war medal[s], each man grasping his spear, [the] shaft decorated with goats' hair, dyed red and yellow and also fringed with the long black hair of a woman telling the story of bloody deeds. (Clark 1978: 1)

Clark never tired of calling these hill people 'sturdy and savage tribes' who were 'slow and phlegmatic' in nature. Whenever she looked into the 'hard faces of these hill people', she had no hesitation in believing they were 'head-cutters'. The missionaries S. W. Rivenburg and V. H. Sword were amazed at the ease with which these 'fierce and untameable tribes' severed heads from a human body. Rev. E. G. Phillips agreed that some of the tribes were 'blood-thirsty savages'. He even found them 'most desperate and incorrigible' (Phillips 1992). For others like D. E. Jones, the fact that some tribes detested excessive labour and would even 'laugh too much' was a sign that they were uncivilised.

In his first letter, Thomas Jones described the people of the Khasi hills, among whom he had come, in the following words:

> A more pitiful lamentable and at the same time a more inviting field for the Christian cannot be found. Here are multitudes upon

> multitudes of untutored heathen, naturally lazy and sluggish, living in filth and rags, afraid to wash a rag lest it should wear out sooner, depriving themselves of proper clothing, niggardly hoarding up every price (farthing) they can get and if asked the reason why they answer that they may have something to sacrifice when they or their friends are ill. (Jyrwa 1980: 26)

The missionaries described their life amidst the tribals as 'living in horrors of savage warfare' which the tribals indulge in. In fact, they were constantly haunted by the fear of being headhunted. When Dr Clark went up the Naga hills, the Magistrate of Sibsagar asked his wife, 'Don't you expect to see your husband with his head on his shoulders?' During their subsequent stay in the hills, Clark's cook was repeatedly warned not to let the fire blaze too brightly lest the villages of the surrounding peaks take notice of the new settlers and adorn their skull stores with new heads (Clark 1978: 14).

The missionaries in their writings constantly referred to the region as 'beyond the boundary of civilisation', 'unknown jungle', 'outside the civilised world'. S. W. Rivenburg expressed his shock that a man was not admitted to his tribe formally 'until he participated in the taking of human life'. In addition, 'after a war between villages, conquerors hang the skulls of their enemies on their fence posts as Americans hang deer heads on their front walls' (Rivenburg 1941: 4). Sword described the Garo tribe as a 'fierce and untameable tribe' (Sword 1935: 93). Similarly, Rev. P. H. Moore (1997) talked of the natives as 'born in heathenism and brought up in a poisonous atmosphere and in their earliest childhood were taught by their own parents [to] lip all forms of lying and deceit and filthy communication—slander, backbiting and reviling abuse' (Moore 1997: 159).

Tribals were often associated with liquor and drunkenness, which the missionaries detested. The Mizos were said to be 'lazy, cruel, superstitious and very prone to drunkenness' (Lloyd 1930: 24). Thomas Oldham (1856: 79) mentioned about the Khasis that of their bad qualities 'dissoluteness of manners and drunkenness were the most prominent.' Of the Tangkhul Naga, Pettigrew wrote disapprovingly of their addiction to *zu* (rice beer) (Solo and Mahangthei 2006). In his annual report, he stated that the Meithei was reckoned to be 'a liar' but the Tangkhul Naga could easily beat the former in the art of lying (Dena 1988: 35).

The missionaries also detested the tribal culture of breaking out into community festivities, with singing, dancing, drinking and a big feast where animals were sacrificed and spirits worshipped. The missionaries in their efforts towards evangelisation tried to discourage such performances perpetually. In fact, the missionaries reported that the opposition and hostility towards Christianity and the tendency to revert to 'heathenism' by the tribals was manifested through these elaborate dance and song performances by the community. These performances were also often done deliberately in order to spite the missionaries. It may be mentioned here that eventually this community singing and dancing was adopted as a part of Christianity in these tribal areas. Adoption of local practices was something common to all religions, be it Buddhism or Islam.

While tribalism was condemned as 'savagery', the missionaries justified their advance in the area by saying that they were ordained to bring the words of the saviour to the tribals. Thanzauva wrote:

> Wherever we go and the more we hear of the customs, habits and lives of the people, the more we are convinced of their need of the Saviour ... we want the coming of the great light of the world who shall pour forth His eternal light upon these people who sit in darkness and in the valley of the shadow of death. We wait for the coming of Him who bringeth life to those who are perishing for want of truth. (Thanzauva 1997: 11)

In fact, even the official Simon Commission referred to some of the tribes as 'backward'. Interestingly, reacting to this description, Cadogan, one of the Commission members, said in the House of Commons in May 1935 that 'It is true that some of these tribesmen eat food which, if you or I eat, would give us ptomaine poisoning at once' (Yonuo 1974: 134).

But overall, the missionaries were convinced of one thing: 'Once civilized and Christianised' these tribes will make a 'manly, worthy people' (Thanzauva 1997: 11). Thus began the long painstaking efforts of the missionaries to bring the tribals into manhood and civilisation.

COLONIAL TRANSFORMATION AND METAMORPHOSIS OF THE TRIBAL

By the 1940s there was a metamorphosis in terms of the image of the tribals as well as their reality. The tribals realised and resented the fact that not only were the British leaving but it was the plainsmen who were going to replace them as rulers. A century of colonial rule, detribalisation, Christianisation and exclusion had changed the tribals too. They had mellowed down, their ideas about and images of others had changed and now they had a Western-educated middle-class leadership to lead them. They had not fought a war since the one against the British invaders. Head-hunting and raiding on the plains had been stopped.[12]

The missionaries and the British administrators had made them aware that it was not the plainsmen but the tribals themselves who were backward and savage. The constant reference to them as 'tribal' and to their 'primitive ways' made them conscious of this. The introduction of modern hygiene, medicine, dress, haircut, schools, churches and so on by the missionaries (Downs 1991: 1–76) and their effectiveness in modernising the hill people were noteworthy. But being conscious of their primitiveness made the tribals insular. The hitherto confident tribals who had considered themselves 'mighty and superior' vis-à-vis the plainsmen now acted differently while dealing with them.

Another case of their diffidence was that the missionaries and colonial administrators constantly referred to the plainsmen as 'hostile people' (Yonuo 1974: 134). The representation of the plainsmen as different from everything that the tribals were—from their looks to their food habits—had a devastating impact. The tribals could not visualise themselves as 'equal' and did not believe that they would be 'able to adjust in mainstream Indian society and polity'.[13] The civilisational discourse that the British and the missionaries applied on the tribals had a devastating impact on them. They internalised this discourse and began to apply it on themselves. As a result, they were convinced that they were indeed primitive and savage as opposed to the British and the Indian plainsmen who were civilised and far more advanced. In fact, the raids, plunders and headhunting that they were so proud of earlier were now considered by them to be features of savagery. The tribals now wanted to be rid of the 'savage' tag and be counted as civilised people. Therefore, they accepted Christianity, went for a modern education, discarded their traditional religions, attires and looks. They had haircuts, covered their bodies with clothes like the white men, learnt to be shy and embarrassed of nakedness and ate food which was not seen as 'savage'. But despite this transformation, they were made to be aware of their 'shameful' history, of their raids, of their nakedness, of their headhunting, of their fratricidal warfare, of their traditional customs, religions and cultural practices, of their mode of living, their lack of hygiene, among others. They were still considered unfit to be treated as equal to other civilised races of the plains. The tribal community was completely demoralised and lost the confidence to deal with the plains people adequately.

Despite having been transformed to meet the demands of the civilisational discourse, the tribals were not accepted as equals in the comity of civilised nations. Thus, these once-proud and valorous tribes entered the postcolonial phase with a sense of shame and embarrassment of their pasts, and they lost their valour and bravery to modern education, a 'civilised' attire and a new religion, trying desperately to cope with the demands of modernity. Yet their postcolonial compatriots continue to refer to them in relation to their pre-colonial past. 'Tribal' is what they are described as, and their cultures frowned upon; the community that was once far more powerful than the plains people had to seek protection and mercy from the same plains people who became the arbiters of their destiny. This was the postcolonial predicament of the tribes of Northeast India.

NOTES

1. Memorandum to the Indian Statutory Commission from the Naga Club, *Indian Statutory Commission Report*, Vol. XIV: 109–10, London, 1930.

2. Ibid.

3. Naga National Council Memorandum to His Majesty's Government and the Government of India, 20 February, 1947. Manipur State Archives, Imphal.

4. A name given to him by the local Lushais. '*Sap*' refers to a white man or an Englishman and '*Upa*' here refers to a respectable elder but not necessarily one who is advanced in years.

5. A name given to him by the local Lushais. The prefix '*Pu*' has two meanings. It is either used to denote a grandfather or a person of respectable status in the society. '*Buanga*' means a person with a fair or milky complexion.

6. Lorrain, J. H. 'Logbook', Manuscript, p. 27. Calvinist Methodist Archives (CMA), National Library of Wales.

7. Ibid., p. 46.

8. Ibid., p. 46.

9. Ibid., p. 56.

10. While this can be attributed to ignorance, it must be noted that it was a common practice during this time that all capable persons should work in the fields, and this category included mothers who had just given birth.

11. Lorrain, Logbook, p. 92–93.

12. J. P. Mills Report on Naga Hills, Census of India, 1931.

13. This was clearly evident in the Naga Club Memorandum to the Indian Statutory Commission and the early NNC Memorandum to the Government of India.

REFERENCES

Clark, Mary M. 1978[1907]. *A Corner in India*. Philadelphia: American Baptist Publication Society. (Reprint, Guwahati, Assam: Christian Literature Society).

Dena, Lal. 1988. *Christian Missions and Colonialism*. Shillong: Vendrame Institute.

Downs, Frederick. 1991. 'Study of Christianity in North East India'. *NEHU Journal of Special Sciences and Humanities* July–September: 1–76.

Jones, D. E. 1998. *A Missionary's Autobiography*. Aizawl: H. Liansailova.

Jyrwa, J. F. 1980. *Wondrous Work of God: A Study on the Growth and Development of the Khasi-Jaintia Presbyterian Church in the 20th Century*. Shillong: M.B. Jyrwa.

Lloyd, J. Merion. 1930. *On Every High Hill*. Liverpool: Foreign Mission Office. (Reprint, Aizawl: Synod Publication Board, 1984).

Moore, Rev. P. H. 1997. 'Need of a Native Ministry'. In *Papers and Discussions of the Jubilee Conference of the American Baptist Missionary Union Held in Nowgong, December 18–29, 1886*. Guwahati and Delhi: Spectrum Publications.

Morris, J. M. 1910. *History of Welsh Calvinist Methodist Foreign Mission*. Liverpool: LMS.

_____. 1930. *The Story of our Foreign Mission*. Liverpool: LMS.

Morris, John Hughes. 1996. *The History of the Welsh Calvinistic Methodists Foreign Mission, to the End of the Year 1904*. New Delhi: Indus Publishing Company.

Oldham, Thomas. 1856. 'The Geological Structure of Part of the Khasi Hills, with Observations on the Meteorology and Ethnology of that District'. *Calcutta Review* XXVII(July–December): 55–93.

Phillips, Rev. E. G. 1992[1887]. 'Historical Sketch of the Garo Field'. In *Papers and Discussions of the Jubilee Conference of the American Baptist Missionary Union Held in Nowgong, December 18–29*. Guwahati and Delhi: Spectrum Publications.

Rivenburg, N 1941. *The Star of Naga Hills: Letters from Rev. Sydney and Hattie Rivenburg, Pioneer Missionaries in Assam, 1883–1923*. Philadelphia: The American Baptist Publication Society.

Solo, Rev. Jonah M., and Rev. K. Mahangthei. 2006. *Forty Years Mission in Manipur: Mission Reports of Rev. William Pettigrew*. Imphal: Christian Literature Centre (CLC).

Sword, V. H. 1935. *Baptists in Assam: A Century of Missionary Service.* Gauhati: Spectrum Publications.

Thanzauva, K. 1997. *Report of the Foreign Missions of the Presbyterian Church of Wales on Mizoram 1894–1957.* Aizawl: Synod Literature and Publication Board.

Yonuo, Asoso. 1974. *The Rising Nagas: A Political and Historical Study.* Delhi: Vivek Publishing House.

Yule, H. 1894. Notes on the Khasi Hills and People. *Journal of Asiatic Society of Bengal* 12(2): 603–612.

Interrogating India's Northeast as an Object of Knowledge Production

Papori Bora

Given the colonial administrative significance of the category of 'tribe' in the Northeast, the discipline of anthropology has historically dominated the study of the Northeast in terms of the study of the 'other' who lacked 'coevalness' with the nation (Bora 2011, based on Fabian 1983). This framework of anthropology and the ethnographic method have been predominant in producing knowledge about the Northeastern tribes. This can be seen in the official colonial initiative to produce several ethnographic monographs on the Northeastern tribes written by scholar-administrators.

These early writings were mostly accounts of soldier-administrators written in the form of travel diaries and military reports, but later developed into detailed surveys and ethnographic reports to meet the administrative demands of the colonial state. Most of them were published in the *Journal of Asiatic Society of Bengal* in the mid-nineteenth century. The late nineteenth century and the beginning of the twentieth century saw the emergence of various ethnographic articles on the tribes which began to be published in journals like the *Journal of the Royal Anthropological Institute*, *Folklore*, *Man*, *Journal of Society of Arts*, *Anthropos*, etc. This ethnographic work reflected nineteenth-century concerns about race and racial difference, origins and migrations of people and links between the racial families of mankind that dominated ethnology (Lotha 2007: 26).

In 1901, the colonial Government of India took up the suggestion of the British Association for Advancement of Science to set up the Ethnographic Survey of India. As a part of this initiative a scheme was initiated in Assam by Sir Bampfylde Fuller, the then Chief Commissioner of Assam, that led to the writing of several monographs on some of the important tribes of the province, which are still considered to be authoritative texts on the topic: P. R. T Gordon's *The Khasis* (1906), Playfair's *The Garos* (1919), John Shakespear's *The Lushei Kuki Clans* (1912), T. C. Hodson's *Naga Tribes of Manipur* (1911), J. H. Hutton's *Angami Nagas* (1921) and *The Sema Nagas* (1921), J. P. Mills' *The Lotha Nagas* (1922), *The Ao Nagas* (1926) and *The Rengma Nagas* (1937), amongst others. These ethnographic monographs were instrumental in classifying the various tribes, placing them within the category of the Mongoloid racial type. The research demonstrated a comparative method and argued for diffusionism, which explained how particular cultural traits came through diffusion because of migration (Lotha 2007: 32). The comparative method was a way to find out the similarities and differences between different tribes in the Northeast and trace their links to other tribes of the Indo-Chinese family, say in Indonesia or the South Pacific area. Trained anthropologists were few in the region. A notable exception was Christopher von Fürer-Haimendorf who conducted fieldwork and used functionalist theory (1969).[1] These ethnographic works created a sense of difference between the categories of caste and tribe, as has often been pointed out by scholars (Nongbri 2006). Thus, tribes were seen in isolation from the so-called castes living in the plains of colonial Assam and this also set up a hierarchy between the categories of caste and tribe. Instrumental in setting up this hierarchy was, of course, colonial anthropological discourse.

In this regard a foundational historical text on Assam, *A History of Assam* (1906) written by Edward Gait, is very significant as he introduced modern historical writing in colonial Assam. I discuss this text in detail elsewhere,[2] but here in the interest of brevity, I will merely touch upon the major implications of reading Gait's text in the context of the present discussion, i.e., in terms of the ways in which knowledge about colonial Assam and (postcolonial) Northeast is constituted. Gait attempted to preserve the royal chronicles or *Buranji*s of the Ahom kingdom, and used them as a source to write history. He thus introduced modern methods of historical research in the region.

An important aspect of Gait's contribution to historical writing was his emphasis on ethnography. He was the Director of Ethnography and Census Commissioner in Assam in the last decade of the nineteenth century. He wrote the Census Report of Assam for the census of 1891 and was the Census Commissioner for the 1911 Census of Eastern India. He was also a collaborator of Herbert Risley, the Census Commissioner for the 1901 Census of India, who introduced ethnological surveys in India in the late nineteenth century. Thus, Gait's text is a good example of the interaction between historical and anthropological discourse in the Northeast, which continues in the contemporary period.

Gait's text enables the use of empirical anthropology as a lens to analyse India's Northeast. The consequences of this colonial empiricist identity formation in postcolonial India continue to shape the region's sense of identity and its difference from the Indian nation-state. Especially in Assam, the question of history is foregrounded in the discourses of the sovereignty movements, in part because colonial administrators like Gait argued that Assam was unique because it had a historical sense—evidenced in the availability of the royal chronicles of the Ahom Kingdom. Early nationalist historians in Assam welcomed Gait's work. Gait's text was particularly important to dispel negative representations of Assam by intellectuals in the neighbouring region of Bengal.

I position *A History of Assam* within the discourse of Orientalism produced about India—Indology. Gait made great efforts to establish himself as a scholar of Indology by publishing works on Assamese history in the *Journal of Asiatic Society of Bengal* (JASB), beginning in the late nineteenth century, thereby establishing himself as the preeminent official historian of the region. Gait's text provides an illustration of how colonial 'Assam' is reproduced as an exception within the context of Indological discourse. As the Northeastern part of the British Empire, Assam (especially the hill areas) was one of the last regions to come under British control in the Indian subcontinent. By the time of Assam's annexation to the British Empire, Orientalist scholars had already established a concrete discourse on India. In Gait's text there is a temporal distancing of Assam from this discourse on India. Given that the classificatory schemes under which Indology had organised India were already in place by the time Gait's text was written, his task in this book became one of comparing Assam to India within Indology's classificatory schemes. He makes two kinds of comparisons: an absolute one, of comparing Assam as a whole to India; and the second, a relative one, of comparing the differences of categories within Assam, again with India as the yardstick (Bora 2011). What emerged were both similarities and differences with India. The differences were given a temporal sense—where differences existed it was assumed that the current state of the tribes were a reflection of an earlier stage in the Indian evolution, that is, the difference of these tribes from contemporary India was considered a difference in stages of historical time. This temporal distance is also spatialised as a physical distance from India where the tribes are understood as immigrants who need more time to tightly fit into the classificatory schemes that define India (ibid.).

Thus, through a reading of Gait's text I show how colonial Assam emerges as the 'Mongolian other' to and as an immigrant in India. I show how Indological discourse enables the contemporary binary of India/Northeast[3] and how Gait's text tries to both place colonial Assam within this Indological categorisation as well as mark it as different. I also argue that the equating of *Buranjis* to history marks an epistemic violence and shows how Gait's work marks the beginning of empirical anthropology and historical discourse in knowing the Northeast. I also show how hierarchies of language and ethnicity place the different ethnic groups in opposition to each other and as existing in a perpetual state of conflict. Suffice it to say here that Gait's text marked a dominant way in which the region and its people were studied and understood: India and colonial Assam as binary opposites, which established the superiority of the categories of India such as religion, caste and language. Thus, while India was understood as caste-based, predominantly Hindu, speaking languages belonging to the Indo-Aryan and Dravidian language families, colonial Assam was understood as non-Hindu, tribal and belonging to the Mongolian race. This also set up a hierarchy within colonial Assam where Hindus, the plains people, speakers of Indo-Aryan languages, were considered to be superior to the hill tribes. In other words, the former group was considered nearer to the category of India—culturally and politically.

While Gait established colonial Assam as one of the few places which had a historical sense in India, the tribes were predominantly understood and studied through the framework of ethnography and anthropology, as seen in the colonial initiative to produce ethnographies on these tribes written by scholar-administrators, as mentioned above. Also, as Abraham Lotha has argued in the context of ethnography of the Nagas, this knowledge produced by the colonial administrators was a form of political domination that enabled the colonial state to know more about the Nagas than the Nagas themselves, by producing definitive knowledge about Naga culture and their way of life (Lotha 2007). This knowledge also enabled the colonial state to claim a protectionist stand towards the tribes insisting on shielding them from the rapid changes of civilisation, which according to them meant that the hills be administratively separated from the plains districts. This ethnographic work also functioned as a way of writing about people 'who do not have history', whose cultures are defined by orality and not by texts (Khongreiwo 2009; Zou 2005). Thus, ethnography became the predominant framework as opposed to studying history through textual sources, and the lack of a primary textual source for writing history led to the tribes being termed as primitive and an 'other' that was to be studied from an anthropological perspective. A form of 'salvage ethnography' thus took hold where anthropologists were bent on documenting the society and culture of the tribes before the communities were fundamentally transformed by social change (Zou 2005). The tribes of the Northeast were thereby kept in an anachronistic time and space (McClintock 1995), as primitive people who were yet to join the contemporary time of the colonial state and later the modern Indian nation. In contrast, the people living in the plains were understood to have history, as argued above through Gait's text, and the right characteristics to qualify as modern subjects. The rest of the chapter will consider how postcolonial social sciences have understood and studied the Northeast and the disciplinary and institutional trajectories within which it has been done.

POSTCOLONIAL SOCIAL SCIENCES AND THE NORTHEAST

In academic work, ways of understanding the Northeast in the postcolonial period revolved around the definition of the category 'tribe'. In the context of Northeast, two ideas about how to incorporate tribes within the nation developed in the postcolonial period, which can be demonstrated by the debate between G. S. Ghurye and Verrier Elwin. Ghurye, who taught in Bombay University and headed the Department of Sociology there, is considered the founder of sociology in India. Ghurye argued for an assimilationist position regarding the tribes, who he understood to be backward Hindus (1943). This is the argument he had initially made about tribes in mainland India, or what he calls 'hither' India, but later he made similar arguments about the assimilation of tribes in the Northeast as well. Ghurye made this argument despite the fact that he considered tribes in the Northeast to be culturally different from tribes in the rest of the country and the Hindu community. As regards tribes in the Northeast, he was concerned about what he called fissiparous and anti-national tendencies that could break up Bharat or India. To articulate his nationalist credentials he calls India 'Bharat' and Northeast India as 'Northeast Bharat'. Of particular importance to him in terms of the tribes in the Northeast was the issue of national security, as demonstrated in the Indo-Chinese War of 1962 in which the Indian army was routed. The war brought renewed attention of scholars and administrators on NEFA (North-East Frontier Agency) and the rest of the Northeast. Until then Verrier Elwin's recommendation in NEFA was accepted and his policy of isolation and incremental development of the tribes so that they were not overwhelmed by social and economic change was implemented. These two positions came to be understood as the assimilation vs. isolation debate. What is problematic about Ghurye's position is that he merely reiterates colonial discourse in his understanding of the Northeastern tribes and this was also the case with the way he understood India, that is, in terms of colonial knowledge production which he merely Indianised. Thus, he gives undue attention to the practice of headhunting prevalent among several Northeastern tribes to justify his fear of anti-national sentiments in the region, such as supporting hostile neighbouring nations as he accused the 'Mongolian' tribes of having racial affinities across the border (Ghurye 1980; Zou 2005).

This formed the basis of Ghurye's argument about the cultural difference of the Northeastern tribes from the rest of India. What we see with Ghurye is the perpetuation of Orientalist perspectives that organised sociology in postcolonial India. As Sujata Patel argues, 'colonial processes and its institutions together with "derivative" nationalist ideas organised the growth of the disciplines of anthropology/sociology in India' (Patel 2013: 107). While Ghurye was critical of these Orientalist constructions of India, he reframed the same Orientalist ideas within an understanding of Indian culture, which was equally problematic as it associated Indian culture and civilisation with a Hinduness. His work was thus a combination of Indology and anthropology (Upadhya 2002). The brand of sociology advocated by Ghurye defined the study of sociology in Indological and empirical terms, or in other words, as a study of 'traditional' India, of castes, tribes and races but reframed in the context of the new nation (Savur 2011).

In Euro-American academia, sociology was conceived as a study of modern industrial society (of the Self) and anthropology as a study of primitive societies (of the Other). However, in the case of former colonies like India, the academic disciplines of sociology and anthropology were intertwined from the beginning (Srinivas 1972; Srinivas and Panini 1973). Recent scholarship in India has highlighted the artificiality of the division between the two disciplines in the Indian context (Uberoi et al. 2007: 7). Sujata Patel in a recent book argues that even though Indian scholarship has been critical of the link between colonialism and its 'hand maiden' anthropology in general, there hasn't been enough critical reflection on the link in the Indian context (Asad 1979; Patel 2011: xv; Srinivas and Panini 1973). As Carol Upadhya writes,

> to understand the trajectory of post-colonial social thought it is not sufficient just to point to the reproduction of colonial discourses. Rather, what is required is a comprehensive mapping of the reconstitution of the modern social science disciplines as they emerged in the context of wider social, political, and economic processes, such as the nationalist movement and the Nehruvian paradigm of economic development. (Upadhya 2002: 28)

This becomes particularly important in the context of the Northeast, where the discipline of anthropology and anthropological framing takes centre stage in understanding 'tribes' within an Indian nationalist framework.

In the Indian context the critique of colonialism or the colonial state was replaced by an affirmation of the Indian nation-state. In sociological literature this trend of prioritising the nation, nation-state and nationalism within sociological theories while claiming to speak a universal language has been termed methodological nationalism (Beck 2007). In the Indian context this can be understood as a form of epistemological nationalism (Patel 2011).[4] Patel argues that 'territorialization' and 'naturalisation'[5] became interlinked and formed the dominant strain of sociology in India (Patel 2011). This is because the discipline was closely associated with the official nationalist discourse on nation, nation-state and modernity and saw its role as tied to helping the nation-state in achieving its goal of planned development (Srinivas and Panini 1973).

Thus, while methodological nationalism led to the growth of Eurocentrism in the Euro-American world, the same methodological nationalism also plagued India. This is particularly pertinent in the context of writing from the margins of the nation, be it Dalit studies or studies on the Northeast. As Visweswaran notes, two strains of nationalist sociology which failed to take account of caste are one with a focus on the Hindu Sanskritic civilisational paradigm and the other a secular sociology comprising Marxist and other classically trained sociologists who in arguing against the Indological paradigm have advocated the category of class as a category of sociological analysis (Visweswaran 2010: 145). In recent decades Dalit sociology has emerged as a challenge to this nationalist sociology, which cannot adequately explain caste oppression (Guru 1999; Selvan 1999). Scholars have called for Dalitisation to move away from the consequences of Brahmanic Hindu civilisational paradigms and Sanskritisation.[6] However, critique of the ways in which the Northeast is studied is scant and it has to do with the fact that the Northeast is not understood as an epistemic category (Bora 2011). This also has to do with the dearth of critical scholarship on the epistemic and political category of the 'tribe'. The colonial distinction between caste and tribe had framed the two in a hierarchy where tribes were understood to be separate from the Hindu Sanskritic tradition. Hence, tribes have been understood as backward Hindus in need of assimilation into the caste system, a position espoused by

Ghurye, and thus thought of as castes in the making (Nongbri 2006; Xaxa 1999).

However, even though postcolonial scholarship has since then taken a step away from the assimilationist perspective of Ghurye, it continued to be enmeshed within the nationalist perspective of integration. In this regard consider the critique of Elwin by Srinivas and Panini. They have argued that Indian nationalists were critical of anthropology as they associated it with the colonial policy of 'divide and rule' and segregation of the tribes. Thus, even though they are appreciative of Elwin's ethnographic work on various tribes, they are critical of his role as adviser of tribal affairs to the Indian government. According to them,

> He [Elwin] wanted the tribes to be protected from the more advanced sections of the populace and their art, song, dance, clothing etc., to be 'preserved'. One could understand the need for protecting the tribals from exploitation by traders, contractors and money lenders but any policy other than their integration with all other sections of the population is unfair to tribals and unrealistic considering the forces released since Independence. (Srinivas and Panini 1973: 193)

They are of the opinion that Ghurye's position on tribes did something to rehabilitate anthropology in the eyes of the nationalist through his opposition to the thesis of Elwin (Srinivas and Panini 1973: 195). But unlike Ghurye's assimilationist position, they advocated an integrationist perspective.

The framework of integration has historically dominated studies of the Northeast in the postcolonial period, in terms of what is understood as 'Tribal Studies'. To illustrate this point let me briefly discuss a few aspects from the book *Tribal Situation in India* (1972) as an example of the concern of social scientists, anthropologists, sociologists, political scientists and social workers about the tribal situation in India. A majority of the articles in this book focuses on the tribes in the Northeast. The seminar[7] on which the book is based was organised with the objective to understand the 'tribal situation' after the Indo-Chinese War

(Ray 1972). What was brought to the fore with the Indo-Chinese War was the need to understand the border regions for the sake of national security and national development. In the introductory address, Ray sets the tone for the seminar through an attempt to go beyond the colonial understanding of tribes by arguing that the term 'tribe' refers to *janas* who are similar to the *jatis*. What distinguishes the former from the latter is the socio-economic system to which the latter, jatis, belong. Thus, for him, jati does not just refer to caste or a socio-religious system. The historical process of assimilating janas into jatis is no longer possible as this mode of production has been taken over by a new mode in the post-Independence period. Instead, he argues for an assimilation of the so-called tribal peoples into the mainstream Indian life. For him the four things that constitute mainstream India are '… the sovereign, independent territorial unity of India, democracy, secularism and planned economy of which industrialisation is the means and socialism is the goal' (ibid.: 24). As S. C. Dubey says in his inaugural address, 'the tribes have to find for themselves a place in Indian society consistent with their conception of honour, but this must be done without detriment to the integrity or strength of India as a nation' (Dubey 1972: 33). This inability of secular nationalist sociologists to take tribality or caste into account is very much in accordance with the methodological or nationalist epistemology as mentioned earlier.

One person who takes a different stand is the anthropologist B. K. Roy Burman who argues for an integrated area approach with regards to the hill tribes of the Northeast, especially NEFA. His approach includes geopolitical, socio-cultural, political-administrative and economic perspectives. He argues that merely focusing on economic development will not be enough. He says,

> the dominant focus in dealing with the tribals of the region seems to be that they are primitive people. But this is not right. The primitive complex of the tribal communities of the country as a whole, and of North East India in particular, is rapidly giving place to the minority complex. While at the beginning of the

> 1950s, a welfare approach was the appropriate one, now welfare approach should only play a subsidiary role to the integrated political, economic and social approach. (Roy Burman 1972: 97)

As I will go on to show in the next section, this welfare imperative has now changed to a development approach.

DISCIPLINING THE NORTHEAST

Unlike other parts of India where some sociology and anthropology departments emerged in the pre-Independence period (Bombay, Calcutta and Lucknow), in the Northeast the first Department of Sociology came up in Dibrugarh University, Assam in the mid-1960s. Until then, anthropology was taught at Gauhati University, Assam, which was set up in 1948. Till Independence, Calcutta University was the nearest centre of higher learning for the region, which had a Department of Anthropology. Unlike elsewhere in the country, these departments of sociology and anthropology mainly focused on Northeast India. University of Delhi's Departments of Sociology (Delhi School of Economics) and Anthropology and Ranchi University however are two exceptions (Kumar 1999). The Department of Sociology of Delhi University had set up a special programme called the North East Hill Area Programme on the recommendation of the University Grants Commission (UGC) (Kumar 1999; Srinivas 1972). Students from the Northeast were admitted to this programme and trained at the Postgraduate and Doctoral levels in Sociology (Kumar 1999). The Department of Anthropology of University of Delhi too paid special attention to the training of students from the Northeast (Kumar 1999). It would seem that given the limitations of nationalist sociology mentioned above in terms of its Hindu civilisational approach (that is, an Indological approach) and the secular sociologists' inability to move beyond the paradigm of abstract citizenship, the only way the Northeast could be studied was as an area studies programme. It is interesting to note here that area studies programmes such as those in the US would comprise mostly American scholars studying other societies and nation-states important for national security issues (the Middle East, South Asia, etc.).[8] In this context, it is not surprising then that Delhi University's Sociology department conceived of an Area Studies Programme focusing on the Northeast, since after all it is a region vital for India's national security surrounded by several foreign countries, some even hostile to India and inhabited by Mongolian tribes, in stark contrast with the population of Aryan and Dravidian India (Bora 2011). And similar to the Orientalist and Eurocentric conceptions of the Middle East or the Orient, which were framed by a directional reference to Europe as the centre, the Northeast has been termed the Northeast from an older Indological perspective, a perspective shared by the centre of power in India, that is, New Delhi.

In the 1970s efforts were made to expand access to higher education in the Northeast. In the first central university of the region, the North-Eastern Hill University (NEHU), established in 1973 in Shillong, Meghalaya, a combined department of Sociology and Anthropology was set up in 1976.[9] Around the same time the ICSSR set up the North-Eastern Regional Centre of ICSSR in Shillong, which gave a fillip to research on the Northeast in the 1970s. This happened in response to one of the main complaints in the 1969 seminar at Indian Institute of Advanced Study, Shimla (see note 7), where several scholars argued that knowledge produced on the Northeast was outdated by almost fifty years and one could not rely on old colonial texts of ethnography. Now instead of the colonial state requiring ethnographic information to govern the Northeast, the postcolonial Indian state needed this knowledge to govern the Northeastern subjects as citizens. New knowledge was required by the new independent Indian state about the society and culture of the Northeast so that it could be taken on the path of planned development and social change. As noted earlier, the seminar was mainly framed as a response to the Indo-China War and the vulnerability that it exposed India to in its border regions. Sanjib Baruah argues that the Indian state's response to this vulnerability was to nationalise space in Arunachal Pradesh (formerly NEFA) through the construction of various kinds of infrastructure and setting up of a strong governmental body that could establish the physical presence of the Indian state and in the process develop the region (Baruah 2005). Thus, development discourse in the region has been used to nationalise space. The nationalist discourse hoped that an 'emotional integration'[10] would come about from this process of state-induced development and integration. Efforts to develop the region have continued to this day. Consider the newly constructed bridge on the Brahmaputra connecting Assam and Arunachal Pradesh, which was inaugurated in June 2017. The Act East Policy (formerly Look East Policy) has a similar framework of politically integrating Northeast India with the rest of India while economically opening up the region to Southeast Asia.[11]

Since higher education in India in the period immediately after Independence was supported by the enormous rise in universities around the country, university departments of the social sciences closely worked with the state of India in its path towards planned development. However, there were differences between central and state universities, with the former being more 'national' in character and thus better funded with more resources, while the state universities were not as well-funded and catered to regional agendas. Besides NEHU, which was the first central university in the Northeast, the region now has other central universities, most of which have come up in the last two decades.[12] The universities are governed by governmental institutions such as the UGC which standardise the organisation, curriculum and other institutional aspects of the different universities in the country. The Council of Social Science Research also plays an important role in nurturing research in social sciences.[13] It would be beyond the scope of this chapter to discuss the institutional history of these various university departments in the region. But an examination is necessary to understand how the field of studies on the Northeast may develop in the future.[14] One has to wait and see whether nationalist sociology and anthropology are transformed in the region and how.

In conclusion, one can argue that the Indian nationalist discourse construes an image of the Northeast as a region that is always lagging behind India both in history and in modernity. This idea of a lagging Northeast is maintained also by the discourses of nationalist counter-insurgency and social sciences disciplines such as history and anthropology, which often analyse the Northeast as an other from the perspective of the Indian self. While colonial sociology identifies caste as the basis of predominant social structure of India, the Northeast is framed by the category of tribe. Thus the discipline of anthropology frames the region as culturally different from India, which in the postcolonial period emerges as both cultural and political difference.

The realisation that the dominant frames within which the Northeast has been analysed are problematic has led to the attempt to move beyond the most persistent ways of seeing the Northeast—i.e., through the national lens—and understand the violence of colonial cartography (Zou and Kumar 2011), cross-border or translational links between the Northeast and Southeast Asia, and an attempt to see the hills of the Northeast as part of a larger 'non-state space' as articulated by James Scott (2009) based on the concept of Zomia[15] first developed by Willem van Schendel (2002). The introduction to a recently edited book by Saikia and Baishya (2017) gives a good contemporary summary of the new literature emerging on the Northeast.

This production of critical knowledge on the Northeast has also kept pace with new institutional formations such as the interdisciplinary North East India Studies Programme at the Jawaharlal Nehru University (JNU) and studies on the Northeast have seen an upward trend. At the moment in Delhi, JNU and Jamia Millia Islamia University have two such centres with different goals and objectives in terms of teaching, research, pedagogy and engagement with public policy. The Department of Sociology in Delhi University is in the process of setting up a North East India Studies Programme.[16] While it is too early to evaluate these formations given their recent origins, one notices that the field of Northeast studies is conceived of in two ways—either from a critical perspective or as a study of just another region of India that has to be analysed in order to better integrate it into the nation. There is a tussle between these two imaginations and this has to do with the way the idea of the Northeast has been historically conceived as a binary of the nation-state, as articulated through this chapter. I would argue that unless we form a postnational[17] perspective, it would be impossible to truly engage with the Northeast. Social sciences and other disciplines in the post-colony are very enmeshed in the ideas of the nation, so much so that any critique of these ideas is seen as a challenge to the sovereignty of the nation-state. At the same time, there cannot be an easy position that transcends the nation (Chatterjee 1998). To reframe a debate in Indian sociology on the question whether it is a sociology of India or a sociology for India, the question for Northeast studies is whether it is a study of Northeast India or a study for the Northeast, a debate which highlights both challenges and linkages, and questions of both identity and differences, without losing sight of a relational politics.

NOTES

1. Unlike evolutionism and diffusionism, functionalist theory, popularised by the anthropologist Bronislaw Malinowski, emphasised the understanding of culture as an integrated whole where different elements had functions necessary for the maintenance of society. Methodologically, empiricism and fieldwork were important components of this anthropological approach, popularised later as 'participant observation'.

2. Discussed in detail in Bora 2011. This chapter refers to the second edition of this book published in 1926. The first edition was published in 1906.

3. To use the term 'Northeast' is not to homogenise differences within the Northeast. Nor is it to condone its use, or suggest it as the appropriate

category of enquiry. Rather, it is to acknowledge that the term has an intellectual and political history marked by the projects of colonialism and nationalism, which limits and defines the contemporary politics of the region (Bora 2011, 2014).

4. Sujata Patel wonders if it would be more appropriate to call methodological nationalism in the Indian context epistemological nationalism and leaves it as a question (Patel 2011: xxxv, fn 17). I would like to accept her suggestion that this is an epistemological nationalism.

5. Wimmer and Schiller (2002), building on Beck (2007), divide methodological nationalism into three strands: first, being blind to the importance of nation and nationalism in the framing of a universal sociology; second, naturalisation—taking for granted the official discourses; third, territorialisation—limiting sociology within the boundaries of the nation-state.

6. According to M. N. Srinivas, Sanskritisation refers to the process in which the low caste or tribe take on the customs and practices of the higher castes.

7. The Indian Institute of Advanced Studies, the Department of Sociology and the Centre of Advanced Study in Sociology of Delhi University organised this seminar in 1969 in Shimla.

8. This does not mean that scholars from these regions did not study in these Area Studies Programmes.

9. Later this changed to the Department of Cultural Anthropology in 1981, which was again renamed as the Department of Anthropology in 1983. The older formation became the Department of Sociology. A detailed study of this institutional history is beyond the scope of this chapter.

10. According to Srinivas and Sanwal (1972: 120),

> Emotional integration involves the acceptance of a common and consistent set of values, norms and attitudes by most, if not all the sections, of a country's population. The intensity of the integration depends on the extent of institutional areas in regard to which value consensus exists. Emotional integration provides the only stable condition for the emergence of healthy and lasting nationhood.

11. See Ramesh (2005).

12. Three of these were set up in 1994 (Assam, Tezpur and Nagaland Universities), while the other four were set up in the 2000s: Mizoram (2000), Manipur (2005), Rajiv Gandhi (2007) [this was formerly known as Arunachal University, set up in 1985, and converted to a central university

in 2007] and Tripura Universities (2007). In addition, Sikkim which has been recently added to the Northeastern category got its central university, Sikkim University in 2007. See www.mhrd.gov.in.

13. For instance, the Northeast wing of the ICSSR (Indian Council of Social Science Research - North-Eastern Regional Centre (ICSSR-NERC) commissioned the *Survey of Research in Sociology and Social Anthropology in Northeast India* edited by Nikhlesh Kumar (1999).

14. For a brief history, see *A Short History of Social-Cultural Anthropology in North-East India* (Ali 2012).

15. Zomia refers to the uplands in Southeast Asia that, historically, could not be incorporated within structures of the state. Here, it refers to the hill areas of Southeast Asia which includes India's Northeast.

16. The Hill Area Programme of the Department has since become defunct.

17. '… the postnational can be instantiated only by suspending the idea of the nation as a prior theoretical–political horizon, and thinking through its impossibility, even while located uncomfortably within its bounds' (De Alwis et al. 2009).

REFERENCES

Ali, A. N. M. Irshad. 2012. 'A Short History of Social-Cultural Anthropology in North-East India'. In Tanka Bahadur Subba (ed.), *North-East India: Handbook of Anthropology*, 302–315. Hyderabad: Orient BlackSwan.

Asad, Talal. 1979. 'Anthropology and the Colonial Encounter'. In Gerrit Huizer and Bruce Mannheim (eds), *The Politics of Anthropology*, 85–94. Berlin, New York: De Gruyter Mouton.

Baruah, Sanjib. 2005. *Durable Disorder: Understanding the Politics of Northeast India*. India: Oxford University Press.

Beck, Ulrich. 2007. 'The Cosmopolitan Condition: Why Methodological Nationalism Fails'. *Theory, Culture & Society* 24(7–8): 286–290.

Bora, Papori. 2010. 'Between the Human, the Citizen and the Tribal: Reading Feminist Politics in India's Northeast.' *International Feminist Journal of Politics* 12(3–4): 341–360.

———. 2011. 'The Nation and its Margins: Reading Gender and the Politics of Sovereignty in India's Northeast'. PhD Dissertation, University of Minnesota.

———. 2014. 'Speech of the Nation and Conversations at the Margins of the Nation-State'. *Interventions: International Journal of Postcolonial Studies* 17(5): 669–685.

Chatterjee, Partha. 1998. 'Beyond the Nation? Or Within?' *Social Text* 56: 57–69.

De Alwis, Malathi, Satish Deshpande, Pradeep Jeganathan, et al. 2009. 'The Postnational Condition'. *Economic and Political Weekly* 44(10).

Dubey, S. C. 1972. 'Inaugural Address'. In K. Suresh Singh (ed.), *Tribal Situation in India*, 28–33. Indian Institute of Advanced Study.

Elwin, Verrier. 1957. *A Philosophy for NEFA*. Gyan Publishing House.

Fabian, Johannes. 1983. *Time and the Other: How Anthropology Makes Its Object*. New York: Columbia University Press.

Fürer-Haimendorf, Christoph von. 1969. *The Konyak Nagas: An Indian Frontier Tribe*. Holt McDougal.

Gait, Edward Albert. 1906. *A History of Assam*. Calcutta: Thacker, Spink & Company.

Ghurye, G.S. 1943. *The Aborigines—'So-called'—And Their Future*. Gokhale Institute of Politics and Economics.

———. 1980. *The Burning Cauldron of North-East India*. Bombay: Popular Prakashan.

Guru, Gopal. 1999. 'The Dalit Movement in Mainstream Sociology'. In S. M. Michael (ed.), *Dalits in Modern India: Vision and Values*, 165–85. New Delhi: Sage/Vistaar.

Khongreiwo, Rammathot. 2009. 'Understanding the Histories of Peoples on the Margins: A Critique of "Northeast India's Durable Disorder"'. *Alternatives* 34(4): 437–454.

Kumar, Nikhlesh. 1999. *Survey of Research in Sociology and Social Anthropology in North East India (1970 90)*. Regency Publications, ICSSR-NERC.

Lotha, Abraham. 2007. *History of Naga Anthropology, 1832–1947*. Dimapur: Chumpo Museum.

Lasuh, W. (ed.), V. K. Nuh (comp.). 2002. *The Naga Chronicle*. Regency Publications, ICSSR-NERC.

Misra, Udayon. 2000. *The Periphery Strikes Back: Challenges to the Nation-State in Assam and Nagaland*. Shimla: Indian Institute of Advanced Study.

McClintock, Anne. 1995. *Imperial Leather: Race, Gender, and Sexuality in the Colonial Contest*. New York and Oxon.: Routledge.

Nongbri, Tiplut. 2006. 'Tribe, Caste and The Indigenous Challenge in India'. In Bengt G. Karlsson and Tanka B. Subba (eds), *Indigeneity in India.*, 75–96. London: Kegan Paul.

Patel, Sujata. 2011. 'Introduction: Ruminating on Sociological Traditions in India'. In *Doing Sociology in India,* xi–xxxviii. New Delhi: Oxford University Press.

_____. 2013. 'Orientalist-Eurocentric Framing of Sociology in India: A Discussion on Three Twentieth-Century Sociologists.' In *Decentering Social Theory: Political Power and Social Theory* 25: 105–128. Emerald.

Ramesh, Jairam. 2005. 'Northeast India in a New Asia'. *Seminar* June 550.

Ray, Niharranjan. 1972. 'Introductory Address'. In K. Suresh Singh (ed.), *Tribal Situation in India*, 3–25. Indian Institute of Advanced Study.

Roy Burman, B. K. 1972. 'Integrated Area Approach to the Problems of the Hill Tribes of the North-East India'. In K. Suresh Singh (ed.), *Tribal Situation in India*, 39–50. Indian Institute of Advanced Study.

Saikia, Y., and A. Baishya (eds). 2017. *Northeast India: A Place of Relations.* Cambridge University Press.

Savur, Manorama. 2011. 'Sociology: The Genealogy of the Discipline in Bombay'. In Sujata Patel (ed.), *Doing Sociology in India: Genealogies, Locations, Practices*, 3–28. India: Oxford University Press.

Schendel, Willem van. 2002. 'Geographies of Knowing, Geographies of Ignorance: Jumping Scale in Southeast Asia'. *Environment and Planning D: Society and Space* 20(6): 647–668.

Scott, James C. 2009. *The Art of Not being Governed: An Anarchist History of Upland Southeast Asia.* Yale University Press.

Selvan, S. 1999. 'Sociology of India and Hinduism: Towards a Method'. In S.M. Michael (ed.), *Dalits in Modern India: Vision and Values*, 165–85. New Delhi: Sage Publications.

Sharma, Jayeeta. 2011. *Empire's Garden: Assam and the Making of India.* Duke University Press.

Srinivas, M. N. 1972. 'Chairman's Address'. In K. Suresh Singh (ed.), *Tribal Situation in India*, 25–27. Indian Institute of Advanced Study.

Srinivas, M. N., and M. N. Panini. 1973. 'The Development of Sociology and Social Anthropology in India'. *Sociological Bulletin 22*(2): 179–215.

Srinivas, M. N., and R. D. Sanwal. 1972. 'Some Aspects of Political Development in the Northeastern Hill Areas of India'. In K. Suresh Singh (ed.), *Tribal Situation in India*, 117–124. Indian Institute of Advanced Study.

Uberoi, Patricia, Nandini Sundar and Satish Deshpande. 2007. 'Introduction: The Professionalization of Indian Anthropology and Sociology'. In Patricia Uberoi, N. Sundar and S. Deshpande (eds), *Anthropology in the East: Founders of Indian Sociology and Anthropology.* New Delhi: Permanent Black.

Upadhya, Carol. 2002. 'The Hindu Nationalist Sociology of GS Ghurye'. *Sociological Bulletin* 51(1): 27–56.

Visweswaran, Kamala. 2010. *Un/common Cultures: Racism and the Rearticulation of Cultural Difference.* Duke University Press.

Wimmer, Andreas, and Nina Glick Schiller. 2002. 'Methodological Nationalism and Beyond: Nation-State Building, Migration and the Social Sciences'. *Global Networks* 2(4): 301–334.

Xaxa, Virginius. 1999. 'Transformation of Tribes in India: Terms of Discourse'. *Economic and Political Weekly* 34(4): 1519–1524.

Zou, David Vumlallian. 2005. 'Raiding the Dreaded Past: Representations of Headhunting and Human Sacrifice in North–East India'. *Contributions to Indian Sociology* 39(1): 75–105.

Zou, David Vumlallian, and M. Satish Kumar. 2011. 'Mapping a Colonial Borderland: Objectifying the Geo-body of India's Northeast'. *The Journal of Asian Studies* 70(1): 141–170.

II

Colonialism and Northeast India

3

Colonialism and History Writing

The Mizo Experience*

Malsawmdawngliana

A recurrent theme in history has always been how colonial rule affected the process of textualisation of oral sources. Orality has always been perceived as a poor method in the construction of history. In the West, the discipline of history considers people without '*logos*' as people without history. This logocentric vision of human history led to the sixteenth-century bloodthirsty Renaissance debate at Salamanca in Spain, after which millions were decimated in the Spanish Americas as they were considered people with no logos, and therefore not humans as the West understood the term (Mukherjee 2003). Nineteenth-century Northeast India had also witnessed a similar situation in which the people without a text were considered 'savage', perfect subjects for the project of the evangelising mission. Existence of a state and text were considered prerequisites for writing history.

The central focus of this chapter is twofold: one, to locate the sources of Mizo history in the context of historiography, beginning from the colonial period that marked the Mizos' entry in recorded history and two, to examine the limitations of the use of these sources. This chapter will study how these limitations are reflected in historical scholarship with special reference to the construction of the history of the region in the pre-colonial period. We will

*An earlier version of this essay was published as 'Sources of Writing Mizo History and their Limitations' in Rila Mukherjee and M. N. Rajesh (eds), *Locality, History, Memory: The Making of the Citizen in South Asia* (2009) by Cambridge Scholars Publishing, Newcastle, UK.

further explore historiography in the postcolonial period during which Mizo society rapidly transformed from a pre-literate society to one with the second-highest literacy rate in India. We will be looking at the hidden agenda in the 'transcreation' of 'orality' into 'textuality' and how these projects of textualisation have been carried forward by the local writers who have internalised these Western ideas of historiography in their writings. These projects point not to a stage of 'advance' but to a stage where the soft power of colonialism penetrated via texts and by extension through governmentality.

PROTECTING THE COLONIAL VASSALS

Initially, the British Indian government did not give much importance to the hill tribes even after the occupation of Cachar in 1832 (Malsawmdawngliana and Rohmingmawii 2016: 92), especially in the Lushai hills, as they were of the opinion that those territories were not worth penetrating as no wealth was to be found there. However, the frequent raids upon the plains territories by the Mizos became a matter of concern for the British who now felt a need to protect their economic vassals: the tea estate owners who earned huge profits in the Cachar and Sylhet borders. There are conflicting views on the cause of these raids. Some scholars believed that the raids conducted by the Mizos were connected with headhunting, while others were of the opinion that it was due to the lust for wealth and procurement of slaves, an interest they shared with the colonial power (Zochungnunga 2004: 58). There are no reports of headhunting during the pre-colonial period. It was a matter of importance to the government officials to keep records of their surroundings especially when there were frequent raids on areas under their jurisdictions. These officials' reports and documents carry information about the land and the people which became an important source of historical records. One such example is Alexander Mackenzie's book *The North-East Frontier of India*. These official reports became instrumental in changing the attitude of the government towards the hill people. Finally, to punish the Mizos for their repeated raids and also to set an example for the other hill tribes so that they dare not encroach upon British land, a series of expeditions were conducted. As a result of these expeditions, the Lushai Hills came under the British Empire. In early historical records, Mizo society is seen as an example of a 'different' society, with the emphasis on difference as 'ungovernable'.

FENCING WITH RECORDS

The British had some knowledge about the Lushai Hills even before they occupied the land and this information was determined by their nature of contact with the Mizos.

> The inhabitants (of the Lushai Hills) were regarded by the few Europeans then residing in Bengal as the fieriest and most barbarous of all the Hill tribes within the province, notorious for their head-hunting expeditions to the neighbouring plains. The object of these raids was to obtain skulls with which to adorn the graves of their ancestors. (Morris 1990: 77, cited in Remruatkimi 2015)

The initial task of the officials was to familiarise themselves with the rugged terrain, the land and the people. This was done for ease of administration. As a result, a large number of works has been published about the Mizos, the earliest of which were done by military and administrative officers who had some involvement in the annexation and administration of the area by the British government. The earliest historical and anthropological account on the Mizos can be seen in the three books written by Thomas Herbert Lewin: *The Hill Tracts of Chittagong and The Dwellers Therein* (1869), *Wild Races of the South-Eastern India* (1870), and *A Fly on the Wheel: Or, How I Helped to Govern India* (1885).

Another work on this period is C. A. Soppitt's *A Short Account of the Kuki-Lushai Tribes on the North-East Frontier with an Outline Grammar of the Rangkhol-Lushai Language and A Comparison of Lushai with Other Dialects* (1893). The officers of the British Army too, like other British administrators, wrote accounts of their military operations in the Chin-Lushai Hills that were then published as books. Some other notable books of this period are R. G. Woodthorpe's *The Lushai Expedition, 1871–72* (1873), A. S. Reid's *Chin-Lushai Land: Including a Description of the Various Expeditions into the Chin-Lushai Hills and the Final Annexation of the Country, with Maps and Illustrations* (1893), and L. W. Shakespear's *History of the Assam Rifles* (1929).

Besides all these useful records, the establishment of the Tribal Research Institute (under Art and Culture Department) sponsored by the Government of Mizoram has brought out many useful sources some of which are confidential reports of the government. One of these, *Foreign Department Report on Chin Lushai Hills, September 1892*,[1] describes the intense efforts made by the British government to bring the Chin Hills of Burma and the North and South Lushai Hills districts of India into a single administrative unit. The follow-up efforts resulted in the publication of two important books. The first of these was Bertram S. Carey and H. N. Tuck's *The Chin Hills: A History of the People, Our Dealings with Them, Their Customs and Manners, and a Gazetteer of Their Country, Vol. 1* (1896, reprinted in 1976) and the other is John Shakespear's *The Lushei Kuki Clans, Parts I and II* (1912). The original purpose of these books was to further the proposed agenda of combination of the three districts into one. Although the proposal was not accepted in the end, these books nevertheless made an important contribution to our understanding of the essential unity of the people concerned. To these should be added William Shaw's *Notes on the Thadou Kukis* (1929) and G. A. Grierson's monumental work, *Linguistic Survey of India, III, Part 3* (1904), both of which arrive at the same conclusion from different perspectives. These books based on a certain degree of anthropological analysis show us the nature of Mizo society and culture when the area was beginning to come under alien administration. Also providing an outsider's glimpse of the Mizo culture is N. E. Parry's book *A Monograph on Lushai Customs and Ceremonies* (1928).

The first sources of Mizo history writing were limited to the accounts of the British officials and Christian missionaries who had a superficial understanding of the society. As a result they have uprooted many aspects of Mizo society and replaced them with colonial categories. Their writings were in the same vein as that of anthropologists who considered the model of Western society as the measuring scale of advancement. There is no denying the fact that these writings rendered valuable information about the land and the people, even though their aim was to maintain records for convenient and effective administration by familiarising themselves with the customs and traditions of their colonial subjects. Moreover, they served to justify British rule over the hill tribes. Their method of writing gradually affected the process of history writing in India's Northeast. Owing to the highly politicised nature of history, society has been studied mostly under the rubric of political history. This method of ethnographic study is one of the vestiges of colonialism.

THE COMING OF ZOSAP MISSIONARIES

During the initial interactions between the British and the hill people, the Mizo were hostile and conducted frequent raids, clouding the atmosphere of the hills with violent and aggressive counter-military operations. The missionaries were not allowed to enter the hills till 1893. When the tense situation subsided, permission was granted to the two missionaries who had waited more than two years to work in the hills. They were allowed access on the condition that they would not interfere in the governmental affairs of the region. The two Christian missionaries were F. W. Savidge and J. H. Lorrain, both members of the Highgate Road Baptist Church in London. They were sent to Lushai Hills in 1894 by the Arthington Aborigines Mission (commonly known as Arthington Mission) (FMPCW: 25). Lorrain and Savidge introduced education among the Mizo in 1894 mainly to facilitate the propagation of Christianity amongst them.

INTRODUCTION OF AN ALPHABET

Before the advent of these pioneer missionaries, two Mizo chiefs, Suaka and Thangphunga, tried learning the Bengali alphabet through their acquaintance with military personnel but they found it very difficult. The missionaries asked them to learn the English alphabet. The script with Roman characters was thus introduced and this was the stepping stone for the existence of literature among the Mizo. At first the Mizos were taught the alphabet, reading, and writing. After a while a good number of adults as well as children began attending the school. They would return home after a month or two having learnt to read a little. The administrative report on the Lushai Hills also highlighted the commendable work done by Lorrain and Savidge.

TRANSLATION AS A MEANS OF EVANGELISATION

In addition to visiting and preaching the gospel in the nearby villages as part of their evangelising mission, the two missionaries began to write short books in Mizo and translated parts of the New Testament, like St. Luke's Gospel, St. John's Gospel and the Acts of the Apostles. Lorrain and Savidge compiled a *Lushai Grammar and Dictionary* which was published by the Assam Government in 1895. *The Old Catechism* was another book composed by them. They also translated about a dozen hymns to Mizo (Llyod 1991: 29–30).

In June 1899, the first printed copies of some translated books from the Bible, like the Gospels of Luke and John and the Acts came to hand and about 150 copies were sold before the end of the year (Hluna 1992: 22–23). In 1902, Edwind Rowlands, a Welsh Missionary, introduced two new textbooks in Mizo language, *Thu Ro Bu* (A New Reader) and *Hriselna Bu* (A Guide to Health and Wellbeing) for the students. In 1903, some advanced textbooks were brought out by the missionaries that included *Lushai Arithmetic Part I and II* and *Kristian Hla Bu* (Hymn Book; enlarged version with 80 hymns), *An Advanced Reader*, *First Reader*, *Paihte Reader* and *Lushai English Primer*. Translations of the Gospels of Matthew and Mark and the First Epistle of the Corinthians were also completed in 1905. As the number of publications grew, the range of texts published, that had remained limited for a long time, also grew. A new edition of the official monthly journal of *Mizo leh Vai Chanchinbu* started by Major Shakespear (earlier *Mizo leh Vai Chanchin Lehkhabu*) published nine Mizo folktales and one non-Mizo story.

What made these works possible was the introduction of an alphabet by pioneer missionaries and their continuous efforts in the field of literature. The two missions working in the north and south of Mizoram decided that the orthography and punctuation used in the Bible should be followed and taught in all the schools and this served as the model for all other books and writing. On mutual consultation and discussion, the two missions decided on changes in spellings of words whenever they found it necessary. Copies of the Bible would be then printed in accordance with the decision the missions took with regards to language and style. Elements of style used in the Bible such as punctuation, use of capital letters and circumflex accent, and the use of compound words have been the guide for all of Mizo literary culture.

The production of these religious texts, along with the process of their translation, thus effectively served to make loyal colonial subjects out of the Mizos—the missionaries had assumed both control and 'authorship' of the emergent Mizo narratives. This is evident in the literary works of the new converts, which followed the prose style of the missionaries, including the use of ordinary, colloquial words, while translating hymns and composing songs of worship. They shunned poetic and ornate language, which they believed should not be used in sacred hymns, but only in songs sung outside church service. Songs with poetry or lyricism were regarded as 'un-Christian'. The new Christians were also strictly prohibited by the church from singing indigenous traditional Mizo tunes, and those who did were suspended and denied full church membership (Lalzama 2017: 195). Even when the lyrics of a Mizo song were suitable for church service, and better than those of English Christian hymns, it was unacceptable to sing it during worship if its tune resembled that of a traditional Mizo song. Thus the Mizo Christian hymns that were sung were entirely in imitation of the extant English and Welsh hymns, in words as well as melody.

To this day, the standard of Mizo hymns is considered lower than that of Mizo non-religious songs, both in terms of musicality and lyricism. Mizo devotional music could have had a much wider range of melodies and compositions rich in poetry if the missionaries had accepted the original Mizo tunes from the beginning. Until recently the church took disciplinary action against those who sang hymns that resembled traditional Mizo tunes and even now the church is against it. Hymns composed even today for inclusion in the hymn books feature only commonly used words of everyday conversation. Over the years, this enforced style and deliberate stifling of indigenous creativity has left a permanent influence on the newer generations, who now produce plain hymns that lack variety.

EDUCATION AND SCHOOL TEXTBOOKS AS AN INSTRUMENT

To facilitate their evangelising mission, the Christian missionaries began setting up schools, and the colonial government gladly gave them the freedom to run them. The responsibilities of framing curriculum, producing textbooks, and training and recruitment of teachers fell in the hands of the missionaries. They knew that efforts to proselytise an illiterate people would be less effective. They, therefore, started primary schools, comprising classes divided age-wise. The books published during this period were either translated or authored by the missionaries, or written by the mission-educated Mizos who had internalised the mission's agenda. The compiled textbooks included *Zirtanbu* (Lushai Primer), *Zawhna leh Chhana bu* (Book of Questions and Answers) and *Zirtanbu Thar* (New Lushai Primer) in which moral, religious and general knowledge lessons were incorporated. The influence of education on the educated Mizos' young minds was immense. In 1901, Edwin Rowlands prepared an Arithmetical Primer, and a Second Reader was also jointly prepared by D. E. Jones and Rowlands. They also distributed a large number of tracts which had been printed free of cost to the Mission. In addition to the above-mentioned subjects, the rudiments of the art of teaching were introduced in the advanced class. In 1907, Rowlands listed the recommended school textbooks as follows (Lalzama 2017: 201):

Lushai Primer
Lushai Advanced Reader
Lushai Arithmetic Part I (Simple 4 Rules)
Lushai Arithmetic Part II (Compound Rules and Reduction)
Lushai Arithmetic Part III (Rule of Three, Interest, etc.)
Lushai Notes on St. Luke's Parables
Lushai English Primer (printed by the government in Shillong)
Lushai Translation—English Primer
Lushai Annotations—English Primer
Lushai Translation—English First Reader
Lushai Annotations—English First Reader
Lushai History of India
Lushai Catechism
Lushai Advanced Arithmetic
Lushai Geography of Assam

Lushai Geography of India
Lushai Annotations—English Second Reader
Lushai Annotations—English Third Reader
Lushai Adaptation English Grammatical Primer
Lushai Middle Reader I (A lai bu)
Lushai Middle Reader II (Bu lai)

The whole syllabus was designed as an instrument to aid the missionaries in their evangelising mission, and to support the colonial agenda. It was thus mandatory for students to study the scriptures as at least one subject. The writing and the teaching of history were adversely affected as well. Trained under the Western system, Mizo writers like Rev. Liangkhaia, V. L. Siama started viewing the process of history writing as linear and progressive as opposed to the tribal, cyclical worldview. Mizo oral traditions, oral histories, narratives, myths and legends were all systematically textualised, rationalised, formalised and reproduced under the Western paradigm. The period before the arrival of the British was looked upon as 'dark' to justify the presence of the coloniser and the need for colonisation, and to make it clear within the context 'from darkness to light'. For instance, popular Mizo singer Lalsangzuali wrote *My Father Was a Head Hunter*, in which she proudly explains how Christianity was instrumental in changing the attitude and behaviour of her tribe. Similarly, a textbook designed for training nurses, by Gladys Mary Evans of Durtlang Hospital, involved creating a Victorian model of the ideal woman that a Mizo woman should emulate.

Sunday School

In Mizoram the first Sunday School was started by pioneer missionaries at Aizawl and it began to hold a regular service of worship in Mizo Language from 2 October 1895. It has been serving a dual role as a centre of learning as well as a means to propagate Christianity among the tribals. The Sunday school became an alternative institution for those who were unable to attend regular school. Sunday schools were set up even in villages where there were no schools. This resulted in the growth of literacy among the Mizos. The following table shows the percentage of literacy in Mizoram against the all-India percentage as shown by the census figures from 1901 to 2011.

Table 3.1: Percentage of Literacy in Mizoram in Comparison to Literacy in India, Census 1901–2011

Year of Census	*Percentage of Literacy in India*	*Percentage of Literacy in Mizoram*
1901	5.35	0.93
1911	5.92	3.98
1921	7.16	6.28
1931	9.50	10.71
1941	16.10	19.48
1951	16.67	31.13
1961	24.02	44.01
1971	29.45	53.79
1981	36.17	59.50
1991	52.19	82.27
2001	65.38	88.49
2011	74.04	91.33

Source: Lalzama 2017: 108.

The progress of Sunday schools side by side with church enabled the growth in literacy among the Mizos. The literacy rate in Mizoram is very high in comparison with that of its neighbouring states. For example, the rate of literacy in Assam was 36.2 per cent in 1981, as compared to 59.50 per cent in Mizoram (Lalzama 2017: 108).

A prominent place was given to Biblical teaching in school although other branches of elementary education were not excluded. Lal Dena opines that the education provided by the mission was of a minimum standard and students were taught as much as was necessary to read the Bible as the primary aim of schooling was conversion (Dena 1998). All Mizo students who were in elementary and advanced levels took Scripture lessons and learnt verses, the catechism, and tonic sol-fa,[2] which they were fond of (FMPCW 1997: 10–11). It may be mentioned that a separate school was maintained by the mission for about 20 Hindi- and Bengali-speaking boys without religious instruction (ibid.: 22). Since all the earlier published books were by the missionaries, this gave them an opportunity to influence the mindset as well as the worldview of the locals. The village school masters performed the dual function of the teacher and the pastor, and were generally responsible for Sunday and weekday services. They were the 'only paid executives' and 'the most important persons in the village' (BMS 1993: 163, 173).

The older generation of Mizos who were educated earlier had totally internalised the teachings of the missionaries and imbibed them strongly, allowing them to shape their attitude and actions. The first textbook revised by D. E. Jones in 1915, *Duh-Lian Zir Tir Bu,* built on Edwin Rowlands' theories while introducing the author's biases. While Rowlands' original simply stated, 'There are five kinds of people in the world: Black-skinned, dark-skinned, brown-skinned, yellow-skinned, fair-skinned. But we are all one; the skin colour only differed because of our settlement'; D. E. Jones added, 'yellow-skinned are most numerous; fair-skinned people are [the] wisest and [most] superior'. He had also added, 'you should be [an] obedient servant, you should not hate porterage/impressed labour, [and] it is not good to keep a concubine' (Lalthangliana 2009: 215–216). These ideas influenced the Mizos to unquestioningly accord superior status to the whites and to submit to their colonial authority. Education thus, besides imparting knowledge and improving literacy, paved the way for the emergence of a new class of society: the Western-educated elite, which was largely made up of people who would be the 'commoners' in a traditional social setup, but who now emerged to be the more influential group. Through these colonial exercises, the Mizos were introduced to a new worldview, or to look at it from a postcolonial approach, these caused the 'worlding' of the Mizos as they were now made aware of their place in a larger world where the fair-skinned ones were at the top of the hierarchy.

'CHANGE' AS THE AGENDA

The Christian missionaries' writings mostly focused on the impact of Christianity upon Mizo culture and society, with the primary objective being to facilitate missionary expansion. The earliest of such works are Grace R. Lewis' *The Lushai Hills: The Story of the Lushai Pioneer Mission* (1970), M. E. Bowser's *Light on the Lushai Hills: The Story of our Foreign Mission* (1930), David Kyles' *Lorrain of the Lushais: Romance and Realism on the North-East Frontier of India* (1944). Like most books of this type, these were mainly written to inform Western readers about the successful projects and activities of the missionaries and to solicit support for them. The Mizos in these narratives feature merely as subjects of the missionaries' projects. The descriptions of the moral and religious life of the Mizos in these texts are not reliable as their purpose was not to help readers understand traditional Mizo culture, but to solicit their approval and support in changing it 'for the better'. These texts are therefore wholly inadequate and misleading as both historical record as well as for developing self-knowledge and self-awareness among Mizos as a community. For the colonial agenda, a new Mizo for British audiences was thus discursively created. This tradition has continued till the present and is the cause for the contentious discourses on Christianity in the region.

Some of these early writings also recorded the changes that occurred in the cultural behaviour of the people, that is, the changes brought about by Christianity in their lives. The anthropological study of N. E. Parry's *The Lakhers* (1932) gives us useful information on the Lakhers. Parry wrote in detail about the cultural activities of the Mara clan, since he had contact with the southern part of Mizoram and the aforementioned clan which the Lushai called the Lakher. A. G McCall in *Lushai Chrysallis* (1949) wrote about the traumatic cultural changes that came about as a result of Western contact through the Christian missionaries and government officials. McCall was of the opinion that although the main task of the government may have been confined to the maintenance of law and order, they were obligated to uphold and preserve the customs of the people. Parry also sought to preserve the pristine nature of the Mizo culture. Sharing the same opinion, McCall believed that certain changes were not only inevitable but desirable. While admitting that change was inevitable, he pleaded that it should be indigenously ignited and properly guided, and not forced on the people by 'over-zealous' outsiders. His book attempts to focus on the government policies in this respect, and also to provide guidelines for the moral and economic development of the people. In addition to this, McCall wrote a book, The *Lushai Hills District Cover* (1980), prepared during 1938–39 as an official handbook for the administration of the district, which had the same objective. It advocated the rule of traditional, or slightly modified forms of traditional governance through the chiefs. Parry defended the institution of *zawlbuk* (bachelor's dormitory) and successfully sought to revive it. Similarly McCall defended the *bawi*[3] system but failed. The accounts found in the above books are incomplete and certainly not free of biases. However, although their contribution and understanding of the subject matter is noteworthy, they have not dealt with the subject directly. The reproduction of this colonial agenda of a civilising mission by the different groups of Mizos themselves was an important exercise in mimicry, where the Western order was geared towards the establishment of hegemony. This required a change in subjectivity and it was achieved when the different groups (administrators, Mizos and others) that were part of a shared space were incorporated into the metanarratives of the West.

SOME ISSUES

When dealing with writings by the colonial administrators, one has to be aware that the sources are historical documents. The earlier writers among the Mizos failed to read/interpret these sources, instead passing the documents on as they were. Instead of transcribing them to interpret history or locate them in the historiographical context, they followed in the footsteps of the British. This act of mimicry perpetuated the same colonial mindsets and practices. Here, the 'worlding' of the Mizo as colonial subject is biased towards reproducing the Mizo as imagined by the coloniser. An in-depth analysis reveals that almost all of these studies on the Mizo are biased towards an ethnography of the community and seldom go beyond ethnographical details. Most studies are devoted to describing the community and its practices rather than carrying out an explicit analysis and interpretation of the Mizo society.

DEBATABLE 'MIZO'

The encounter between the colonisers and the colonised brought in a new method of writing history based on written records. The written materials which were available to the educated elite made the Mizos re-think and reconstruct their identity. This was enhanced by their exposure to the outside world, especially after the Second World War. For the first time, life beyond the hills became a matter of interest. The introduction of literacy, a new language, written literature and a new religion changed the world of the Mizos. This produced a kind of hybrid culture with the adoption of elements of Western culture while retaining one's ethnic culture. With this reorientation, the community successfully created a new identity under the banner of 'Mizo'.

However, recent Mizo scholars have questioned the sources and debated the formation of this common generic term. The people living in Myanmar have opted for the term 'Zomi', people living in Manipur opted for 'Zo' and the majority of the people living in

Mizoram opted for 'Mizo'. Those who are against the use of this generic term are of the opinion that Mizo was constructed under the banner of the Lusei[4] clan. The Britishers are to blame since most of their writings patronise a single culture, that is, that of the Lusei's, over the other clans. This has undermined the composite nature of tribal societies and at the same time instilled a false sense of 'superiority' in the psyche of the Lusei clan. In this case, the patronisation of only the Lusei resulted in the false conception that the Lusei dialect and cultural practices are yardsticks for Mizo identity. This has led to further confusion and the other clans feel that they are being marginalised or alienated. In building a common identity, one has to take into account the different clans within the Mizos who have diverse cultural practices and dialects. The Mizos are not a homogenous group with a single culture: there are different clans within the Mizos, and the cultural practices of these clans vary. Thus, the process of history-writing should reflect these differences and avoid the use of terms which paint a homogenous picture and conceal local diversities. The varying strands cannot be hidden away and are needed to make the Mizo tapestry richer. Such an exercise of homogenisation thus created a uniform whole rather than examining the mosaic of cultures that constitute the Mizos.

While tracing the ethnic background of the Mizos, there arises confusion over the question of common nomenclature and origin. This is mainly because the oral sources have not been systematically studied and compared with the relevant information from prevailing archaeological findings such as memorial stones. For example, protected monuments such as Lung Au and Lungphunlian reveal valuable information about the Mizo past. However, the literary sources of the Mizos today belong to the British period, produced by British officials during their brief rule in Mizoram. Mizo history can thus be accurately reconstructed only with a fair use of the oral literatures and by employing indigenous concepts and categories which are in tune with the latest methodology. This reconstruction of history would accomplish two things: first, it negates the biased colonial historiography; and second, it rehabilitates Mizo history through readings based on a combination of modern methods which are also rooted in the Mizo cultural tradition.

CONCLUSION

Constructions of the history of the Mizos excluded orality, thus erasing an entire worldview grounded in a specific cultural matrix. This resulted in the production of a Mizo subject who was the product of colonial desire and thus imbued with attributes that were at a considerable distance from the indigenous worldview. The incorporation of the Mizos into the larger world or the 'worlding' of the Mizos created a subjectivity that mimicked the Western agenda and the few existing traces of resistance were not mapped by the colonial writers and historiographers. It is possible to recover these through a process of conscientious cultural translation that employs oral history and situating it in context with other sources. Through this exercise, one can rewrite and re-right the rich and diverse history of the Mizos.

NOTES

1. *Foreign Department Report on Chin Lushai Hills, September, 1892*. Aizawl: Tribal Research Institute. Available at https://indianculture.gov.in/ebooks/foreign-department-report-chin-lushai-hills-september-1892 (accessed May 2023)

2. Tonic sol-fa notation, also called Solfége, is a system of learning music where the tones are called do, re, mi, fa, so, la, ti. A hand gesture is assigned to each syllable.

3. A person who surrendered himself, his life or those of his or her family members to a Mizo chief was known as *bawi*. They were interpreted to be a category of slaves by the missionaries. Dr Peter Frazer, a missionary and physician, made an attempt to end the bawi system in Mizo society. A series of appeals had been made to the British government to end the same.

4. The native Mizos refer to themselves as 'Lusei' in the local dialect whereas outsiders to the community like the British colonisers have termed them 'Lushai'.

REFERENCES

Baptist Missionary Society (BMS). 1993. *Reports by Missionaries of Baptist Missionary Society, 1901–1938*, The Mizoram Gospel Centenary Committee (comp.). Serkawn: Baptist Church of Mizoram.

Bowser, M. E. 1928. *Light on the Lushai Hills: The Story of our Foreign Mission*. London: The Carey Press.

Carey, Bertram S. and H. N. Tuck. 1976[1896]. *The Chin Hills: A History of the People, Our Dealings with Them, Their Customs and Manners, and Gazetteer of Their Country, Vol. 1.*

Dena, Lal. 1998. *Christian Mission and Colonialism*. Shillong: Vendrame Institute.

FMPCW (Foreign Mission of the Presbyterian Church of Wales). 1997. *Reports of the Foreign Mission of the Presbyterian Church of Wales on Mizoram 1894–1957*, K. Thanzauva (comp.). Aizawl: Synod Literature and Publication Board.

Grace R. Lewis. 1907. *The Lushai Hills: The Story of the Lushai Pioneer Mission*. London: Baptist Missionary Society.

Grierson, G. A. 1904. *Linguistic Survey of India, Part III*. Reprint. Delhi: Motilal Banarsidass.

Hluna, J. V. 1992. *Education and Missionaries in Mizoram*. Guwahati: Spectrum Publications.

Kyles, David. 1944. *Lorrain of the Lushais: Romance and Realism on the North-East Frontier of India*. London: Sterling Tract Enterprise.

Lalthangliana, B. 2009. *Mizo Chanchin: A Short Account and Easy Reference of Mizo History*. Aizawl: Gilzom Offset.

Lalzama. 2017. *Mizo Language and Literature: Emergence and Development (Contribution of Christian Missionaries from 1897–1947*). Aizawl: KL Offset Printers.

Lewin, T. H. 1869. *The Hill Tracts of Chittagong and the Dweller Therein, with Composition Vocabularies of the Hill Dialects.* Calcutta: Bengal Printing Company.

———. 1978[1870]. *Wild Races of the South-Eastern India*. Reprint, Aizawl: Tribal Research Institute.

———. 1885. *A Fly on the Wheel or How I Helped to Govern India*. London: W. H. Allen & Co.

Llyod, J. M. 1991. *History of the Church in Mizoram: Harvest in the Hills*. Aizawl: Synod Publication Board.

Mackenzie, Alexander. 1979[1884]. *The North-East Frontier of India*. Delhi: Mittal Publications.

Malsawmdawngliana and Rohmingmawii. 2016. *Mizo Narratives: Accounts From Mizoram*. Guwahati: Scientific Publications.

McCall, A. G. 1949. *Lushai Chrysallis*. London: Luzac & Co.

———. 1980. *The Lushai Hills District Cover*. Aizawl: Tribal Research Institute.

Morris, John Hughes. 1990[1930]. *The Story of Our Foreign Mission*. Aizawl: Synod Publication Board.

Mukherjee, Rila. 2003. *Europe Transformed: 1350-1789*. Calcutta: Progressive Publishers.

Parry, N. E. 1928. *A Monograph on Lushai Customs and Ceremonies*. Shillong: Government Press.

———. 1932. *The Lakhers*. Aizawl: Tribal Research Institute.

Reid, A. S. 1976[1893]. *Chin-Lushai Land: Including a Description of the Various Expeditions into the Chin-Lushai Hills and the Final Annexation of the Country, with Maps and Illustrations*. Aizawl: Tribal Research Institute.

Reid, Robert. 1942. *The Lushai Hills*. Aizawl: Tribal Research Institute.

Remruatkimi, C. 2015. 'Colonial Accounts of the Mizos'. In Rohmingmawii and Malsawmdawngliana (eds), *Mizo Narratives: Accounts from Mizoram*, 83–91. Guwahati: Scientific Book Centre.

Shakespear, J. 1975[1912]. *The Lushei Kuki Clans, Parts I and II*. Aizawl: Tribal Research Institute.

Shakespeare, L. W. 1977[1929]. *History of the Assam Riffles*. Aizawl: Tribal Research Institute.

Shaw, William. 1929. *Notes on the Thadou Kukis*. The Asiatic Society of Bengal on behalf of the Government of Assam.

Soppitt, C. A. 1976[1893]. *A Short Account of the Kuki-Lushai Tribes on the North-Eastern Frontier with An Outline Grammar of the Rangkhol-Lushai Language and A Comparison of Lushai with Other Dialects*. Aizawl: Tribal Research Institute.

Woodthorpe, R. G. 1873. *The Lushai Expedition, 1871–72*. London: Hurst and Blackett.

Zochungnunga. 2004. 'Survey of the Pre-Colonial Mizo Economy'. In Sangkima (ed.), *A Modern History of Mizoram*. Guwahati: Spectrum Publications.

4

Census and Identity Politics among the Plains Tribes in Colonial Assam*

Suryasikha Pathak

Many historical studies of the census use the corpus of demographic knowledge as a part of ethnographic inquiry. But recent studies have brought into focus the politics of numbers, or the political arithmetic, because unlike in the nineteenth century, quantitative approaches are no longer enmeshed in a naive scientific attitude now regarded as empiricism (Kreager 1997: 154). The census, that started in India from the middle of the century, 'because of its methodology and agenda—was a unique project', as is often argued (Samarendra 2011: 52). The census is admittedly a document of great ethnographic value and the '1881 census was the mother of colonial ethnography' (Singh 2011: 57). But the question of numbers also became important from the censuses of the twentieth century onward. Early colonial censuses were of course primarily 'ethnographic classificatory exercises', originating 'in the need for information about people to facilitate their governance and to expedite the exploitation of their skills and resources' (Singh 1996: 138). But ethnographic concerns did not begin, as is often presumed, with the census. These issues and ideas were already a part of administrative thinking by the 1850s. The consolidation of colonial rule over an agrarian society of great diversity gave rise to systematic revenue collection and required a comprehensive land register, which ensured maximum collection

*Previously published as 'Census as a Site of Contestation: Identity Politics among the Plains Tribes in Colonial Assam' in the Indian Sociological Society e-journal, *Explorations* 5(2): 105–124.

of land revenue at a very local level (Kreager 1997: 165). Colonial knowledge production geared towards governance of a large, diverse territory was the reason that 'census was symptomatic of the Victorian urge to "know", "classify" and "count"' (Meeto 2007: 43). Hence the colonial census held within itself 'an unresolved contradiction: its schedules attested to the heterogeneity of Jatis, its processes demanded homogeneity from communities to be counted' (Samarendra 2011: 53).

The ethnographic aspect of the census was always most dominant, and a number of studies draw extensively upon the census data. George Abraham Grierson, who compiled the Linguistic Survey of India, 1903, claimed that it was essentially based on figures from the census of 1891 (Samarendra 2011: 166). As Bernard Cohn remarks in his seminal essay, 'It would not be an exaggeration to say that down until 1950 scholars' and scientists' views on the nature, structure and functioning of the Indian caste system were shaped mainly by data and conceptions growing out of the census operations' (Cohn 1990: 242). While the census has been an important historical source as a part of ethnographic inquiry, it is also necessary to inquire into the relationship between quantitative and qualitative definitions of population.

There have been numerous detailed studies on census classification and enumeration, its effect on the indigenous population, and its 'consciousness of caste and the use of census for validation of claims to new status within the caste system' (Cohn 1990: 241). As observed by Kenneth Jones, there was an increasing realisation that a critical relation between the census and political identity cannot be denied. The census was used in various ways by the subjects of the colonial state who were in fact the subjects of the census itself. The census and the subject were involved in a complex relationship where each defined the other and attempted to control it. But as mentioned by Arjun Appadurai and others, such an exercise was totally appropriated, or conversely, 'democratic' politics came to be 'adversely affected by the idea of numerically dominated bloc voting…' (Appadurai

1993: 331). So, although the census did lead to a considerable rigidity in defining collective identities, it also set into motion 'a controversial mobility of nationalist, ethnic, communal and other identities' (Kreager 1997: 166). But these trends concretised into a politics that depended on 'representation' and 'representativeness' and established the ground for present-day communal and ethnic conflict in South Asia. On the question of identity politics—caste-based or communalised or tribal—'the most significant moment in the formation of fixed identities in the subcontinent was the introduction of the colonial census' (Meeto 2007: 128). The focus of Appadurai and others is caste, which is a crucial category to understand Indian reality. This chapter attempts to understand a similar situation within this framework of the politics of numbers: the contemporary ethnic situation in Northeast India, particularly the demands for autonomy and separate statehood among the tribal communities. Here too, along with other means of articulation, census enumeration gave rise to an identity where demographic numerical strength played a determining role in the emerging notion of politics and identity. As mentioned by Appadurai, identities constructed by such a process, necessitated by the colonial state, 'transformed not just into imagined communities but into "enumerated communities"' (Appadurai 1993: 332).

Notions of identity emerged with the first census because of its classificatory and enumerative role. This is evident in the increase and decrease in the numerical strength of the 'tribal' communities, seen through markers of religion and language. Census officials took an interest in the changes that they observed and were curious to find out how other communities related to the caste Hindu hierarchisation. As remarked by K. S. Singh, census officials were 'prone to describe tribal religion as raw material for Hinduism' (Singh 1996: 142). They focused on the process of socio-cultural assimilation of tribal societies into Hinduism. Hinduism was a primary category for understanding 'tribal' societies and Herbert H. Risley and others saw such a process as a negative marker for authentication of such communities. Risley and Edward A. Gait, who had defined the basic principles of categorisation, thought that tribes all over India were gradually losing their identity and becoming 'Hinduised' in a movement from 'tribe' to 'caste'. The officers of the colonial administration presumed that the phenomenon of Hinduisation was an inevitability in the tribal world, but as B. B. Chaudhuri points out, the process was far more complex, especially in regions where it was immediately linked with the radical agrarian movement (Chaudhuri 2002: 34).

CONSTRUCTING 'TRIBE' AND 'CASTE' IN COLONIAL CENSUS

> I have laid stress on the fact that caste is not necessarily connected with occupation, because in Assam Proper it is almost entirely a matter of race. (Census of India 1901: 115)

The situation was much more complex in the province of Assam, where the diversity of communities was much larger and there was a remarkable fluidity in demographic structure. The region had experienced migrations both from the east and the west for centuries, and it was a trend predicted likely to continue. In fact, it was quite difficult to pin down communities, as admitted by B. C. Allen in the 1901 census. He says, 'There is, in fact, no absolute test by means of which we can divide the inhabitants of Assam into those who are Assamese and those who are not' (Census of India 1901: 17). The ambiguous or fluid identity of the Assamese indicated that there was a thin line of differentiation between the Hindus and the non-Hindus or between tribe and caste. Hence in the Brahmaputra Valley, in order to differentiate between various communities—the caste Hindus and the 'tribal' communities—the colonial census authorities resorted to indices like religion and language, qualified by notions of purity, prescription, and proscription. Therefore, the question of 'Hinduisation' and Hindu influences was critically intertwined with the decrease in numbers of followers of animistic practices within these communities. This was especially the case in the Brahmaputra Valley where the colonial officials felt the tribal communities were particularly susceptible or vulnerable to such influences. Simultaneously, they accepted that it was possible to classify the animistic tribes of the province, adding the comment that even to 'the most casual observer the Assam range must be an object of interest' ethnographically (ibid.: 120). Animism itself was a negative category for classification, because, only 'those who had no recognized religion were shown in the column of the schedule for religion under the name of their tribe' (Census of India 1911: 36).

Since there was an ambiguity of definition and the census officials perceived 'Hinduism' and 'animism' as two opposite ends of a spectrum of faiths connected by the path of conversion, the problem of classification was compounded. 'A large number of such people have already been converted to Hinduism and many of them now are so near the border line that it is difficult to say what they are' (Census of India 1911). The problem was not as easily resolved as observed by the census enumerators because religio-cultural practices co-existed and these communities were reluctant to give up their old customs and food habits, and proscriptions were not usually successful. Therefore, certain differences in lifestyles and practices persisted, which demonstrated the nature of still extant community identities and challenged the construct of a homogenous 'Assamese' identity.

Gradually, the numerical strength of communities changed with the growth of political consciousness among various communities. Also any seeming ethnographic clarity among the colonial officers was of course coupled with a certain political idea about interplay of communities in the fluid demographic situation that existed in the Brahmaputra Valley during the early decades of the twentieth century.

The first regular census of Assam was attempted in 1872 and at that time the several districts forming the Chief Commissionership of Assam were under the Bengal government. By 1878 the question of taking a new census was mooted by the government. The 1881 census marks the debate regarding the understanding of tribe and caste in colonial Assam, under the guidance of the Superintendent of Census, Denzil Ibbetson. There was no clear distinction established between tribe and caste before the 1901 census and that led to confusion regarding categories and their enumeration. The category 'hill tribes' was used to

> arbitrarily to designate certain of the non-Aryan tribes, which are more decidedly hostile to Hinduism than others. Tribes like Abors, Daflas, Garos, Khasis, Syntengs, Kukis, Mikirs, Miris, Mishmis, and Nagas are included under this head; while many other tribes which are classed as aboriginal, such as Kacharis, Hajongs, Lalungs, and others, were entered in the Religion tables as Hindus. (Census of India 1881: 34)

The Hindus in the hills, 'Kacharis' or Dimasas of North Cachar, according to the 1881 census were 'hardly more right to be classed among Hindus than Kukis or Mikirs' (ibid.: 35). It marked the increase in the numbers of 'hill tribes' and as communities, these were no longer classified as Hindus but as 'aboriginal races'.

CATEGORISING RELIGION: HINDUISM AND ANIMISM, CASTE AND TRIBE

> Accretion to the ranks of the Hindus from the aboriginal tribes has continued steadily, but by no means evenly in all districts. In the case of some plains Kacharis of the Brahmaputra Valley and hill Kacharis of North Cachar difficulties were reported about orthodox Hindu enumerators being disinclined to write the whilom Animists as Hindus ... In any case the border line is so vague and primitive practices so often continue side by side with Hindu ceremonies ... (Census of India 1921: 50)

The 1891 census acquired importance since religion was classified separately from caste and tribe to remove the confusion regarding 'Hinduised' tribals. In the 1881 census, the classification had simplistically assumed that the 'tribes on the frontier which were altogether beyond Hindu influence were…Animistic, and those which were beginning to come under that influence… Hindu' (Census of India 1891: 82). So, classification was hinged on the hills–plains divide, further influenced by the biases of the local enumerators. The later census too was not objective in its classification but segregation led to contestation and claiming of certain categories. Animism was characterised as 'a religion of a very low type' thought to be 'professed by the most backward tribes of the province' (ibid.: 94). Though the absence of comparative figures showing the spread of Hinduism since 1881 leaves a lot of ground for speculation, Gait claimed that the work of proselytisation was steadily going on (ibid.: 83). And the twin processes of the spread of education and the influence of Hinduism gradually affected the number of people clinging to 'their (ancestral) superstition of their forefathers' (ibid.: 94).

The difference between the 1901 and the 1911 censuses was an increase in the numbers of animists by 16 per cent. In the Brahmaputra Valley, this increase was attributed to greater accuracy of recording religions; in Darrang, the increase registered was 38 per cent, in Sibsagar nearly 42 per cent, and in Lakhimpur nearly 32.7 per cent. Nowgong, where immigration was not a factor, showed an increase of over 35 per cent. However, in Kamrup the growth was less than 12 per cent, and conversions to Hinduism were presumed to be the cause. There was a sharp decrease in Goalpara, which was due to conversion to a new faith, the Brahma, which should not be confused with the Brahmo Samaj (Census of India 1911: 37).

Conversely, it was claimed that the percentage of growth for Hindus was not as encouraging. Colonial officials established an inverse relationship between Hinduism and animism. As was stated explicitly in the census, 'we see that in every district of the Brahmaputra Valley except Goalpara the proportion of Hindus has fallen owing to the increase of animists and, to a small extent, of Muhammadans' (Census of India 1911: 39). All this information was juxtaposed mainly against the Muhammadans and, to a lesser degree, against the Christians to locate the demographic transformations. However, the census also acknowledged that there was a certain ambiguity in defining Hindu and Hinduism. The 1911 census quoted Sir Alfred Lyall, lecturing in Cambridge in 1891:

> If I were asked for a definition of Hinduism, I could give no precise answer...For the word Hindu is not exclusively a religious denomination, it denotes also a country, and to a certain degree a race...religion, parentage and country... (ibid.: 40)

According to colonial officials, such ambiguity gave rise to complexities and fluidity. Though there was an accepted idea of mobility among the people in the plains, it was difficult to ascertain when new converts 'definitely became Hindus'. Even the latter censuses abound in examples of the ensuing confusion. As J. Mcswiney comments in the 1911 census, 'In the Brahmaputra Valley it is hard to say when the new converts definitely become Hindu, especially as many of them cling to their old habits of eating and drinking' (Census of India 1911: 41). This kind of impression was drawn primarily from the 'tribal' communities, who progressively became 'Hinduised'. For example, the Mishings he encountered in the east of Darrang had continued eating fowl and drinking liquor, though they had come under the tutelage of a *Gosain.* The proscription of such food was strictly adhered to when the Gosain was present. The reasons stated for the conversion were mostly social and economic: 'that they were strangers in a strange land, and unless they made some arrangements with the gods of the place or their representative, there was no knowing what evil might befall them,' meaning that they were attempting to adjust to the environment to avoid alienation (ibid.). So, they placed themselves under the religious patronage of a Gosain and 'paid him his annual fee in order to be on the safe side' (ibid.). He also remarked that during that period the missionary efforts of the Vaishnava Gosains of the Brahmaputra Valley had been very successful among the tribal communities.

In the 1921 census it was reported that 'accretion to the ranks of the Hindus from the aboriginal tribes has continued steadily but by no means evenly in all districts' (Census of India 1921: 50). Of course, many of these claims and counter claims were individual and subjective, and some of these were also influenced by the local enumerators and by politics. Though the Hindu Mahasabha was not active in Assam during the early 1920s and the Tribal League was not formed, the Satradhikars were strong spokesmen of Hinduism and equally active were the nascent associations among the tribes, especially the Kacharis.[1] But there were also instances when orthodox Hindu enumerators refused to enumerate some animist plains-Kacharis of the Brahmaputra Valley as Hindus. Similarly, a section of the Kacharis in Nowgong aiming for caste mobility and inclusion as 'regular Hindus' wanted to be classified as Saktas (ibid.).

The local belief systems were fluid and since 'primitive practices so often continued side by side with Hindu ceremonies', uniformity could not be maintained by the enumerating staff (Census of India 1921). So the census officers attempted to simplify the enumeration process by stating that if subjects claimed so, they must be entered as Hindus. In other cases, people who paid rent to a Gosain were to be entered as Hindus, according to customary definitions (ibid.).

Political and social movements for the annihilation of caste and tribal barriers were, as observed by the census authorities, at most, superficial and were 'still in domain of talk and not of practice... And it is noteworthy that Hindu and aboriginal recruits to recent advanced political views had generally to be obtained by promises of material benefit...' (Census of India 1921: 51).

COMMUNALISATION OF NUMBERS: THE 1930s AND 1940s

> There was energetic propaganda by the Hindu Mahasabha which practically amounted to an advocacy of returning as Hindu every

> person whose religion could not be found to have been originated outside India ... regardless of whether the followers of other Indian religions wished to be returned as Hindu or not ... (Census of India 1931: 385)

The issue of conversion to Hinduism among tribes becomes more important in the context of the relative increase and decrease in the Hindu and Muslim populations. In 1921 there was an increase in the numbers both of Hindus and Muslims. And again, it was observed that in 'Kamrup, Darrang and Nowgong [a large increase in Hindu population] corresponds [to a] decrease among the Animists; the new converts are chiefly [Plains-Kacharis], Karbis and Mishings' (ibid.: 52). Therefore, in the Brahmaputra Valley, the increase had sharply dropped from the 1911 figures of animists.

The changing numbers of Hindu and Muslim populations and regional politics led to a growing fear among the Assamese caste-Hindu middle class of a 'Muslim invasion' and communalisation in the 1930s and 1940s. The numbers of the plains tribes were essential to the Hindus to maintain a majoritarian position in the province, and it was also a political necessity for the Congress, who considered its mass base—the caste Hindu peasantry—essential to counter the Muslim League. The Muslim population had increased by 16.8 per cent by 1921 in the province.

The 1931 census laid the base for further communalisation of demographic politics. It traced the growth of the immigrant population in the province, especially of the East Bengal peasants from Mymensing district. According to C. S. Mullan (Superintendent of Census, Assam), the figures 'illustrate the wonderful rapidity with which the lower district of the Assam Valley are becoming colonies of Mymensing' (Census of India 1931. 50). The immigrants with their hunger for land were compared to vultures attracted to a carcass.

The 1931 census and the period prior to it saw the emergence of very strong efforts to disseminate propaganda by the Hindu Sabha of Assam, which strengthened the movement of the

Vaishnava Gosains and Satradhikars. The census authorities saw it as an extension and reflection of a nation-wide movement, like the missionary efforts of the Hindu Mahasabha, or the Hindu Mission, whose activities were confined among the tribals of Bihar, Bengal, Orissa and Assam laying claims on the 'aboriginal'. Perceiving changes in the numbers of the census, the Superintendents felt that the propaganda work of the Hindu Mission was certainly a great success in Assam and had an enormous influence on the tribal people occupying the grey area between Hinduism and animism. It was felt that such a claim was a recent development in the practice of Hinduism, and was an effect of the census. Unlike the earlier efforts, there was no attempt to formally convert or admit people to the Hindu fold and caste hierarchy. The Assam Provincial Hindu Sabha presumed that the tribes of Assam, like the Garos, Khasis, Mundas, Santals, Karbis, Mishings, Mishmis, Lushais, Tiwas, Rabhas, Kacharis, Meches were 'really Hindus' (Census of India 1931: 188). It protested that the 1921 census classified such communities as well as castes like Kaibartas, Chutiyas, and Koches as animists. The notice was issued in the interests of those who loved the Hindu religion. It was the Hindu Mahasabha's response to the threat that was felt by the 'tide of conversion to Christianity.'[2] By being 'saviours' to these communities, to the 'the simple men and women' who were being converted to Christianity by various missionary societies, the Mahasabha claimed to have brought back the aboriginal within the fold of Hinduism. Their arguments were drawn largely from the notion of unilinear influence of Hinduisation, which considered these communities to be 'naturalized Hindus by long and close contact with their Hindu neighbours' (ibid.). They claimed that the misleading propaganda by Christians and colonial notions about caste and tribe gave rise to misconceptions. This propaganda encouraged the 'animists' to return as 'Kshatriyas', and claimed that the absorption was more than what was shown in the census report of 1931. 'The newly initiated Animists wanted to be returned as Kshatriyas but as mentioned earlier, enumerators, who were mostly upper caste Hindus were not convinced of such claims and returned them as animist' (ibid.). So there were instances of claims and counter claims on the issue of enumerating and classifying such communities and the fluidity of practices led to complexities and sometimes even oversimplification of the situation. The census Superintendent and District Commissioners always presumed the naivety of these 'tribal' communities and suspected that enumerators, nearly all of them being Hindus, were naturally biased. As the Deputy Commissioner of Darrang commented:

> the Hindu enumerators (and they are nearly all Hindus) tend to record all animistic and aboriginal tribes, such as Kacharis, Karbis, Mishings, Mundas and Santhals, as Hindus. Even if the enumerator fails, the supervisor or checking officer tends to keep him up to the scratch. An instance was brought to my notice at Halem where the enumerator had written Mishing, but the checking officer changed it to 'Hindu Mishing'. (ibid.: 190)

The official categories and classification were often questioned and checked by the agency of and consciousness among these people, 'animists' and 'aboriginals'. Mullan himself claimed to have 'received several petitions from Kacharis in Kamrup stating that they had [been] returned as Hindus in the census schedules and that they objected to the action of the enumerators recording their religion as Hindu' (Census of India 1931). The propaganda campaign by the Hindu Sabha produced many effects—some Kacharis willingly returned as Hindus, others were convinced by the enumerators to accept that category, and in some cases the enumerators took advantage of their confusion or ignorance to record them as Hindu. In cases where a particular indigenous faith had no definite name, there was genuine confusion. Some Tiwas came to see Mullan in Nowgong in January 1930 and asked for his advice as to 'how they should return their religion' in the census. After questioning them, Mullan ascertained and was convinced that theirs was a 'purely tribal religion' and advised the Tiwas to tell the truth (ibid.). Thereafter the Tiwas resolved in a meeting that the community should identify their religion as Tiwa. But during enumeration, 'in spite…of this resolution the vast majority of Tiwas returned themselves as Hindus, in many cases, voluntarily' (ibid.). Mullan suspected that enumerators routinely entered as 'Hindu' the names of 'tribal' people 'who found it difficult to state precisely what their religion was and often in such cases Hinduism got the benefit of doubt' (ibid.). The relative success of Hindu propaganda was evident in the increase in the number of Hindus, which was conflated 'owing to the inclusion of animists such as Kacharis, Mishings and aboriginal tea garden coolies' (ibid.).

Goalpara, among all the districts in the Brahmaputra Valley, showed remarkable increase (38 per cent) in the numbers of animists. A large number of people in the Kokrajhar thana of that district returned 'both their religion and their caste as Boro' and many Santhali settlers did the same (Census of India 1931: 193). This could be attributed to a growing political consciousness. It is interesting to note that in the same area in the earlier decades there was an attempt of religious reformation among the Boros or Bodos and it was a primary location for the various associations of the Bodos.

TRIBAL IDENTITY AND THE CENSUS

A reaction to the enumerators recording tribal identities as Hindu saw the emergence of revivalism that strongly articulated the notion of a tribal identity. The Census of 1931 quotes Rupnath Brahma, an accepted spokesperson of the Bodo community, saying that the Bodos should speak for themselves (Census of India 1931: 194). He claimed that Boros or Bodos had 'a distinct state of civilization of their own…also a distinct form of religion which they have been retaining' and that they were definitely not 'idol worshippers' (ibid.). Brahma asserted that despite Hindu influences, 'the Bodos had a separate society of their own and never allowed their tribal peculiarities to be merged into the Hindu society'. They did not recognise the Brahmanical supremacy of caste hierarchy either (ibid.).

Those who followed Vedic religion cannot be treated as animists. But Rupnath Brahma also stated that proximity of religious practices was overridden by other considerations, because 'according to their views, they would be losers thereby in the *social and political spheres*' (Census of India 1931, emphasis added). Therefore, political consciousness was critical to their decision to be enumerated and recognised as Bodos. By the 1930s the administration too had clearly accepted the discourse of the tribal politics:

> They are in favour of having a separate representation of their own in councils and other government departments and they are not in favour of allowing their tribal interests to be merged with those of the Hindus. With these objectives in view many of the Bodos, especially those of the Kokrajhar thana, returned themselves as Boro by religion and Boro by caste. They say that considering the strength of their population in the whole province they have a rightful claim to have a separate category as Boro or Bodo in the census report. (ibid.)

The question of numerical strength of communities had become important by then and the Bodos had been officially striving towards 'separate representation' since the arrival of the Simon Commission. So the 1931 census had an instrumental role in furthering the franchise reforms that were to be constituted later. The assertion of the plains' tribes was also very evidently attributed to processes initiated by representative communitarian politics. The intensity was perhaps not equal to the Hindu–Muslim tension because of the 'autochthonous' status of these communities and also because of the fluidity of identities that existed. But there was mounting pressure on the question of identities and politics, which led to colonial policies regarding various communities in the sphere of representational politics and this affected the balance of political power in the province.

Maintaining a 'tribal' identity had become important for that purpose mainly. By the 1931 census the connection between political power, representation and community identity was very obvious. Census Superintendents were also asked to compile lists of the Depressed and Backward Classes and for Assam, Mullan compiled a list of communities based on social divisions:

(a) Hindu exterior castes
(b) Indigenous backward tribes
(c) Tea garden coolie castes

The indigenous backward tribes of Assam were the aboriginal communities 'either living in the hills like the Naga tribes—quite untouched by Hinduism' or 'living in the plains—like the Tiwas or Mishings—and influenced to a greater or less[er] degree by Hinduism' (Census of India 1931: 204). The criteria of qualification for this category, especially in the case of aboriginal tribes living in the Brahmaputra plains, was that 'such tribes should still be aloof from the main body of Hindus and should still be generally regarded as a separate community rather than as a Hindu caste. In deciding this the fact that they still speak a Tibeto-Burmese tribal language may be of importance' (ibid.).

Therefore, the colonial state did widen demographic fissures in the Brahmaputra Valley, particularly with regard to representation in various institutions and more generally in social and political spheres.

LANGUAGE AND TRIBE: SPEAKING ASSAMESE AND 'BEING TRIBAL'

> There is probably no country in the world which affords a richer field for the philologist than Assam, for, though the population barely exceeds six millions, no less than one and sixty-seven different languages were returned at the last census. (Census of Assam 1901: 87)

Another interesting aspect of identity was language—dying tribal dialects, growing bilingualism and the convergence of the use of 'Assamese' language with emerging notions of a monolithic 'Assamese' identity. In fact, the task of classifying was not easy when the marker of being a backward and depressed 'tribe' was indigenous religion, as accepted by various officials. The Tiwas, Rabhas, Kacharis, Meches, and Mishings were under various degrees of Hindu influence and it was generally agreed upon that, 'in spite of partial conversion to Hinduism they still remain tribal people' (Census of Assam 1901: 21). Even the caste-Hindu Assamese middle class, though eager to include them in the fold of Hinduism, found it difficult to accept them as 'proper' Hindus because they kept 'pigs and fowls' (ibid.). Therefore, the question of tribal identity hinged not only on the definition of religion and the movement of tribal to caste by conversion, but segregation from the caste-Hindu hierarchy and language was considered important too. By this logic, the Kacharis were a backward tribe but the Ahoms were not, because the latter, 'though in many ways a separate community—[had] been for so long completely Hinduised' that they [were considered] a racial caste (ibid.). The Kacharis though 'nominally Hinduised' were considered 'more a tribe' than 'caste'. Preservation of one's own language and also the social and cultural distance maintained from the 'general development of Assamese culture' distinguished 'tribe' from 'caste' and therefore 'backward' from the privileged. Therefore, the backward tribes of Assam were divided into two sections, 'the real hillmen and those living principally in the plains who have been Hinduised to a greater or less extent,' the latter including the Kacharis, Mishings, Tiwas, Rabhas, Hojongs, Tiparas of Sylhet and Deoris of upper Assam, who had preserved their tribal languages (ibid.).

As observed above, adopting the Assamese language was often not perceived as a mere linguistic shift, but often signified conversion to 'Hinduism', ushering in a transformation in one's culture and mother tongue. The 1891 census thought that the Bodo (Kachari) language was dying out because the Bodo (Kacharis) were 'gradually being converted to Hinduism, and when this process is completed, many adopt Assamese as their parent tongue, at least as soon as they drop their distinctive racial name' (Census of India 1891: 159).

There was a general concern about the disappearance of various languages of the Bodo group as was evident in the decrease when compared to the 1881 figures. The comparison shows a sharp decrease especially in the case of Tiwas and more so for the Rabhas. The loss was in favour of Assamese, because these tribes, which had for centuries retained their languages, had been rapidly taking to speaking in Assamese. The colonial authorities expressed surprise and thought that changes like 'better communication… and greater amount of trade and travel' put people to greater exposure. As observed by E. A. Gait,

> Thousands of Kacharis, & C. leave their homes for a few months annually to work on tea gardens and roads … they must perforce speak Assamese … The process will doubtless continue at an annually increasing rate, and the entire extinction of all these languages … is probably only a matter of a very few years. (Census of India 1891: 163)

From 1910 to 1921 the trend of decrease continued, but the indigenous tribal languages continued to survive and did not disappear as predicted thirty years back. The decrease continued because of 'contact with others, i.e., practically, contact with the Aryan languages of the plains' (Census of India 1921: 122–123). Aryan languages did not mean Assamese alone; in many cases Bodos and Dimasas who registered their caste as Kshatriya, also declared their language as Bengali, as it happened in the North Cachar Hills and Goalpara (ibid.). But the languages most affected by external influences in the plains were the Chutiya, Tiwa, Kachari and Rabha. The period till the 1920s experienced a gradual but penetrative influence of Hinduism. But as acknowledged by J. W. Mcswiney, the 'superior Aryan civilization' continued to exert influence and pressure, and according to the 1921 census, there were many who may not have had lost their mother tongue, and a great number of them were bilingual, although 'the usual feeling of superior civilization conferred by Aryan speech must have influenced them concurrently with the move towards Hinduism' (ibid.: 123).

By 1931, officially there was a more organised effort to enumerate languages and dialects more accurately and scientifically by collapsing the social, ethnic map with the linguistic map. And so by 1931, political awareness among certain tribal communities led to a consciousness about the need for asserting distinctive identities at the time of enumeration. Therefore the 1931 census showed a 9.5 per cent increase in the speakers of the Assam-Burmese branch, i.e., the Bodo group, comprising the Garo, Rabha, Chutiya, Boro or Bodo (Kachari), Dimasa (Hill Kachari) and Tiwa communities (Census of India 1931: 172). Mullan remarks:

> In 1911 the number of Rabha speakers numbered 28,000, so that the 1921 census figures for this language were apparently too low (Rabha speakers now [in 1931] number 27,000 against 22,000 in 1921). Chutiya speakers who now number 4,315 show a slight increase over the 1921 figure.... Bara, Bodo, Mech or plains Kachari which showed a slight decrease in 1921 shows a considerable increase at this census in the number of its speakers—from 260,000 to 283,000. (ibid.)

In the earlier two censuses, i.e., 1911 and 1921, the question was whether the tribal languages were disappearing as a result of contact with others and this had caused some alarm. But it was evident that those languages were not dying, and as mentioned earlier, there has been an increase in the number of their speakers. Therefore, the notion that Assamese was successful in establishing hegemony over other dialects was erroneous. These communities were undoubtedly the only real bilingual people but they were conscious of 'holding their own in a wonderful manner' (ibid.: 181).

THE TRIBAL LEAGUE AND THE 1941 CENSUS

Though the ethnographic aspect was mostly left out in the 1941 census, the ideas of caste and tribe as enumerated and contested categories had already been established in political and public spheres at both regional and national levels, and so, even in the absence of the surveys of the census, the ideas of caste and tribe were sustained.

Therefore, though the 1941 census was not an elaborate ethnographic exercise like the 1931 census, with data presenting only a limited number of communities at the district level such as the Scheduled Castes, Scheduled Tribes and other castes, it created political tension regarding number (Singh 1996: 143). It generated controversy about categories and numbers, particularly because by then representation in the Legislative Councils and Assemblies was totally driven by the logic of the politics of numbers and it was an ethnographically defined communitarian politics.

The 1941 census evoked strong responses from various sections of the Assamese society and led to a debate in the Assembly, which was heavily reported and discussed in the newspapers. The Congress criticised the government for manipulating the census operation so as to conceal the correct figures of the followers of different religions. The Congress moved an adjournment motion to discuss the census operation.[3]

The cause of discontent and tension was the changed basis of classification, a shift from religion as a matrix of classification to one based on community. Compilation for communities was done with reference to 'race, tribe and caste' and not religion as it was in the case of the 1931 census. The Congress and few others accused the United Party government of tampering with date compilation and deviating from the rules followed by the census authority of India. It was under the Assam provincial government's instance that K. W. P. Marar, the Census Superintendent, issued a special circular to the Deputy Commissioners and Census Officers in Assam to compile data on the basis of 'community'. He wrote:

> The basis for community is answer to question 3, but generally the communities are unavoidably mixed up and where community cannot be ascertained in answer to question 3, answer to question 4 will be the basis; e.g., If a Kachari has not in answer to question 3 mentioned that he is a Kachari, and is returned under question 4 as Hindu, Muslim or Christian, he will be shown as Hindu, Muslim or Christian as the case may be, but if he is returned as a Kachari against question 3 he will be entered [as] such irrespective of his religion. (ibid.)

The government stated that the purpose of clubbing communities professing different religions was to create a 'separate entity under the constitution for the purpose of franchise.'[4] Siddhi Nath Sarma, for instance, clarified that as the tabulation would be done on the basis of 'community', and not on religious lines, it would simplify the problem of classification of the primitive tribes. He added that in this way their total number regardless of their religion could be recorded.[5] These efforts on the part of the colonial government to seek out community identity corresponded to the Tribal League's own efforts to project community identity as one unified tribal people. And for this purpose, the Tribal League disseminated propaganda. Bernard S. Cohn (1990: 249) has observed such active interference in the process of census enumeration and how the growing 'consciousness of the significance of the census operation had reached a point where Indians were not merely content to petition and to write books: some group set out to influence the answers which people would give in the census'. A bulletin of the Tribal League was taken out in 1940 with the main objective of instructing the 'tribal' people—Bodo, Kachari, Mech, Rabha, Tiwa, Mishing, Karbi, Deuri, etc.—about the politics of census enumeration (The Assam Tribal League 1940: 1). The importance of the census for preservation of tribal identity and interests was reiterated. The political aspirations of the Tribal League were moulded by government policies, which were correspondingly influenced by these political aspirations.

There was a growing reliance on the census as a support for articulating political aspirations, which resulted in the convergence between the census and the world it sought to describe. By 1941 the census became very closely interlinked with political issues such as attempts to prove the existence of a community to validate the creation of a separate constituency. 'Enumeration on the basis of community would show [us] as a distinctive community which would enable us to demand special provisions in education and in the socio-economic spheres' (The Assam Tribal League 1940: 4). It was also emphasised by the Tribal League that if special measures were not taken to ameliorate their conditions, they would remain backward forever. The Tribal League's definition of 'tribals' was broad and included those who were otherwise classified as 'Hinduised'. Religion was a secondary aspect of tribal identity. The essence of 'tribalness' was the existence of distinctive rituals and customs, rules and regulations, which were retained, therefore aiding the preservation of a distinctive lifestyle often in totality and in some cases partially (ibid.).

Further, the Tribal League also emphasised the separateness and differences in the social structure of the 'tribals' and the caste-Hindu Assamese. It persistently opposed various moves by the more conservative circles and the Congress to categorise tribals under Hindus and to show them as a part of Hindu society. It is difficult to judge the extent to which the 'tribal' leaders understood the complexity and the political motivations behind creating the notion of two polarised societies. But in giving it a concrete shape, at least in politics, the census aided the crystallisation of identities.

The census enumeration made the identity of the plains tribes a political reality, while simultaneously creating a site for contestation and redefining of identity through the official legitimacy it conferred on communities. The apparent connection between the census and political rights contributed to the communitarian politics of the 1930s and 1940s. However, it also demonstrated that identities are not fixed and often situationally motivated and that there are layers to any visible and tangible identity.

NOTES

1. The nomenclature Kachari was loosely used for various communities like the Bodos, Dimasas, Sonowals and others.

2. As stated in the pamphlet quoted in the Census of India, 1931, page 189.

3. Assam Legislative Assembly Proceedings (ALAP), 4 December 1941: Adjournment motion in connection with the conducting of the last census operations in Assam brought by Siddhi Nath Sarma. Available at Central Secretariat Library, New Delhi.

4. Classification of communities according to Appendix II of ALAP, prepared by the Assam Government, was as follows: (1) Assam Valley Hindus; (2) Assam Valley Muslims; (3) Surma Valley Hindus; (4) Surma Valley Muslims; (5) Scheduled Castes; (6) Tribal People, Hills; (7) Tribal People, Plains; (8) Europeans and Anglo-Indians.

5. Speech by Siddhi Nath Sarma at Legislative Assembly of Assam on 4 December 1941. Available at Central Secretariat Library, New Delhi.

REFERENCES

Appadurai, Arjun. 1993. 'Number in the Colonial Imagination'. In Carol A. Breckenridge and Peter van der Veer (ed.), *Orientalism and the Postcolonial Predicament*. Philadelphia: University of Pennsylvania Press.

Census of India, 1881. Report on the Census of Assam. Calcutta: Office of Superintendent of Government Printing, 1883.

Census of India, 1891. Vol. I, Assam, Report by E. A. Gait. Shillong, 1892.

Census of India, 1901. Vol. IV, Assam, Part I, Report by B. C. Allen, ICS, Superintendent of Census Operations. Shillong, 1902.

Census of India, 1911. Vol. III, Assam, Part I, Report by J. W. Mcswiney. Shillong, 1912.

Census of India, 1921. Vol. III, Assam, Part I, Report by G. T. Lloyd. Shillong, 1923.

Census of India, 1931. Vol. III, Assam, Part I, Report by C. S. Mullan. Shillong, 1932.

Census of India, 1941. Vol. IX, Assam Tables, Report by K. W. P Marar, Superintendent of Census Operations, Assam. Shimla: GOI Press, 1942.

Chaudhuri, Binay Bhushan. 2002. 'Society and Culture of the Tribal World in Colonial Eastern India: Reconsidering the Notion of "Hinduisation" of Tribes'. In Hetukar Jha (ed.), *Perspectives on Indian History and Society: A Critique.* New Delhi: Manohar Books.

Cohn, Bernard S. 1990. 'The Census and Objectification in South Asia'. In Bernard S. Cohn, *An Anthropologist among the Historians and Other Essays.* Delhi: Oxford University Press.

Kreager, Philip. 1997. 'Population and Identity'. In David I. Kertzer and Tom Fricke (eds), *Anthropological Demography: Towards a New Synthesis.* Chicago: University of Chicago Press.

Meeto (Kamaljit Bhasin-Malik). 2007. *In the Making: Identity Formation in South Asia.* Gurgaon: Three Essays Collective.

Samarendra, Padmanabh. 2011. 'Census in Colonial India and the Birth of Caste'. *Economic and Political Weekly* XLVI(33).

Singh, K. S. 1996. 'Census and Ethnography'. In S. P. Mohanty and A. R. Momin (eds), *Census as a Social Document.* New Delhi: Rawat Publications.

_____. 2011. *Diversity, Identity, and Linkages: Explorations in Historical Ethnography.* New Delhi: Oxford University Press.

The Assam Tribal League. 1940. *Bulletin 2.* Assam: Bhimbar Deuri.

III

Race, Ethnicity and Migration

5

Northeastern Migrants in Delhi

Racial Discrimination, Violence and State Response*

Hoineilhing Sitlhou and Salah Punathil

This chapter primarily deals with two issues: First, it gives a brief account of the racial discrimination and violence that Northeasterners have experienced in the metropolitan city of Delhi in the recent past. Second, it deals with the state response to the problem of discrimination and violence in the form of the Bezbaruah Committee, 2014, and the reception and perceptions about its implementation among migrants in Delhi. The data presented in this chapter is part of a survey that was conducted with 95 respondents to understand the problems of the Northeast populace outside the Northeast region, taking the case of New Delhi and using the snowball sampling method. The data is supplemented with interviews of key resource persons who are directly involved with the issues of Northeast migration to metropolitan states of India.

The survey comprised elaborate questions seeking the respondents' view on all contours of discrimination and violence persisting against Northeasterners in Delhi. For the snowball sampling it was ensured that the sample represented the following

---

*An earlier version of this essay was published as 'Racial Discrimination and Violence against North Easterners and Bezbaruah Committee Report' in *Explorations* 1(1): 91–102. This essay is based on the project 'Archiving Marginalities in North East India', jointly undertaken by the Department of Sociology and the Centre for Regional Studies, University of Hyderabad, and funded by UGC-UPE Phase II. Both the authors have contributed equally in the writing of this chapter.

internal categories of subjects under study: members from all states in the Northeast, men, women, students, informal labourers, professionals, and government employees. Attention was given to the residential settlements of Northeasterners to understand the spatial differences in experiencing discrimination. The study also highlights the significance of the internal differences within the category of Northeasterners in terms of region, class, gender, physical appearance and culture in mapping the divergent experiences of discrimination and violence. Finally, the rich empirical data presented in the work contributes to a new theorisation of race and violence in India today.

THE NORTHEAST INDIA

The Northeast of India comprises eight states—Arunachal Pradesh, Assam, Manipur, Meghalaya, Mizoram, Nagaland, Sikkim and Tripura. The region is home to numerous ethnic communities that have migrated from all points of the compass, the majority of them belonging to the Indo-Chinese Mongoloid racial grouping (Downs 2011: 223).

> A large segment of the population is made up of the mongoloids of the Sino-Tibetan linguistic family who came into the region from north-western China, northern Burma, Thailand, Cambodia and Laos at different points of time, and the Caucasoids belonging to the Aryan linguistic family. (Nongbri 2014: 4)

In fact many of them trace their lineage to Southeast Asia with a few centuries of acculturation in between (McDuie-Ra 2012a: 27), but its strategic location is at the confluence of South, Southeast and East Asia (Nongbri 2014: 5). In accordance with general contemporary usage of the term 'Northeast India', the region lies to the north and east of Bangladesh, between approximately Latitude 20° to 29° North and Longitude 90° to 98° East (Pachuau 1998: 1). It spans over an area of about 2.6 lakh sq. km, covering nearly 8 per cent of the land area of India and less than 4 per cent (3.8 per cent) of its population (39 million according to 2001 census) (Nongbri 2014: 3).

MIGRATION OF NORTHEASTERNERS OUTSIDE NORTHEAST INDIA

Internal migration from one part of the country to another is a common occurrence in India. There has been constant movement of population across regions, and such movements vary from to time to time depending on the socio-economic circumstances. However, in the recent past, there has been a tremendous flux of population from rural localities to cities under the circumstances of globalisation. The large-scale migration from Northeast India towards metropolitan cities like Delhi in the last two decades makes Northeasterners a visible category in the so-called mainland of India. The survey conducted by the North East Support Centre and Helpline (NESCH) in early 2011 puts the number of migrants outside the Northeast at 4,14,850. Out of this, 48 per cent have migrated to Delhi, making for a population of around 2,00,000 (McDuie-Ra 2012b: 70). Moreover, the same study has confirmed that 86 per cent of people from the Northeast face racial discrimination in Delhi (NESCH 2011: 19). Duncan McDuie-Ra (2012a) argues that the migration of Northeasterners to places like Delhi has blurred the prevailing boundary between the Indian nation state and its perceived essential Other, the Northeast. Poor infrastructure, unemployment and political turmoil in the Northeastern states push the people to move out of their states. The employment opportunities that came up in the neoliberal regime attracted them to cities like Delhi. While many of the youth are employed in informal sectors, many migrate for education or employment in the government services and private companies.

Over a period of time, Northeasterners became outsiders in the minds of average Indians, and they began to be addressed by various derogatory terms because of their different physical and cultural characteristics. As a mode of discourse, the function of a stereotype is to exaggerate the differences of the 'Other', and as a mode of identification, it operates through a series of mutually exclusive categories differentiating the 'Self' and the 'Other' (Bhabha 1994). These occurrences are not just contemporary social phenomena but something that has historical relevance. 'Ignorance about the history, mores and values of the Northeasterners and deeply internalised ideas about homogenised "Indianness" are responsible for this form of racism' (Ngaihte 2014: 15).

During the colonial regime, the hegemonic discourse wanted to construe the native as a decadent population and the colonisers created certain stereotypes on the basis of racial origin in order to justify conquest and establish systems of administration and instruction. Therefore, race was a means of differentiation done for the convenience of classification. To a sociologist, race is not determined by physical characteristics alone. Rather, race is a social concept that may vary from one society to another depending upon how individual members of a society perceived physical differences among fellow human beings. The idea of race itself and the actual divisions of persons into groups based on selected hereditary features like skin colour, facial features and hair textures are social constructs (Banton 1987).

It must be noted that earlier discourse on racism in India was mainly framed around caste-based discrimination (*see* Ghurye 1999). However, such a discourse was marginal and racial violence is not often understood as an Indian experience in mainstream academic and political discourse in India (NESCH 2011). Race is always perceived as an alien thing. The experience of Northeastern migrants in Delhi and other cities in India invokes the problem of racial violence in India today more seriously than ever. Arjun Appadurai brings attention to how ethnic differences are articulated in everyday life and that the internalised notion of the 'Other' plays a significant role in such racist behaviour in a globalised society (Appadurai 1998). According to McDuie-Ra,

> India contains many communities earmarked as "others" based on religion, caste and even ethnicity, yet the nationality and origin of these communities are not questioned at every turn. They can "blend" into the heartland (rarely completely) in ways that Northeast migrants cannot. This is not to argue that these "others" do not face discrimination and violence; rather, Northeast migrants feel that their experiences of racism are distinct'. (2012b: 71)

The recent campaign for anti-racism legislation in India throws in an array of sociological questions and debates on prejudice, discrimination, identity and racism. The practice of racism against people from the Northeast in mainland India is of a different order in which their identity as an Indian is questioned (Ngaihte 2014). To add to the long list of deaths, cases of physical atrocities and physical assault against Northeasterners, a 29-year-old Manipuri BPO employee was beaten to death by five youth in South Delhi on 21 July 2014. Six months prior to this incident, a 19-year-old student from Arunachal Pradesh, Nido Tania, died after being beaten with iron rods and sticks by some men. This happened after an altercation with a shopkeeper who allegedly made fun of his clothes and hair (*Time* 2014). A committee called the Bezbaruah Committee was set up following the attack and murder of Nido Tania in 2014.

RACE AND ETHNICITY: THE CONCEPTUAL FRAMEWORK

It is important to reflect on the generic term that has been frequently employed in recent studies in social sciences, that is, the concept of 'ethnicity'. The consciousness, identification and mobilisation around a particular cultural identity that leads to boundary-making and exclusion of other cultural identities, can be called ethnicity. Conflicts and violence based on 'ascriptive' group identities like race, religion, language, tribe or caste are broadly ethnic in nature (Varshney 2002). The framework of 'ethnicity' is meant to capture the cultural core of the 'groupness', both imagined as well as real. Ethnic groups gain currency and existential traction in a society when it acquires an organisational form that is mostly political. In this way, two aspects are quite central to the idea of ethnic differences: the ascriptive cultural identity and its organisation, and its mobilisation for various social, political and economic reasons. According to Fredrik Barth, 'ethnic categories provide an organisational vessel that may be given varying amounts and forms of content in different socio-cultural systems' (Barth 1969: 43). The seemingly objective cultural differences of ethnic groups are often articulated in such a way that organisation of behaviours, social relations, symbols of differences, etc. generate boundaries and exclusivity. Barth in his seminal essay warns that what defines the ethnic nature of a group is the boundary it defines and not the cultural ideas or ideals it encloses or claims to uphold and build upon (ibid.).

Roger Brubaker in his study on ethnicity says:

> I want to suggest that ethnic conflicts—or what might better be called ethnicised or ethnically-framed conflicts—need not, and should not, be understood as conflicts *between ethnic groups*, just as racial or racially framed conflicts need not be understood as conflicts between *races*, or nationally framed conflicts as conflicts between *nations*. (Brubaker 2004: 9–10; emphases added)

'Race and ethnicity function as code-shorthand, if you will, reminding us and telling others who "I" am, who "we" are, what we do, how we live and what we value, not to mention what we look like' (Caliendo and McIlwain 2011: xxii). Biological notions of race have functioned as an accepted truth about the nature of human difference. The tendency is to consider 'race' to be a social construction rooted in physical differences, among the most prominent of which is skin colour or tone (ibid: xxiii). For instance, Johann Friedrich Blumenbach in 1775 created a racial classification system that divided humans into five races: Caucasian (white), Mongolian (yellow), Malayan (brown), Ethiopian (black) and American (red).

One important characteristic of racial and ethnic relations as expressed by Michael Banton (1987) had to do with everyday circumstances. He argued that groups are identified by signs, such as those of phenotype (outward appearance), language and religion. In the same vein, the construct of 'what an Indian ought to look like' has been an important subject of debate. Sanjoy Hazarika asserts that there is a tendency to have a preconceived notion of how a Northeasterner would look like. When people say they are from the Northeast, immediately the person is construed to be a tribal with a certain kind of feature(s), look and attire. The majority of people in the Northeast—or the region we call the Northeast—are actually non-tribals like Hazarika. He continues, 'We are actually a majority but most of the Indians do not know that. I [have] not faced discrimination in Delhi and many of my friends do not face it because [we look] similar to the description of what an Indian looks like'.[1] Alana Golmei reiterated the same point made by Hazarika. When Northeasterners are endowed with physical features such as a mongoloid face, it is difficult for mainland Indians to accept them as citizens of India.[2] Udayon Misra recalled that when the name of a prominent tribal politician from the Northeast came up for an important national post, he was considered unfit for the post because his Mongolian features were unacceptable to the 'Indian peasants' (Misra 2014: 5).

The above discussion shows that both the generic category of ethnicity and the specific category of race become salient when group identities are constructed under socio-political circumstances and discrimination, conflict and violence become inevitable in such ethno-political projects. The dichotomised notion of Northeasterners versus mainstream society is built upon a construction of a racially framed national core and its margin, the Northeast. The racially framed margin is further imagined as less integrated to the core because of differences of cuisine, attire, and values and this denies substantial citizenship to people of the Northeast. The quandary is very concisely summed up in the following poem titled, 'What Does an Indian Look Like?' by Cherrie L. Chhangte, a Mizo poet:

> You look at me, and you see
> My eyes, my skin, my language, my faith.
> You dissect my past, analyse my present
> Predict my future and build my profile.
> I am a curiosity, an 'ethnic' specimen.
> Politics, history, anthropology, your impressive learning,
> All unable to answer the fundamental question—
> 'What does an Indian look like?'
> An Indian looks like me, an Indian is Me. (as documented in Misra 2014: 6)

VIOLENCE AGAINST NORTHEASTERNERS IN DELHI

We perceive the problem of violence against Northeasterners as multifaceted as opposed to conventional violence. The *Oxford Dictionary* defines violence as 'behaviour involving physical force intended to hurt, damage, or kill someone or something; it is the unlawful exercise of physical force or intimidation by exhibition of such force'. Collective violence can be defined as physical force being indulged in by two or more individuals, acting on behalf of themselves or on behalf of the group to which they belong and such deeds always stem from a strong antagonistic attitude (Parthasarathy 1997). However, the idea of violence is a contested one in social sciences. Though violence is generally perceived as infliction of physical harm, this notion of physical injury is not acceptable to many as violence can be symbolic, physical, everyday, and so on. The concept of the everydayness of violence gives us the insight that such acts are a routine part of day-to-day living. The mundane nature of violence can be understood only by looking at the everyday interactions of the local social and cultural realms. Such studies explain the hidden, routine forms of conflicts operating beneath the surface that act as the ground for larger national or regional phenomena (Das 1990).

The narratives of Northeastern migrants in Delhi expose different forms of such racial violence in various arenas of life in Delhi. To understand the problem of racial violence against Northeastern migrants and its multiple manifestations, it is important to explain how Northeasterners are seen as 'different' and the 'essential other' of mainland India. The increasing levels of migration of people from various Northeastern states to Delhi in the recent past is due to the backwardness in their respective homelands and in contrast, better opportunities for education and employment in Delhi. Events of the recent past have brought to the forefront the need to discuss themes of intolerance and violence rather than diversity and accommodation in the city. The geographical belongingness of being placed at the outer edge of India's territorial map, besides the physical and cultural differences, marks the Northeasterners in Delhi as a visibly different and social category. However, the problem lies in the fact that this difference is hierarchised racially, and Northeasterners often meet with violence. The experiences of discrimination by and violence from non-Northeasterners ranges from verbal abuse to physical attacks such as killings and frequent instances of raping of Northeastern women. Nandita Haksar's recent book (2016), *The Exodus is Not Over: Migrations from the Ruptured Homelands of Northeast India*, features first-generation youngsters from the Northeast who have migrated to Delhi, Bengaluru, Goa and other places in search of work. Mostly, they find jobs as low-rung workers in retail, the hospitality industry or call centres. She relates the stories of a few Tangkhul Naga migrant workers from Ukhrul district of Manipur. Haksar writes that it has taken enormous courage for Ngalatim Hongray, Ngalatim's brother Yaokhalek Hongray, and Livingstone Shazia as well as R. S. Mayori to narrate stories of the humiliation and racism that they have faced and the absence of workers' rights that they have experienced (*Civil Society* 2017).

A study, *Migration from North East to Urban Centres: A Study of Delhi Region*, was conducted by V. V. Giri National Labour Institute (Noida) in 2012 (Remesh 2012). The study listed the various kind of issues confronted by migrants from Northeast India in the city which formed the basis of their insecurities and vulnerabilities: the cultural gap in terms of food habits, faith, and social systems; discrimination on the basis of physical features and personal traits; daily harassment from landlords, overcharging of rent, rejection as tenants; and denial of voting rights, verbal abuse, discrimination and harassment at the workplace (Remesh 2012). Similarly, the study conducted by the North East Support Centre and Helpline between 2009 and 2011 confirms that racial discrimination is meted out to Northeast Indians in varied forms, which include: violence against women, molestation, rape and attempt to rape, trafficking of women, physical violence against men, murder, non-payment of salary, non-refund of rental deposit, and media bias (NESCH 2011).

The following sections show how violence emerges as the most disturbing concern in the narratives of migrants as is evident from the field work we conducted in Delhi. Most of the respondents, irrespective of their profile, have experienced at least one instance of violence to narrate either from their own lives or as something that their friends, relatives or acquaintances have gone through. The concept of 'symbolic violence', introduced by Bourdieu, is useful while analysing varied forms of violence that Northeasterners experience in Delhi. According to Bourdieu, symbolic violence is 'gentle, imperceptible and invisible even to its victims, and is mostly exerted though purely symbolic channels of communication and cognitions (more precisely misrecognition), recognition, or even feeling' (Bourdieu, cited in Holdt 2013: 115). Symbolic violence is practised through 'durable dispositions' internalised in the minds and bodies of the victim or the dominated. It is through symbolic violence that ideologies, hierarchies and structures of authority are imposed on individuals and groups. The force of the dictator through 'durable dispositions' is practised only with the consent of the dominated. Symbolic violence, he says, is the crucial method through which social order, and hierarchies and structures of power endure and reproduce over time. While the modern state is the centre of the construction of symbolic order as it holds 'the monopoly of legitimate symbolic violence', dominant communities often exert power over the weaker ones through symbolic channels. By producing and reproducing symbolic violence, the dominant sections give legitimacy to hierarchical practices and effectively hide the continuing power relations at play (Holdt 2013). It becomes increasingly difficult for the subjects of symbolic violence to realise and fight back as this type of violence is invisible and pervasive. In the case of Northeasterners in Delhi, symbolic violence through verbal abuse is something that many respondents have experienced at least once in their life in the capital city. Derogatory words such as 'Momos' and 'Chinkees' are very frequent and directly deployed in public. These are racially stigmatised ways of addressing a population which has distinct physical features and cultural practices. Northeasterners are also often called Nepalis, Bahadurs, Firangis, Japanese and Chinese—all of which identify them as foreigners. To be called a foreigner in India despite actually belonging to the Indian nation generates an identity crisis in them.

The narratives from the field reveal many other everyday forms of discrimination and violence that Northeasterners encounter in Delhi. Most of the respondents report that they are forced to pay higher fares while travelling by auto-rickshaws and this often results in verbal abuse and quarrel. Many respondents agreed that they are subjected to discrimination and humiliation when it comes to finding accommodation in Delhi. They are denied accommodation by house owners as they are deemed unfit as tenants because of their lifestyle and food practices. Northeastern cuisines often include meat such as pork and beef, and this leads to conflict, which ends in the Northeasterners being humiliated by the landlords and neighbours. The culture of socialisation among Northeasterners, especially celebrations where boys and girls mingle, is routinely misinterpreted as sexual promiscuity and 'immoral' behaviour by others. There have been several instances which show how these notions lead to abuse and violence. Instances of Northeastern migrants being denied access to rental properties and being forcefully evicted are also not uncommon. However, the direct physical attacks are the most overt expression of racial discrimination in Delhi. This has given rise to a strong sense of fear among Northeastern migrants of being targeted by others in Delhi. The recent instances of violent attacks have intensified their sense of insecurity. According to Alana Golmei, 'there are also many cases which go unreported, cases of physical assault and molestation. Even our boys are not spared when they protect their sisters and friends. They also get beaten up and are assaulted.'[3]

The everyday violence that occurs in both private as well as public spaces is often rooted in patriarchy and this gender violence has been explored ethnographically.

> In everyday life gender codes are usually mixed with other attributes of identity. The intersectional approach points to considering simultaneously all the axes of subordination that women experience and incorporate… [and] accounts for the form of inequality affecting the symbolic constructions and shared representations of gender and 'race', sexual orientation, age, legal status, class and culture. (Toffanin 2012: 21–22)

The field insights highlight the specific vulnerability that each Northeastern woman experiences, as a woman and as a migrant, as they are more prone to physical and symbolic violence. The high number of rape cases in Delhi makes it unsafe for women, and especially Northeastern women, to travel at night. Many women migrants have reported that they are verbally harassed by men because there is a stereotypical perception about their sexuality. Sharmila Rege in her study on caste and gender talks about a similar discourse prevailing among Brahmins about Dalit women (Rege 1998). The visibility of Dalit women in public is interpreted among the upper castes as moral impurity and that they are sexually 'available' (ibid.). Northeastern women, because of their appearance and visibility in public life, are often sexually objectified.

Most of the respondents, irrespective of their gender, say that they avoid confrontation with people and act submissive in order to avoid potential violence. They are less assertive and often ignore light abuses to avoid violent attacks from others. Some of the narratives reveal how they are subjected to verbal abuse and even physical threat when they resist these everyday forms of violence. Most of the respondents think that their hometown is safer than Delhi despite all the political and social turbulence in the Northeast. However, many female respondents agree that going out at night is risky for women in both the places. Some respondents, especially those from Manipur, think Delhi is safer than their home state. The ethnic conflicts, army violence and poor governance make life in states like Manipur extremely difficult and insecure. Thus for migrants from states like Manipur, Delhi is not merely a place for better educational and employment opportunities, but a place where life is comparatively safer. This indicates that the experience of being a migrant in Delhi varies significantly among people from the Northeast depending on where in Northeast they come from. For example, many migrants from Assam say that they encounter fewer problems in Delhi as they are geographically and culturally more in proximity with the mainland and many of them look physically similar to the people of the mainland. Most of the Nagas think that their homeland is safer and more comfortable than Delhi but that Nagaland lacks the opportunities available in Delhi.

THE BEZBARUAH COMMITTEE, 2014

There is often a performative dimension in public documents prepared by the state in the sense that they are intended to preserve the myth of rationality and neutrality of the state (Hansen 2001). The legitimacy of the state can be ensured through performative governance. The government's reason for appointing committees thus is often an attempt to protect the myth of rationality of its own actions (Hansen 2001; Das 2006). While this is true to a certain degree, Das points out that such commissions of inquiry are also put up in reaction to the anxiety produced and pressure created by civil rights groups and victims seeking accountability (Das 2006). In the following section, we analyse the contours of a major report submitted on the problems of Northeasterners living outside the Northeast.

The Ministry of Home Affairs had constituted a committee under the chairmanship of M. P. Bezbaruah, retired IAS officer and member of the North Eastern Council, to look into the various concerns of the citizens hailing from the Northeastern states living in different parts of the country and to suggest suitable remedial measures including legal measures which could be taken up by the government. The eleven-member committee headed by M. P. Bezbaruah then submitted its report on the discrimination faced by and racial attacks on members of the Northeastern community in metropolitan cities of India. The eighty-two-page report paints a grim picture of the nature and extent of discrimination and attacks against the Northeastern community and provides a comprehensive list of short-term and long-term measures that must be taken by the government to counter this injustice. The report estimates that over two lakh people from the Northeast have migrated to Delhi between 2005 and 2013 and that about 86 per cent of them have faced discrimination in some form or the other. It also finds that Delhi is the worst offender among the metro cities when it comes to racial discrimination against people from the Northeast (*Firstpost* 2014).

The government responded favourably towards the following points under the Bezbaruah Committee recommendations:

(1) The insertion of new sections of 153C and 509A in the Indian Penal Code to strengthen the legal framework against racial discrimination

(2) Setting up of a special helpline number (1093) for people from the Northeast
(3) Setting up a panel of seven lawyers out of which five would be women lawyers to provide legal assistance to people from the Northeast
(4) In order to educate people about the Northeast, universities have been advised that history of the Northeast and its participation in the freedom movement of the country should be taught at graduation level and post-graduation level, and for this purpose, curricula should be changed.
(5) Appointment of a nodal police officer and a new police station for Northeasterners for immediate registering of FIR
(6) A relief fund for helping victims of hate crimes to be given under Delhi Victim Compensation Scheme, 2011

Implementation of the Recommendations

The field response to the report and its implementation will provide a better picture of the scenario. Methodologically, juxtaposing policy and response from the field will unravel the gap that exists between policy-making and the everyday reality. In the survey we conducted, there were two questions specifically on the Bezbaruah Committee:

(1) The Bezbaruah Committee which was set up in 2014 had recommended the act of reaching out to Northeastern people via social media, such as Facebook groups (e.g., Northeast India Against Racism) and WhatsApp groups, via a special helpline for Northeastern people (1093) which is synchronised with the helpline number 100, via email support, etc. Have you found these useful? Do you think these have solved the problem faced by the Northeast migrants to an extent? Comment.

(2) Among the Bezbaruah Committee recommendations that the government responded favourably to, which of the following according to you are the most relevant, most active and most effective as a long-term solution to the problems faced by Northeasterners in Delhi? (See Table 5.2). Please mark the options in decreasing order of priority. Please narrate your experiences.

Table 5.1: Feedback on the Success of Recommendations Made by the Bezbaruah Committee

Has the implementation of the recommendations made by the Bezbaruah Committee succeeded in solving the problems faced by the Northeasterners?	*No. of Respondents*	*Percentage*
Yes	65	68.4
No	12	12.6
Not aware	14	14.7
No answer	4	4.3

Source: Survey conducted as part of a project entitled 'Archiving Marginalities in North East India' spearheaded by the Department of Sociology and Centre for Regional Studies under the UGC-UPE Phase II, University of Hyderabad.

As the data given in Table 5.1 shows, a clear-cut majority of 68.4 per cent of the respondents gave credit to the efforts made by the government through the implementation of the recommendations of the committee in solving many of the issues faced by the Northeasterners in Delhi. Even those who had not really made use of the provisions felt that their very presence—like the helpline number 1093 which can be easily dialled in case of an emergency—gave a sense of security and comfort. A few were sceptical about these provisions, while a few were not aware of these but believed they would be useful if utilised effectively. The need to promote awareness about the laws was brought up by a post-graduate from Shillong working with Convergys, an information management company. He suggested that the various

Table 5.2: Feedback on the Effectiveness of Recommendations Made by the Bezbaruah Committee

Bezbaruah Committee Recommendations	*No. of Respondents That Considered the Recommendation Effective*	*Percentage*
(1) The insertion of new sections of 153C and 509A in the Indian Penal Code to strengthen the legal framework against racial discrimination.	14	14.7
(2) Setting up of a special helpline number 1093 for Northeasterners.	21	22.1
(3) Setting up a panel of 7 lawyers, out of which 5 are women, to provide legal assistance to people from the Northeast.	5	5.3
(4) In order to educate people about the Northeast, universities have been advised that history of the Northeast and the region's participation in the freedom movement of the country should be taught at graduation level and post-graduation level, and for this purpose, curricula be changed.	32	33.7
(5) Appointment of a nodal police officer and a police station for Northeasterners for immediate registering of FIR.	4	4.2
(6) A provision for a relief fund for helping victims of hate crimes as given under Delhi Victim Compensation Scheme 2011.	0	0
No. of respondents that did not answer: 19 (or 20% of the total)		

Source: Survey conducted as part of a project entitled 'Archiving Marginalities in North East India' spearheaded by the Department of Sociology and Centre for Regional Studies under the UGC-UPE Phase II, University of Hyderabad.

Northeast student associations in Delhi should work together with the Delhi Police in spreading awareness about the helpline number 1093 and other means of availing police assistance.

The respondents narrated many incidents where they had first-hand experience of relying on the various laws implemented under the Bezbaruah Committee recommendations. A 45-year-old government employee from Manipur who had been staying in Delhi for twenty-four years said that the very fact that the committee had come into existence proved that the authorities have taken cognisance. The fear of the law inculcated in the minds of the people prevents the abuse of and violence against the vulnerable to a great extent. It also enabled people to approach the concerned authorities and seek more prompt redressal than before. The setting up of a helpline number 1093 was the fastest medium to reach the authorities.[4] In one instance, the salary of a call centre employee from Manipur was withheld for a long time on the ground that his residential proof certificate was considered invalid. He approached the police who ignored him initially but responded when he warned them that he would be contacting the North East Support Centre and Helpline.[5] There are stories of respondents using the helpline in cases such as harassment by landlord who refused to give back the security deposit, molestation and fights with locals (non-Northeasterners), etc. Community support is however strong and people from the region have a tendency to reach out to their friends, members of the community (student organisations/church groupings) and relatives. They usually used the law as the last resort to solve their issues, as is common practice in Northeast India. Instead of solving the problem, this often aggravates the situation and thus there is a need to create awareness to make Northeasterners trust the law of the Indian state—alongside making active efforts to build that trust.

Table 5.2 shows the respondents' choice as to the most relevant and effective recommendations of the committee in solving the problems faced by Northeasterners. We can see that 33.7 per cent of the respondents supported the inclusion of Northeast India in the national-level curriculum at the graduate and post-graduate level with the purpose of bridging the cognitive gap and enhancing knowledge of the diversity in Indian society.

A 34-year-old respondent from Manipur residing in Munirka (New Delhi) opined that money or relief fund is not as important as they are perceived to be. She also doubted the efficiency of 'insertion of new sections 153 C and 509 A in the Indian Penal Code' because culprits always have a chance to bargain their way out of the rule of law, as had happened in the case of Jessica Lal.[6] Another respondent from Manipur who stays in the same locality in New Delhi highlighted how language becomes an obstacle in dealing with policemen. According to him,

> ...the appointment of a nodal police officer and a special police station for Northeasterners will definitely make approaching the law easier. Educating the people about the rich and relevant history of Northeast states will [help] others realise that we are also Indian[s] just like them. They always look upon us as Chinese or Nepali due to our physical appearances... But we always perceive them as Indians. This is because we [have always been] much aware of them through the national news, movies, or learnings in textbooks since high-school.[7]

A 25-year-old research student from Jawaharlal Nehru University was positive that education is the answer to the problems faced by people from Northeast India. She said, 'Education is important as it is the first thing moulding the mindset of children. Knowing the history of Northeast India, and to be more precise, [the fact that] Northeast is in India, will really help in connecting people from different regions [as citizens of] one nation.'[8] However, a member of the Bezbaruah Committee, Alana Golmei, opined that the results are far from satisfactory.

> We are still waiting for the recommendations to be implemented. The insertion of new sections of 153 C and 501 A in the Indian Penal Code to strengthen the legal framework against racial discrimination is not yet done. The [...] special helpline number 1093 for North[easterners] is already there. We are asking for

> it to be made a national helpline instead of it being operational in Delhi alone ... The plea for the insertion of the history of Northeast and [its] participation in the Indian freedom movement in NCERT and CBSE textbooks is ongoing. A request was also made for a multi-purpose building so that our boys and girls can learn and do something. Initially, the Delhi State Legal Services Authority (DSLSA) had empanelled 7 lawyers and later [the number was] increased to 11 [who represented the] 8 states of the region but most of the Northeastern community is not aware of this.

CONCLUSION

This chapter has attempted to address the question of racial discrimination and violence against Northeasterners in India by providing insight into theoretical issues as well as policy implementations. The increasing discrimination and violence against Northeasterners can be seen as a consequence of the construction of this population as racially and ethnically marginal to the nation-state in postcolonial India. The study we conducted found that the reality of increasing migration from the Northeast translates to hierarchical constructions of 'mainstream' Indians and its socio-spatial 'other', the Northeasterners, which is accompanied by routine violence.

The Bezbaruah Committee has promised much and delivered some, but its guidelines still need to be fully implemented before it can be called successful. It has nonetheless improved the situation for the Northeasterners by providing ways of immediate redressal of the problems they faced in Delhi. Full-fledged implementation of the Bezbaruah Committee's recommendations will go a long way in providing a long-term solution to the racial discrimination and violence experienced by Northeasterners.

The evidence presented in this chapter reveals that such violence is multifaceted—it is symbolic, physical, and frequent.

While there is a general pattern of experience, it is found that internal differences within the category of Northeast in terms of state, class, gender, physical appearance and culture are crucial in mapping the divergent forms of discrimination and violence among the Northeasterners in Delhi. However, racism against Northeasterners in general needs to be theorised adequately and discussed in academic discourse more actively. Further, it would be interesting to examine how the experience of Northeastern migrants in Delhi differs from that in other metropolitan cities like Mumbai, Bangalore and Hyderabad and semi-urban locations. Such a study and further data would allow a comparative understanding of racial antagonism against Northeasterners in various regions of the country.

NOTES

1. Sanjoy Hazarika, Director of the Commonwealth Human Rights Initiative (CHRI), interviewed on April 2015 in New Delhi.
2. Alana Golmei, General Secretary of North East Support and Helpline, and Member of the Bezbaruah Committee, interviewed in April 2015 in New Delhi.
3. Alana Golmei, interviewed in April 2015 in New Delhi.
4. Holkhopao Baite, interviewed on 18 June 2016 in New Delhi. The respondent is originally from Manipur.
5. A. Haokip, interviewed in June 2016. The respondent, originally from Manipur, at the time of the interview worked for a private company in New Delhi.
6. Jessica Lal was shot dead on 30 April 1999 by the son of a politician. The accused was initially acquitted by the court, but later sentenced to imprisonment following huge public outcry for justice.
7. Seilienmang Haokip, interviewed on 2 July 2016 in Delhi. The respondent is originally from Manipur.
8. Indrani Nath, interviewed on 7 June 2016 in Delhi. The respondent is originally from Assam.

REFERENCES

Appadurai, Arjun. 1998. 'Dead Certainty: Ethnic Violence in the Era of Globalization'. *Public Culture* 10(2): 225–247.

Barth, Fredrik. 1969. *Ethnic Groups and Boundaries: the Social Organization of Cultural Difference*. Boston: Little Brown.

Banton, Michael. 1987. *Racial Theories*. London: Cambridge University Press.

Bhabha, Homi. 1994. *The Location of Culture*. London & New York: Routledge.

Brubaker, Roger. 2004. *Ethnicity without Groups*. USA: Harvard University Press.

Caliendo, Stephen M., and Charlton D. McIlwain. 2011. *The Routledge Companion to Race and Ethnicity*. London: Routledge.

Civil Society. 2017. 'The Lost Young Migrants from the Northeast', 23 March. Available at http://www.civilsocietyonline.com/books-authors/lost-migrants-from-the-northeast/ (accessed on 10 April 2017).

Das, Veena. 2006. *Life and Words: Violence and the Descent into the Ordinary*. California: University of California Press.

——— (ed.). 1990. *Communities, Riots and Survivors in South Asia*. New York: Oxford University Press.

Downs, F. S. 2011. 'Christian Conversion Movements in Northeast India'. In T. K. Ommen (ed.), *Social Movements: Issues of Identity*, 381–400. New Delhi: OUP.

Firstpost. 2014. 'Bezbaruah Report on North East Community: Five Key Recommendations', 23 August. Available at http://www.firstpost.com/india/bezbaruah-report-north-east-community-five-key-recommendations-1678393.html (accessed on 19 March 2017).

Ghurye, G. S. 1999. *Caste and Race in India*. Bombay: Popular Prakashan.

Haksar, Nandita. 2016. *The Exodus is Not Over: Migrations from the Ruptured Homelands of Northeast India*. New Delhi: Speaking Tiger.

Hansen, Thomas B. 2001. *Wages of Violence: Naming and Identity in Post Colonial Bombay*. Princeton: Princeton University Press.

Holdt, Karl von. 2013. 'The Violence of Order, Orders of Violence: Between Fanon and Bourdieu'. *Current Sociology* 61(2): 226–243.

McDuie-Ra, Duncan. 2012a. *Northeast Migrants in Delhi: Race, Refuge and Retail*. Netherlands: Amsterdam University Press.

———. 2012b. 'The "North-East" Map of Delhi'. *Economic and Political Weekly* XLVII(30): 69–77.

Misra, Udayon. 2014. *India's North East: Identity Movements, State and Civil Society*. New Delhi: OUP.

NESCH (North East Support Centre & Helpline). 2011 (March). *North East Migration and Challenges in National Capital Cities*. New Delhi: NESCH.

Ngaihte, Thangkhanlal. 2014. 'Nido Taniam and the Fraught Question of Racism in India'. *Economic and Political Weekly* Vol XLIX(11): 15–17.

Nongbri, Tiplut. 2014. *Development Masculinity and Christianity: Essays and Verses from India's North East.* Shimla: Indian Institute of Advanced Study.

Pachuau, Lalsangkima. 1998. *Ethnic Identity and Christianity: A Socio-historical and Missiological Study of Christianity in Northeast India with Special Reference to Mizoram*. Frankfurt: Peter Lang.

Parthasarathy, D. 1997. *Collective Violence in a Provincial City.* Calcutta: Oxford University Press.

Remesh, Babu P. 2012. *Migration from North East to Urban Centres: A Study of Delhi Region.* Noida (Delhi): V. V. Giri National Labour Institute.

Rege, Sharmila. 1998. 'Dalit Women Talk Differently: A Critique of Actually Existing Democracy.' *Economic and Political Weekly* 44(31): 31–46.

Time. 2014. 'What the Death of Nido Taniam Tells Us About Racism in India'. 6 February. Available at http://time.com/4876/nido-taniam-india-racism/ (accessed April 2023).

Toffanin, Angela Maria. 2012. 'Research on Violence against Women: A Sociological Perspective'. *Interdisciplinary Journal of Family Studies* XVII: 15–30.

Varshney, Ashutosh. 2002. *Ethnic Conflict and Civic Life: Hindus and Muslims in India.* New Delhi: Oxford University Press.

6

Northeast Youth Migration to Cities

The Kuki Case in Delhi*

Thanggoulen Kipgen

Migration in search of employment has occurred all through history and it is by no means a new phenomenon. Migrations from India, into India, and within India have been analysed by scholars from different fields (see Bates 1985; De Haan and Rogaly 1994; Kapur 2010; Mishra 2016). Although migration studies is a growing field in India, the northeastern part of the country remains at the margin of this discourse. The few studies on migration related to the Northeast mostly focus on in-migration from other states of India and international migration from the neighbouring countries. But the out-migration of the Northeasterners to urban centres in India is an area of migration research that is relatively unexplored.

The rate of migration of Kukis from Northeast India to various metropolises like Bengaluru, Mumbai and Kolkata in search of jobs has increased in the past few decades. Among these cities, Delhi is often the most favoured destination. This needs to be understood in the context of Delhi's transformation into a 'global city' through neoliberal capitalism that has changed the consumer and business landscape of the city. The desire for Northeastern labour in the 'de-Indianised' spaces of global capital draws migrants from the frontier to work in shopping malls, spas,

*An earlier version of this essay was published as 'Migrants and Their Social Networks: A Study of Kuki Migrants in Delhi' in *Sociological Bulletin* 68(3): 342–356.

restaurants, call centres and other commercial centres (McDuie-Ra 2012a: 61). In using the term 'Northeastern migrants', we are referring to 'those people from the Northeast who trace their lineage to East and Southeast Asia and as such are members of ethnic minorities racially distinct from communities in the rest of India…' (ibid.: 29). The unfavourable socio-economic and political conditions prevalent in their places of origin and the demand for Northeastern labour particularly in the service sectors have encouraged migration among Kukis. This chapter discusses the various factors that have contributed to the Kuki out-migration from the state of Manipur to Delhi. We shall confine our scope to the study of Kuki migrants migrating to Delhi for work in call centres, retail outlets, hotels, restaurants, beauty salons, hospitals and other places. The study made use of both secondary and primary sources of data, the latter collected through fieldwork conducted in Delhi using questionnaires and through interviews.

DEFINING NORTHEAST INDIA AND THE KUKIS

The term 'Northeast India' is a politico-geographical expression that refers to eight states: Assam, Arunachal Pradesh, Manipur, Meghalaya, Mizoram, Nagaland, Sikkim and Tripura. The region is home to various ethnic communities that have migrated from various places, the majority of them belonging to the Indo-Chinese Mongoloid racial grouping (as cited in Sitlhou 2017: xxii). The Northeastern region accounts for about 12 per cent of the country's total tribal population, and except for Assam and Tripura, the people in the other five states are predominantly tribal. When we use the term 'Northeast India' or 'Northeastern region' here, we refer to the physical or geographical territory of the nation-state as well as the social facets, which include diverse ethno-linguistic groups, customs, beliefs and practices (Nongkynrih 2009: 368).

The word 'Kuki' is a generic term which includes a number of tribes and clans. Kukis are trans-border tribes scattered across three international boundaries, namely: the Northeast of India, the Northern Provinces of the Chin Hills of Burma, and the Chittagong Hill Tract of Bangladesh. Kukis are identified as the Mongoloid racial stock of the Austro-Asiatic group of the Tibeto-Burman linguistic family. William Shaw, a British civil servant who served in Assam, wrote in his *Notes on the Thadou Kukis* that, 'the Koms, Aimols, Khotlangs, Thadous, Lushais, Chins, Pois, Suktes, Paites, Gangtes and so on are undoubtedly all connected' (Shaw 1929: 16), and 'are Kukis' (Arora and Kipgen 2012: 434). In independent India, the various Kuki tribes are represented or recognised under 'Any Kuki Tribes' in the constitutional Scheduled Castes and Scheduled Tribes lists of 1951 in the states of Assam, Manipur, Tripura, Meghalaya, and Mizoram, and in Nagaland they are simply recognised as Kuki. There are Kukis in all states of Northeast India except Arunachal Pradesh and Sikkim.

DEFINING YOUTH AS AN AGE GROUP

Before we delve deeper into the topic of youth migration, it is necessary to define the term 'youth' with regards to the section of population it refers to. In India, persons aged 15–29 years are considered youth and account for 26 to 29 per cent of the total population. A substantial proportion of them attain some level of education and enter the labour market while they are in the age group of 15–29 years, although some of them may be chronically unemployed or may remain unemployed for a long period. Some others may become intermittently unemployed during some weeks or days of the year due to seasonal fluctuations in the labour market (NSSO 2014: 186). On the other hand, the National Youth Policy (2003: 2) defines youth as 'persons in the age group of 13 to 35 years'. It is acknowledged that since all the 'persons within this age group are unlikely to be one homogenous group, but rather a conglomeration of sub-groups with differing social roles and requirements, the age group may, therefore, be divided into two broad sub-groups viz. 13–19 years and 20–35 years'. Using these two definitions, youth, in this particular case study, refers to those who are in the age group of 15–35 years, taking the minimum age from the NSSO Report and maximum age from the National Youth Policy.

Nongkynrih (2009: 369) argues that the definition of youth is 'a modern construction because a person is a youth on the basis of the birth certificate issued by the authorized bodies of the nation-state'. He further states that there are societies in Northeast India where age is not the basis for defining youth. He uses the term 'generational principle' where social actors or members of society are addressed by specific social terms, and these terms denote their generation. In Kuki society, the term '*khangthah*' refers to unmarried youth who have reached a certain stage of life where their 'physical strength is recognized and utilized in collective activities' (ibid.: 369). Kuki migrants in Delhi fit well in both the modern and generational classifications of youth.

In this case study, the majority of respondents was in the age group of 15–35 years at the time of migration and fits the operational definition of youth (see Table 6.1). Just 5 per cent and 1 per cent of the respondents were in the age groups of 35–40 years and 40 years and above, respectively, and technically do not qualify as 'youth'. However, it is important to note that these older respondents (of ages 35–40 and above) are those

Table 6.1: Age Groups of Kuki Migrants in Delhi (N=130)

S. No.	*Age Group*	*Percentage of Kuki Migrants in Delhi*
1	15–20 years	2.3
2	20–25 years	24.42
3	25–30 years	51.14
4	30–35 years	14.50
5	35–40 years	5.34
6	40 years and above	2.32

Source: Based on the author's primary fieldwork in 2015–2016.

migrants who have been in Delhi for more than 5 to 15 years (see Table 6.2 for more details). This data suggests that these respondents (above 35 years) belonged to the age group of 15–35 years when they had migrated to the capital city. These Kuki migrants were also unmarried at the time of migration and thus they would have qualified as youth according to the 'generational principle' definition as well.

Table 6.2: Duration of Stay in Delhi of Kuki Migrants of Various Age Groups (N=130)

Duration of Stay in Delhi → *Age Group ↓*	*3–5 Years*	*5–7 Years*	*7–9 Years*	*9–11 Years*	*11–13 Years*	*13–15 Years*	*15 Years and Above*
15–20 years	3	–	1	–	–	–	–
20–25 years	29	2	1	–	–	–	–
25–30 years	38	14	13	3	–	–	–
30–35 years	4	2	6	7	–	–	–
35–40 years	–	2	–	2	–	–	3
40 years and above	–	–	–	2	–	–	–

Source: Based on the author's primary fieldwork in 2015–2016.

FACTORS OF KUKI MIGRATION TO DELHI

While reasons for migration may be specific to individuals, migrants in general may share similar experiences. Lee (1969: 50) argues that migration is governed by factors associated with the place of origin and the place of destination. Negative factors at the areas of origin, such as lack of job opportunities, push migrants away whereas positive factors of the destination, such as better chances of finding work and wages, pull them towards it. Revenstein (1885: 199) in his 'Laws of Migration' argues that 'migrants proceeding long distances generally go by preference to one of the great centres of commerce or industry'. Lowell and Findlay (2001: 3) argued that not only has the demand for skilled labour in developed countries (or areas) increased, but pull factors such as better wages and employment conditions, better information and a better chance of recruitment and cheaper transportation encourage skilled migrants to seek jobs in developed regions. Limited or no economic opportunities in places of origin and the lure of better opportunities and lifestyle in developed areas act as the push and pull factors of migration (Parkins 2010: 12). Martin and Zurcher (2008) argue that the factors behind the decision to migrate, and hence also the type of migrant, can be grouped broadly into two categories: economic and non-economic. Further, the factors propelling a migrant to make that final move can be divided into three categories: demand-pull, supply-push, and networks (see Table 6.3).

Table 6.3: Factors which Affect Migration

Type of Migrant	*Demand-Pull*	*Supply-Push*	*Networks/Other*
Economic	Labour recruitment	Unemployment or underemployment and issues such as low wages	Job and wage information flows
Non-economic	Family unification (spouses join each other, children join parents)	Fleeing war and/or civil unrest	Communication; transportation; assistance; organisations; desire for new experience

Source: Martin and Zurcher (2008).

Conditions of Home: Supply-Push

The root causes of migration are generally hypothesised to be those associated with poverty and disadvantage (Schmeidl 1997). High levels of unemployment and poverty in the place of origin often act as a push factor in the decision to emigrate (Wickramasekera 2002). Unemployment and poverty remain the main reasons for the out-migration of youth towards cities across India. In

Northeast India, the states are primarily agrarian with weak economies and underdeveloped industrial sectors. Historically, the region has been one of the most backward in the country due to 'poor infrastructure and lack of democratic governance combined with low productivity and market access, low levels of industrial activity and limited spread of modern service sector... agriculture is the main stay of the region's economy' (Rajan and Chyrmang 2016: 105). The number of educated youth in the northeastern region is increasing, but the growth in employment opportunities is not commensurate (Nongkynrih 2009: 372).

Unemployment and Poverty

Despite having a higher literacy rate than the national average, the state of Manipur remains socio-economically backward. As Sharma (2014) observed, the economy of Manipur is characterised by a high rate of unemployment and poverty, low capital formation, inadequate infrastructural facilities, geographical isolation, communication bottlenecks and practically no industrialisation. Unemployment is alarmingly high particularly among the educated youth in Manipur. As a result, they are increasingly migrating to metropolises like Delhi in search of better employment opportunities (Reimeingam 2011: 137). In Manipur, employment opportunities are mostly based in the public sector. For instance, the total number of persons employed in the organised sector in the state was 80,600 as on 31 March 2005. Out of this, 78,000 were employed in the public sector and the remaining 2,600 were in the private sector. In the public sector, the share of employment in central and state governments were 5.77 and 79.36 per cent respectively, and that in quasi-central and state governments were 5.38 per cent and 4.36 per cent respectively (Government of Manipur 2016: 188). Therefore, state government has the highest share in employment generation. However, the number of persons employed by the state government has been decreasing each year. For instance, persons employed by the state government have decreased from 60,982 in 2006 to 58,171 in 2009 and to 54,181 in 2014 (ibid.: 189).

Though the state provides 87 per cent of all employment, the number of appointments made by the state is minimal. Data from the Employment Exchange shows the number of persons employed by the state government in various governmental departments (see Table 6.4). Accordingly, the number of persons newly registered in the Employment Exchanges in the state during the year 2012–13 was 35,573 as against 22,825 during the year 2007–08, showing an increase of 62.25 per cent. The number of vacancies notified in 2008–09 was 4,667 as against the 3,170 during the year 2007–08. There were two persons placed in appointment during the year 2007–08 and 210 persons in 2008–09 (Government of Manipur 2016: 185–186). Thus we see that though the number of educated unemployed people registered with the Employment Exchange has increased each year over the last few decades, the number of placements is negligible, contributing indirectly to out-migration of educated youth in search of employment.

Table 6.4: Number of Registrants and Placements Effected by Employment Exchanges of Manipur

Year	*Particulars*		
	Number of Persons Registered during the Year	*Number of Vacancies Notified*	*Number of Persons Placed in Appointments*
2007–08	22825	3170	2
2008–09	37033	4667	210
2009–10	31607	2344	3
2010–11	16057	1096	644
2011–12	22059	1365	128
2012–13	35573	2081	Data not available
2013–14	15794	1428	Data not available
2014–15	23861	634	Data not available

Source: Government of Manipur 2016.

It should also be noted that the private sector plays a very important role in employment generation particularly among the youths. However, various factors have hindered the growth of private sectors and entrepreneurship in Manipur. Bandhs, strikes and blockades have directly or indirectly affected the economy of the state. According to the Directorate of Economics and Statistics, Government of Manipur, in 2005–06, state-wide bandhs led to a loss of Rs 24 per head per day, totalling a loss of Rs 6.13 crores per day and the National Highway blockade caused a loss of Rs 11 per head per day, totalling Rs 2.67 crores per day. The worst scenario was witnessed in 2010–11 when 97 days of bandhs and 135 days of economic blockade resulted in a loss of Rs 645.3 crores. On an average, 9 to 10 per cent of the state's NSDP (Net State Domestic Product) was lost due to bandhs and blockades in the last six years (Singha 2013: 8–9).

Table 6.5: Economic Loss in Manipur due to Bandhs and Blockades (Rs in Cr)

Year	*Number of Days of Bandh*	*Loss due to Bandh*	*Number of Days of Economic Blockade*	*Loss due to Economic Blockade*	*Total Loss due to Bandh and Blockade*
2004–05	20	111.4	60	130.2	241.6
2005–06	48	306.24	97	236.68	542.92
2006–07	94	642.96	77	201.74	844.7
2007–08	52	382.2	43	122.12	504.32
2008–09	56	442.4	63	178.91	621.31
2010–11	97	229.5	135	415.8	645.3

Source: Singha 2013.

The frequent and spontaneous imposition of economic blockades and bandhs creates a hostile atmosphere for economic investments in the state. It has led to a state of insecurity of life, of business and employment and has caused a disruption in market connectivity. The economy is also affected negatively in the long term in two ways: (a) brain drain, and (b) discouragement to entrepreneurship (Sharma 2014: 8). One of our interviewees, Lun (28), who is working in a call centre, said,

> After I finished my graduation I worked as an assistant teacher in a private school as I had no other opportunities. My parents had no regular income. They earn from working in the forests and paddy fields during harvesting season. My younger sister [weaves] to help my parents in running the family. My monthly income from the school was Rs 3300 per month. After buying my siblings educational [supplies] such as textbooks, notebooks, pens, pencils, [and paying my] rent, I am left with nothing at all. Many times I couldn't even pay tithe to the church. I heard from friends that I can earn much more in Delhi. That's when I decided to come here.

The unfavourable socio-economic condition in Manipur has an impact on students as well. Chongboi (27) from Vijay Nagar in North Delhi, who is working in a call centre, said,

> See ... you cannot even cover the syllabus due to bandhs and blockades that occur throughout the year. When competition is so high, and you are not allowed to attend classes regularly, there is no other choice but to leave the state for good. I came to Delhi and finished my graduation in 2013. I am now working in a call centre to support my siblings who are staying with me.

Thanks to their cultural capital, the educated youths are the ones in the family who most often undertake the risk involved in the migration process. This is true for all genders, and in most cases it is the elder sibling who takes the risk to undertake the journey first, the reason most often being an obligation to generate income for their family's survival and sustenance. Some elder siblings even give up their own education and migrate to Delhi to earn and support their families back home. A female respondent (27) working in one private company said,

> I am the eldest among five siblings in our family. I was in my second year of college when I came to Delhi. My parents' earnings are not enough to support all of us. I came to learn that people are leaving for Delhi to work in private companies and earning a

> good amount of money. So, I enquired about it and found some people who could help me out. I talked to my parents and they all agreed with my decision. I am now sending money every month to support my siblings' education.

In addition to the socio-economic factors, the unfavourable political scenario in the states of the Northeast, such as insurgency and related violence as well as frequent conflicts, also encourages the Kukis to move out of the state and avail employment opportunities outside. Of all the states in the Northeast that have been affected by insurgency-related violence, Manipur is by far the most adversely affected. There were a total of 63 insurgent groups (both active and inactive) in Manipur in 2016 (SATP 2016). There have been instances where insurgent groups have forced people, particularly educated ones, to join their groups. Escaping such a situation is also often a motivation for the Kuki youth to undertake the journey of migration. For instance, one respondent, Len (28) from Ukhrul district, who studied in Churachandpur district, said,

> I don't want to go back to my village in Ukhrul district because I heard that some underground groups are recruiting youths particularly the educated ones during festivals and social gatherings. I know that if they find me they will force me to join their group. So, after I finished my Class 12, I decided to come to Delhi directly from Churachandpur. Now, I am doing a correspondence course in IGNOU and also working in a restaurant.

Aspirations

Reimeingam (2011: 137) argued that besides social and political unrest, the high number of educated unemployed youth with growing aspirations in the state of Manipur, where job opportunities are limited, leads to out-migration. In recent years, with improved communication and better infrastructure, there is an increased contact between tribal people and outsiders which has led to rising aspirations of the people in the Northeast. Families aspire to provide better education to their children and improve their living conditions. As the traditional occupational systems have failed to provide extra income and the state has limited income generation opportunities, many families have had to send their young members outside the state so they could find work and support the family back home.

There is also corruption, nepotism and bribery in most departmental recruitments under the state government. Singh (2002) argues that even when employment opportunities are available, the youth of Manipur have to resort to paying bribes or depend on their connections and relations to get jobs (cited in Nongkynrih 2009: 391). For those educated unemployed who are among the economically backward and who have no political patronage or links, getting government jobs in the state is a distant dream. With limited opportunities in the private sectors in Manipur, the Kuki youth, with the cultural capital that they have acquired, are pulled towards Delhi for employment in various service and hospitality sectors. As one Mimin (28), a graduate from Manipur University, said,

> I was a fresh graduate when I came to Delhi. After my graduation there was a notification for recruitment of Sub-Inspector in the Police Department. I cleared the Mains exam but I was told that I have to pay at least seven to eight lakhs to some MLAs or ministers to get through the interview. I don't have that much money. So, I didn't get through the interview. I was jobless for many months. Instead of staying home jobless, I decided to come to Delhi to work in private companies.

Opportunities in Delhi: Demand-Pull

The neoliberal transformation of Delhi in the last few decades has created spaces of engagement between Northeasterners and the residents of the Indian capital. Castells' (1991: 108) theory of 'specialty labor', by which he meant not only high skilled labour but labour that is 'in exceptionally high demand', fits to the context of the demand for Northeastern labour in Delhi. The demand for labour in the city's globalised spaces has led to a rapid increase in migration from the Northeast as the youth find work in hotels, restaurants, shopping malls and call centres. The rapid growth of new consumer spaces for the middle and upper classes and the growth of the services sector catering to global capital are the most common sectors where Northeastern labour finds employment in Delhi (McDuie-Ra 2012a, 2012b). It is widely reported that relatively better command over English (among the educated) and friendly attitude of the youth from North Eastern Region (NER) often makes it easier to find a job in the cities, especially in hospitality and service sectors (Remesh 2012: 5). In recent years, with the emergence of new occupations particularly after the liberalisation of the economy, there are growing opportunities in the private sector, especially service sectors (NESCH 2011). Earlier Delhi attracted only the wealthy and the educated from the Northeast. However, in recent years, there has been a dramatic growth in the number of people from other backgrounds coming for work in retail, hospitality and call centres which is most remarkable and visible to residents and visitors of the city. Delhi has been one of the most preferred destinations for Kuki youths as the cultural capital they possess, such as better educational qualification, their sense of fashion and conversational abilities, gives them an edge in availing of job opportunities in the service sector.

Demand for Northeastern Labour in Call Centres

There are various factors that characterise the demands of labour from the Northeast in call centres in Delhi and NCR. The availability of a large English-speaking skilled workforce has attracted many multinational companies dealing with information and communication technologies into the city. Gurgaon has been the site of emergence of a prominent outsourcing and offshoring hub over the past decade, with numerous business process outsourcing (BPO) firms (Dupont 2011: 539). Call centres depend upon access to a relatively low-cost labour force and one that is well educated and fluent in English (McDuie-Ra 2012b: 75). People from the hill states of the Northeast are educated in English-medium schools and many of these hill states have a very high literacy rate. Except in the states of Assam and Arunachal Pradesh, where Hindi is commonly spoken, English is the lingua franca spoken between different ethnic groups in rest of the hill states of the Northeast. In Manipur, Hindi is banned as a result of ethno-nationalist campaigns to restore the Meitei language and resist Indian domination by the Meitei insurgent groups (McDuie-Ra 2012a: 76).[1] Because of their early English education and unfamiliarity with other Indian languages, most people from Northeast India speak English without a heavy accent which is common in speakers from other parts of India (ibid.: 76). It is also widely reported that relatively better command over English and friendly attitude of the youth from NER often help them to easily find a job in the cities (Remesh 2012: 5).

The burgeoning call centre industry offers livelihood opportunities to many of the Kuki migrants. Most of these migrants are young and unmarried which makes it easier for them to work flexible shifts timed to serve American, Australian and European business hours. Given the lack of job opportunities at their home state, the Kuki youth who could not continue their studies due to reasons like poverty, pressure from the family to contribute to the household income, responsibility of supporting younger siblings' education, etc. decide to migrate to as far as Delhi in search of employment. There is thus a large concentration of college dropouts working in the call centre industry, which requires a higher secondary school certificate as educational qualification. There are also a few migrants who have even completed their Master's degrees, indicating the sheer lack of opportunities at their place of origin. Call centres provide a higher monthly income and Delhi promises a better lifestyle to this qualified workforce which makes it a preferred option for educated Kuki migrants. There are also instances where migrants have left their homes while pursuing higher education. One male respondent said,

> I came to Delhi while I was in the second year [of my] Bachelor of Arts [degree]. I am the eldest among three sisters and two brothers in the family. We live in a village, very far from the town in which I was pursuing my graduation. I was renting a house in the town while my parents who earn little income from paddy and forest products supported me by sending money every month. My younger siblings had passed their higher secondary and matriculation while I was in my second year of college. It became an extra burden on my parents. Once my parents came down to town and we had a discussion where we had agreed that I should consider going to Delhi to earn and also support my siblings' education. So, I left my studies and came to Delhi. I am sending home some of my earnings every month.

Opportunities in Shopping Malls

The capital city of Delhi, like many other globalised urban spaces across the world, has seen the growth of malls and shopping centres for many years now. Shopping malls have been described as the 'new temples of India—not dedicated anymore to Gods, but devoted to consumption and leisure' (Detilleux 2007: 78) which house 'numerous outlets of foreign retail chains offering international brand names, cinemas, restaurants, and more' (Dupont 2011: 543). There are 62 operational malls as of April 2011; 16 upcoming malls planned till 2014 and another 5 malls on hold as of April 2011 in Delhi and NCR (Asipac 2011: 4–9). Also, the population of Delhi has been increasing from 9.9 million in 2001 to 16.7 million in 2011 (Census of India 2011). With the increase in population, the demand for malls has also increased and to cater to this demand, an increasing number of malls have come up in Delhi and NCR. Further, with Delhi having the highest average per capita annual income in the country (2.01 lakh as of 2011), the demand for organised shopping spaces like shopping malls will continue to be on the rise in the years to come (*The Economic Times* 2013).

The Northeastern migrants with physical features similar to the East and Southeast Asian people are in great demand in these new global, cosmopolitan markets. 'Their labour is in demand because they reproduce the de-Indianised aesthetic without the need to import foreign labour' (McDuie-Ra 2012a: 73). They are welcome and desired 'because they look, speak, and act un-Indian'. In a country where caste-consciousness is still very strong, the people from the Northeast are regarded as both 'neutral' and 'exotic' since they are not associated with a particular caste, religion or regional group in 'mainland' India (ibid.: 74). Therefore, the Northeastern labour force 'constructs a space that is in India but not of India' and fits perfectly in these cosmopolitan spaces coveted by the middle classes.

Thanks to their looks and fluency in English, the Kuki migrants, especially the women, find opportunities in these spaces without much difficulty. One female migrant (23) working at Saket Citywalk, an upscale mall in Delhi, said,

> Many of the customers [think I am] either from Japan or Korea. Sometimes they ask for photos. Even the children seem to like us. But these are rich people with high-class lifestyles ... They mostly speak English while they are shopping.

Kuki migrants usually do not have to wait long in search of jobs thanks to the huge demand for labour and it is also easy for them to shift from one store, hotel or restaurant to another through networks that the Northeastern diaspora have built. It is common among female migrants to move to a new workplace to be in close proximity to another worker from the same community. One female respondent (19) working at DLF Ambience Mall said,

> I once shifted to another job just because I had a friend who was working there. My friend told me that there was a vacancy in their shop. So, I talked to the HR (Human Resources) and they recruited me. The pay was lesser but I decided to go there because it was boring to stay alone.

Demand for Healthcare Workers in Delhi

Delhi is emerging as a major healthcare hub in the country with a significant presence of the private sector. It has some of the best medical facilities in the country due to its location and its status as the capital city. Not only does it attract large sections of the Indian population but foreigners as well. Many people from developed countries visit Delhi for treatment as medical expenses are much lower when compared to First World countries and also the wait time for appointments is much shorter (DDA 2007). A large number of hospitals have been established to meet the growing demands for health services and this has attracted large numbers of healthcare staff from across the country.

There is a large population of Kuki nurses working both in public and private hospitals in Delhi. The limited number of nursing institutes in the state of Manipur leads to many students leaving the state and moving to various cities, mostly in south India, to pursue nursing training. After completing their courses, they prefer to move to Delhi for various reasons. While there is demand for nursing staff in other cities of India as well, the demand is relatively higher in the NCR and moreover, the salaries offered are much higher. For instance, the starting monthly salary for nurses in cities of South India is around Rs 6,000 to 7,000 whereas it is between Rs 15,000 and 20,000 in Delhi. Another factor that attracts Kuki nurses to Delhi is the opportunity for permanent recruitment in government hospitals. Hospitals run by the local bodies such as New Delhi Municipal Council (NDMC) and Municipal Corporation of Delhi (MCD) are open to all citizens of India irrespective of their state of origin. Kim (30), who worked in Kolkata before coming to Delhi, said,

> I came to Delhi in 2010. I chose Delhi because you don't need to register yourself [with] the Delhi Nursing Board (DNB) to be eligible for government hospitals. In other states of India, you need to register yourself with the respective state's nursing board to qualify as a nurse, which is not very easy. In Delhi, you can use

> your registration number that you already have from your nursing college. So, I decided to come to Delhi.

Therefore, the promise of a higher income and equal opportunities of recruitment and job security in governmental hospitals draw a large number of Kuki migrant nurses to Delhi.

The Role of Social Networks

A social network can be defined as a chain of relations which connect people with one another. It is generally perceived that the more alien a place is, the less attractive it would be to prospective migrants. However, the existence of social networks at the place of destination can encourage people at the place of origin to undertake the journey of migration. These social networks help migrants to overcome feelings of apprehension and insecurity. Various studies on migration have examined the importance of social networks in determining the choice and destination of migration (see Boyd 1989; Haug 2008; Massey et al. 1993; Ritchey 1976; Thieme 2006). Sonja Haug (2008: 588) defines social network as 'a composite of interpersonal relations in which migrants interact with their family or friends'. D. S. Massey et al. (1993: 448) define migrant networks as 'a set of interpersonal ties that connect migrants, former migrants, and non-migrants in origin and destination areas through ties of kinship, friendship, and shared community origin'.

Social networks play a very significant role in making Delhi a popular destination for the Kukis. The pioneer migrants in the city were students who migrated in the early 1980s and enrolled themselves for higher studies in different universities. Delhi as a destination for work, however, only became popular in the post-liberalisation period of the Indian economy as job opportunities grew with the growing market. Especially from the year 2000 onwards, there have been a growing number of Kuki youth who have migrated out of Manipur and have chosen Delhi as a place for education and employment. Many students join part-time jobs in the city to support themselves while preparing for various competitive examinations. According to Duncan McDuie-Ra, Delhi provides the opportunities to work, study, learn the ropes of the Indian bureaucracy, and to do all of these things at once (2012a). The migrants primarily relied on social networks (both ethnic and kinship relations) to obtain requisite support and help as well as to gather information about jobs, accommodation and other essential requirements. Once relations are formed, the network becomes self-sustaining and creates a 'chain of migration' that encourages individuals at the place of origin to undertake the same journey that their predecessors did.

People from the Northeast have always faced various forms of discrimination in 'mainland' India due to differences in terms of their physical features, food habits, lifestyles, and so on (see Kikon 2015; McDuie-Ra 2012a; Sitlhou and Punathil 2017; Wouters and Subba 2013), which can be traced back to colonial times. Northeast India, as a part of Willem Schendel's concept of Zomia—'an upland massif stretching throughout mainland Southeast Asia to the Yunnan province in China, the hill areas of Northeast India, the Chittagong Hill Tracts in Bangladesh, and the Himalayas' (Scott 2009: 4)—has historically been marginal to the state and is regarded as 'uncivilised', 'backward', 'savage' and 'primitive' (ibid.: 100). In postcolonial India, the hill areas of the Northeast were classified as 'backward tracts', and 'excluded from the operation of laws applicable in the rest of British-controlled India' (Baruah 2005: 36). Even the Constituent Assembly Debates in independent India pointed to the fact that the tribal people were given special constitutional provisions in the form of Scheduled Areas 'as museums for purposes of demonstration and exhibition before the world to justify their (British) existence in India' (Corbridge 2000: 68). This reference to tribal museums and exhibitions speaks directly to a policy of isolationism and marginalisation (ibid.: 68).

Postcolonial India is characterised by linguistic, ethnic, religious and racial diversity. This multiplicity is, however, often portrayed or known exclusively within the Indo-Aryan and Dravidian cultural and linguistic frames. The region known as the Northeast has been obscured by various strands of national and international discourses (Pachuau 2014: 2). The Northeast as a region is stereotyped and imagined by the 'mainlanders' as 'backward' and 'dangerous' (Wouters and Subba 2013: 6), and represented as 'a region that lacks peace, one that is volatile and capable of breaking out in unrest at any time' (Pachuau 2014: 51). Then, what ensues when these 'backward', 'primitive', 'dangerous', 'savage' and 'barbaric' tribal people from the Northeastern states move in search of employment and opportunities into the booming urban centres in other Indian states? Northeasterners in Delhi face various forms of discrimination and marginalisation. Physical assault and sexual violence against men and women from the Northeast are frequently reported from different areas in the NCR (NESCH 2011: 20). 'The geographical belongingness of being placed at the outer edge of India's territorial map, but more importantly, physical appearance and cultural differences, marks the Northeasterners in Delhi as a visibly different social category' (Sitlhou and Punathil 2017: 94).

However, despite the discrimination and marginalisation they face, the Kukis find Delhi to be an attractive destination because of the prevailing social networks. The Kuki migrants prefer to stay together as a group and use their social networks as support groups that provide a feeling of community and togetherness against the violence of marginalisation and threat to security. In case of emergencies or other unforeseen crisis, the Kuki community pools its resources together and assists its members. With the growing rate of migration, ethnic clusters or Kuki-majority neighbourhoods have developed in few areas, especially in South Delhi. The popular localities are Munirka Village, Safdarjung Enclave, Kishangarh Village, Masoodpur, Katwaria Sarai and Mahipalpur. Other localities that host Kuki migrants are Dilshad

Garden and Shalimar Garden in the east and Vijay Nagar, Patel Chest, Malka Ganj and others in the north. McDuie-Ra (2012a: 103) in his study of Northeast migrants in Delhi observed that the occurrence of crimes specifically targeting the community, such as murder, rape, mob violence, kidnapping, assault, and sexual harassment, and their reporting across print and electronic media puts tremendous psychological stress on migrants which pushes them to stay together in a close-knit community. The social networks thus allow the migrants to adapt and respond to the various hardships and uncertainties they face in the city.

CONCLUSION

Poverty, unemployment and socio-political instability push many educated youths in Manipur to leave their home state and migrate to large cities that offer a diversity of job opportunities and a better life. With their educational qualification, sophisticated interpersonal and English communication skills, many Kuki youths are able to find well-paying jobs, notably in the globalised private services sector, even in a cut-throat competitive environment like Delhi, and despite the multiple biases that work against Northeasterners.

Other than the lure of lucrative jobs, which enable them to support families back home, the existence of social networks in the city is a powerful incentive that plays a crucial role in the Kukis' choice of destination. The closely-knit community of Kukis is a ready source of friendship and strength and offers wide-ranging support to its members in times of crisis, helping new migrants navigate an uncertain life in the city, characterised by violence both visible and invisible. The social networks are therefore also a vital survival strategy for the migrants. Despite the many forms of discrimination and marginalisation faced by Kukis, and by all Northeastern migrants in general, the capital city of Delhi thus seems to remain one of their most preferred destinations.

NOTES

1. A proscribed outfit in Manipur issued a notification prohibiting the use of Hindi in Manipur in September 2000. Hindi films and television series were banned because they were seen as a threat to the local language and culture.

REFERENCES

Arora, V., and N. Kipgen. 2012. 'The Politics of Identifying with and Distancing from Kuki Identity in Manipur'. *Sociological Bulletin* 61(3): 429–449.

Asipac. 2011. *Demand and Supply of Mall Space in India: Delhi and NCR.* Bangalore: Asipac Mall Services Pvt. Ltd.

Baruah, S. 2005. *Durable Disorder: Understanding the Politics of Northeast India.* New Delhi: Oxford University Press.

Bates, C. N. 1985. 'Regional Dependence and Rural Development in Central India: The Pivotal Role of Migrant Labour'. *Modern Asian Studies* 19(3): 572–92.

Boyd, M. 1989. 'Family and Personal Networks in International Migration: Recent Developments and New Agendas'. *International Migration Review* 23(3): 638–70.

Castells, M. 1991. *The Informational City: Information Technology, Economic Restructuring and the Urban Regional Process.* Oxford: Blackwell.

Corbridge, S. 2000. 'Competing Inequalities: The Scheduled Tribes and the Reservations System in India's Jharkhand'. *The Journal of Asian Studies* 59(1):62–85.

DDA (Delhi Development Authority). 2007. *Master Plan for Delhi 2021.* Delhi: Delhi Development Authority.

De Haan, A., and Rogaly B. 1994. 'Eastward Ho! Leapfrogging and Seasonal Migration in Eastern India'. *South Asia Research* 14(I): 36–61.

Detilleux, C. 2007. 'En marchant dans Gurgaon'. *Revue Urbanisme* 355: 78–79.

Dupont, V. D. N. 2011. 'The Dream of Delhi as a Global City'. *International Journal of Urban and Regional Research* 35(3): 533–554.

Ganguly, J. Baran. 2006. *An Economic History of North East India.* New Delhi: Akansha Publishing House.

Government of Manipur. 2016. *Economic Survey: Manipur 2015–16.* Lamphelpat: Directorate of Economics and Statistics.

Haug, S. 2008. 'Migration Networks and Migration Decision-Making'. *Journal of Ethnic and Migration Studies* 34(4): 585–605.

Kapur, D. 2010. *Diaspora, Development, and Democracy: The Domestic Impact of International Migration from India.* Princeton: Princeton University Press.

Kikon, D. 2015. 'Fermenting Modernity: Putting Akhuni on the Nation's Table in India'. *South Asia: Journal of South Asian Studies* 38(2): 320–335.

Lee, E. 1969. 'A Theory of Migration'. In J. A. Jackson (ed.), *Sociological Studies 2: Migration*, 282–297. London: Cambridge University Press.

Lowell, B. L., and A. Findlay. 2001. *Migration of Highly Skilled Persons from Developing Countries: Impact and Policy Responses.* Geneva: International Labour Office.

Martin, P., and G. Zurcher 2008: 'Managing Migration: The Global Challenge'. *Population Bulletin* 63(1): 1–19.

Massey, D. S., et al. 1993. 'Theories of International Migration: A Review and Appraisal'. *Population and Development Review* 19(3): 431–466.

McDuie-Ra, Duncan. 2012a. *Northeast Migrants in Delhi: Race, Refuge and Retail.* Netherlands: Amsterdam University Press.

______. 2012b. 'The North-East Map of Delhi'. *Economic and Political Weekly* 47(30): 69–77.

Mishra, D. K. (ed.) 2016. *Internal Migration in Contemporary India.* New Delhi: Sage Publication.

National Youth Policy. 2003. Available at http://www.youth-policy.com/Policies/IndiaNATIONALYOUTHPOLICY2003.pdf (accessed on 12 May 2016)

NESCH (North East Support Centre and Helpline). 2011. *North East Migration and Challenges in National Capital Cities.* Delhi: NESCH.

Nongkynrih, A. K. 2009. 'Problems of the Youth of North-East India: A Sociological Inquiry'. *Sociological Bulletin* 58(3): 367–382.

NSSO. 2014. *Employment and Unemployment Situation in India,* Report No. 554(68/10/1), 68th Round (July 2011–June 2012). New Delhi: Ministry of Statistics and Programme Implementation, Government of India.

Pachuau, L. K. 2014. *Being Mizo: Identity and Belonging in Northeast India.* New Delhi: Oxford University Press.

Parkins, N. C. 2010. 'Push and Pull Factors of Migration'. *American Review of Political Economy* 8(2): 6–24.

Rajan, S., and R. Chyrmang. 2016. 'Migration and Marginalisation: A Study of North East Migrants in Delhi'. In Deepak K. Mishra (ed.), *Internal Migration in Contemporary India*, 96–153. New Delhi: Sage Publication.

Reimeingam, M. 2011. 'Unemployment, Job Aspiration and Migration: A Case Study of Tangkhul Migrants to Delhi'. *Eastern Quarterly* 7(III and IV): 128–139.

Remesh, B. P. 2012. *Migration from North-East to Urban Centres: A Study of Delhi Region.* Noida: V. V. Giri National Labour Institute.

Revenstein, E. G. 1885. 'The Laws of Migration'. *Journal of the Royal Statistical Society* 48(2): 167–235.

Ritchey, P. N. 1976. 'Explanations of Migration'. *Annual Review of Sociology* 2: 363–404.

SATP (South Asia Terrorism Portal). 2016. Manipur Assessment - Year 2016. Available at https://www.satp.org/satporgtp/countries/india/states/manipur/2016.htm (accessed on 24 February 2023).

Schmeidl, S. 1997. 'Exploring the Causes of Forced Migration: A Pooled Time-Series Analysis, 1971–1990'. *Social Science Quarterly* 78(2): 284–308.

Scott, J. C. 2009. *The Art of Not Being Governed: An Anarchist History of Upland South East Asia.* New Haven: Yale University Press.

Sharma, S. K. 2014. 'Dynamics of Bandhs and Blockades in Northeast India: A Study of Manipur and the Way Ahead'. *Manekshaw Paper No. 48*. New Delhi: Centre for Land Warfare Studies.

Shaw, William. 1929. *Notes on the Thadou Kukis.* Guwahati: Spectrum Publications.

Singh, M. Amarjeet. 2002. 'A Sociological Study of Educated Unemployed Youth of Imphal East and West Districts of Manipur'. Unpublished PhD thesis. Shillong: North-Eastern Hill University.

Singha, K. 2013. *Conflict and Education in Manipur: A Comparative Analysis,* Working Paper No. 305. Bangalore: The Institute for Social and Economic Change.

Sitlhou, H. 2017. *Deconstructing Colonial Ethnography: An Analysis of Missionary Writings on North East India.* New Delhi: Ruby Press.

Sitlhou, H., and Punathil, S. 2017. 'Research in Progress: Racial Discrimination and Violence against Northeasterners and the Bezbaruah Committee Report, 2014'. *Explorations* 1(1): 91–102.

The Economic Times. 2013. 'Delhi Has Highest per Capita Income in the Country', 12 September. Available at https://economictimes.indiatimes.com/news/economy/indicators/delhi-has-highest-per-capita-income-in-the-country/articleshow/22525222.cms (accessed on 17 November 2017).

Thieme, S. 2006. *Social Networks and Migration: Far West Nepalese Labour Migrants in Delhi*. Münster: LIT Verlag.

Wickramasekera, P. 2002. *Asian Labour Migration: Issues and Challenges in an Era of Globalization*. Geneva: International Labour Office.

Wouters, J. J. P., and T. B. Subba. 2013. 'The "Indian Face," India's Northeast, and "the Idea of India"'. *Asian Anthropology* 12(2): 126–140.

IV

Negotiating Gender, Culture and Identity

7

Alternative Sexuality and Civil Society in Mizoram*

Lalhmingmawii

The acceptance of alternative sexualities has grown over the years in many societies. Research (Vanita and Kidwai 2008; Pattanaik 2000) claims that pre-British India was never a site of contestation of sexualities. Paintings and sculptures in temples, epics, chronicles, and even mythology depict the existence of same-sex sexuality in India (ibid.). British colonisers instilled the ideology of heteronormativity in the minds of the Indian people by adopting a law that criminalises alternative sexuality (Section 377 of the Indian Penal Code). Henceforth, India continued to have stringent laws on alternative sexuality until 6 September 2018, when a five-judge bench partially struck down Section 377, decriminalising same-sex relations between consenting adults (*Supreme Court Observer* 2021).

Economic liberalisation in the 1990s brought about certain changes in the Northeast. According to Henessy (2000: 7), 'Global diasporic connections enabled individuals [...] to initiate sexuality movements in certain ways'. Joseph (2005) affirms that 'factors like cultural globalisation, alliances, HIV epidemic and emerging social movements of the deprived populations have given opportunities to the sexual minorities to articulate their desires, choices and rights in a more powerful manner'. With economic liberalisation, the Lesbian Gay Bisexual Transgender

*An earlier version of this essay was published as 'Transcending Boundaries: Alternative Sexuality and Church Response' in *Senhri Journal of Multidisciplinary Studies* 1(2): 1–13.

(LGBT) communities could gain patronisation and this helped activists bring the issue of criminalisation of and discrimination against alternative sexualities to the forefront and present them before the courts of law. This led to the furthering of rights of transgender persons through their inclusion in the list of genders and reservation under the category of Other Backward Classes (OBC). With these changes, the plight of people of alternate sexual orientations and identities seemed to have improved to a certain extent. Several states have drafted policies and implemented them to give benefits to the sexually marginalised communities. However the impact of legislation and policy-making is distinct in different parts of India. This chapter will focus on the effect of such laws and policies on Mizoram.

METHODOLOGY

This chapter is the outcome of a research on 'men who have sex with men' (MSM) in Mizoram. As defined by UNAIDS, men who have sex with men includes 'not only self-identified gay and bisexual men, but also men who engage in male–male sex and self-identify as heterosexual, or those whose sexual identity is but a part of their cultural self-identification' (UNAIDS 2006). The fieldwork was started in 2013 and carried on till 2022. This ethnographic study focuses primarily on the MSM population in Aizawl, the capital of Mizoram. Semi-structured interviews, participant observations, and recording biographical narratives were the main methods used to collect data.

Interviews and participant observation of people with alternate sexual orientations and identities have been conducted in locations such as Targeted Intervention Centre run by Mizoram State AIDS Control Society, initially funded by François-Xavier Bagnoud (FXB) and later by Zoram Drivers Ramthim Board (ZDRB), government hospitals such as Civil Hospital in Aizawl which also runs the ART Centre for HIV patients, the streets of

Aizawl, local tea shops, private houses, and alcohol shops—or any other place that was convenient for the informant as discretion and confidentiality was a priority. The informants in this research are men who have sex with men, active members and leaders of the Young Mizo Association (YMA), Mizo Hmeichhe Insuihkhawm Pawl (MHIP)—a women's organisation in Mizoram—pastors, church elders and counsellors employed by the Presbyterian Church of Mizoram, the police and social workers.

In Mizoram, the majority of the population profess Christianity as their religion. There are numerous Christian denominations in the state, yet the church leaders interviewed so far belong to the two denominations with the largest number of members in Aizawl. The Presbyterian Church of Mizoram has 6,11,241 members while the Baptist Church of Mizoram has 1,72,254 members.[1] Secondary sources consulted for this research are newspaper reports, blogs,[2] colonial writings in the form of books,[3] church documents such as circulars, and documents procured from FXB such as leaflets and reports.

ALTERNATIVE SEXUALITY AND MIZO SOCIETY

Mizoram was known as Lushai Hills while it was under British rule. Prior to British invasion, each village was administered by a village chief assisted by village elders. The British extended their territory to include this region in the late 1800s and they governed it till India became independent in 1947 (Liangkhaia 2011). Colonisation by the British and the subsequent introduction of Christianity by the British missionaries were initially met with hostility. The Mizos who traditionally believed in the existence of supernatural powers and evil spirits within inanimate objects, in due course of time, adopted the religion introduced by the colonial missionaries (ibid.). As per the 2011 Census record, the population of Christians in Mizoram is 87.16 per cent.

Mizo society has always been a patriarchal and patrilineal society, where the household is usually headed by male members and lineages are traced through the father. If we look at historical writings, we can deduce that majority of the village chiefs were male. Traditional Mizo society had a clear-cut division of labour. Women were engaged in household activities while men were expected to do 'rough' work such as warfare, hunting, and clearing the forest for jhum cultivation. Men who were incapable of performing such activities were labelled as womanly and were often taunted as feminine. In this society, gender non-conformists are given derogatory titles. Attempting to trace their presence in the past is also a challenging task since not many records are available that mention those who do not follow gender norms and do not fit into the heteronormative social structure. Assumption could be made based on oral history[4] that some form of alternative sexuality must have existed in the past before the British colonisation because the Mizos have terms such as *mawngkawluk/mawngkawhur*, *patil* and *tuai*, which may be translated as 'sodomite', 'lesbian' and 'gay' respectively.

We see from historical accounts that in Mizo society, there have always been individuals who exist outside stereotypical gender norms. The first ever mention of alternative sexuality can be found in a book called *Mizo History* written by Hrangthiauva. Here, he wrote that in the 18th century in a village called Saihmar, the chief, Lalkangloa, was *tuai.*[5] He wore skirts and smoked *tuibur*. Tuibur is a type of indigenous smoking pipe used only by women.[6]

When the British colonised the Lushai Hills, they criminalised subversive genders. H. W. G. Cole, who served as the Superintendent of the Lushai Hills from 1899–1900 and 1906–1911, issued a statute, Order No. 3 of 1909. 10, criminalising homosexuality and cross-dressing which made it mandatory for the chiefs to report cases of offence, failure of which resulted in punishment. Further, N. E. Parry, who was the Superintendent of the Lushai Hills during 1924–1928, made it mandatory to report all cases of sodomy. Even today, due to the legacy of the colonial regulations and Christian ideology, alternative sexual behaviour is branded as immoral in Mizo society. Therefore, when the Delhi High Court read down Section 377 of the IPC in 2009, the churches in Mizoram responded by denouncing the verdict.[7] Rinu Varghese reporting for *Christian Today* (Varghese 2009) mentioned the contents of the letter sent to Veerappa Moily, the then Law Minister of India, as:

> Homosexuality is against all religious ethics and the culture of Indian society. We feel that Indian society is safeguarded by the IPC Section 377 from unnatural and anti-social behaviour. Hence we are of the opinion that there is no need of legalising homosexuality in our country. Homosexuality is against the natural order of God's purpose in creating both sexes. Anything that goes against the natural order does not last over time and will have negative impact on the lives of the people and society. The society has the right to consider the ethical and moral aspects [of] an individual's life. We are of the strong opinion that legality should never challenge ethical and moral standard[s] of the society. It is on this basis that the Church finds this judgement unacceptable.

It thus pleaded, '… to seek a thoughtful review of the verdict and retain a good standard of social, ethical values in our country, known for upholding its traditional values for centuries.' Varghese also reported on the church leaders' support of the 1909 order which criminalised homosexuality.

Other reports have also mentioned how the churches joined hands to protest this verdict by their refusal to accept same-sex relationships among their members (*Zee News* 2009). In 2009, the leader of the YMA, Lalbiakzuala Colney, argued that the 1909 order continues to be relevant for Mizo Christians (*DNA India* 2009). In 2022, the leaders of the YMA met the Chief Minister of Mizoram, Zoramthanga, and raised their concern regarding the tender issued by the Government of Mizoram to construct toilet facilities in Aizawl for transgender persons. The YMA deemed this project inappropriate for Mizoram. This could be seen as a denial of inclusivity with regard to even basic necessities for individuals with alternative gender and sexuality.

Queer theorists have rightly pointed out that treating gender as a binary creates rigid psychological and social boundaries that inevitably results in an imbalanced power structure and hierarchy as certain kinds of desires, acts, and identities are excluded from the mainstream, marginalised and made inferior (Seidman 1997). In this day and age, when the world is opening up to embrace same-sex relationships, Mizo society under the watchful eye of the church and the civil society is still unable to recognise and accept alternate forms of sexuality.

HOMOSEXUALITY AND CHRISTIAN IDEOLOGY

The Synod Executive Secretary of the Presbyterian Church of Mizoram had said in the context of legalising homosexuality that 'homosexuality is against the ethics of Christianity and the Bible' (Varghese 2009). The Bible indeed has several passages which condemn homosexuality. In the Old Testament, the Judgment of Leviticus Chapter 18 condemns certain sexual acts including incest and male homosexuality. Chapter 20 adds to the general condemnation of Chapter 18 a specific penalty for sexual relations between men. In Deuteronomy we find the following prohibition:

> There shall be no whore (*kadeshah*) of the daughters of Israel, nor a sodomite (*kadesh*) of the sons of Israel.

In the New Testament, denunciation of homosexuality can be found in Paul's Epistle to the Romans:

> Because of this, God gave them over to shameful lusts. Even their women exchanged natural relations for unnatural ones. In the same way the men also abandoned natural relations with women and were inflamed with lust for one another. Men committed indecent acts with other men, and received in themselves the due penalty for their perversion. (Romans 1: 26–27, NIV)

Studies of historical civilisations and societies such as those in ancient and medieval India, ancient Greece, Rome, Egypt, China, medieval Japan, Western Europe, Persia, Africa and America have revealed that homosexuality was not condemned during that period of time (see Boswell 1980; Crompton 2003; Vanita 2005; Vanita and Kidwai 2008). According to Crompton (2003), the origin of the condemnation of homosexuality lies in the Roman law in which homosexuality is punishable by a death penalty in accordance with the law of the Old Testament. The Roman Empire in the fourth century was highly influenced by Christianity. This Roman law was subsequently adopted by countries like Spain, England, and France who further proselytised a legal system based on the tenets of Roman law in their colonial territories leading to criminalisation of homosexuality. Homosexual individuals thus became the victims of faith-inspired intolerance, and owing to European colonialism, this intolerance spread all around the world (ibid.)

Studies on homosexuality and Christianity reveal the challenging impact immoralisation and criminalisation of homosexuality has on the lives of Christians. Woggon (1981) opines that because of the persecution faced by homosexual individuals, they have developed a 'ghetto' mentality, not unlike other marginalised subcultures that are forced to live away from the mainstream society. Yip (1997) in his research on 60 Christian men who identified as gay revealed that churches have been extremely resistant to progress on the issue of homosexuality. Even the most liberal of positions among the churches merely state that alternate sexual orientations should not be condemned. But there has been no sign of acceptance of homosexuality since non-normative physical relationships are not compatible with Christian moral teachings. A study by Levy and Reeves (2011) explored the conflict experienced by gay, lesbian and queer individuals between their religious and sexual identities. This conflict is dealt with differently by each individual: some reject their sexual identity, some reject their Christian identity, some integrate these two identities, while others compartmentalise their lives or are forced to live with the conflict. An awareness of the conflict between the Christian doctrines and same-sex attraction often left participants confused and fearful. Subhi and Geelan (2012) through their research on homosexuals in Brisbane city area found that such conflict between one's faith and sexuality results in feelings of depression, self-blame, guilt, alienation and suicidal tendencies. The conflict is greater if a person comes from an orthodox or deeply religious family. On the other hand, those who have declared their sexuality and come out in society, and/or forfeited their faith in Christianity, have been able to overcome this conflict to a large extent.

Nevertheless, homosexuality remains 'an important stigma' as Goffman (1963) asserts. He says that in a social interaction, a visibly stigmatised person's actions are always analysed and recorded and considered 'deviant' or unacceptable by others. According to him, stigma is 'an expectation of a discrediting judgment of oneself by others in a particular context'. He mentions how daunting it is for individuals who have to use various tactics to hide the stigma they possess in an attempt to act normal. As Manzo (2004) said, 'Stigma attaches to outcomes that are almost always negative'. Dooley (2009) points out the enormous role that stigma plays in the lives of homosexual persons and how they often relocate elsewhere in an attempt to escape the stigma. They are 'denied access to aspects of the dominant culture' in an environment where 'heterosexuality is the predominant acceptable sexual expression' (ibid.). Boswell (1980) remarks in this context:

> Only when social attitudes are favourable do gay people tend to form a visible subculture. In hostile societies they become invisible, a luxury afforded them by the essentially private nature of their variation from the norm, but one which greatly increases their isolation and drastically reduces their lobbying effectiveness.

This is how Christianity through its stigmatisation of homosexuality espouses heteronormativity among its followers.

It is very difficult to discuss the topics of homosexuality and Christianity in interviews as respondents often prefer to evade questions on these subjects. In a conversation with A,[8] who is a cross-dresser, we could fortunately dwell on this topic. She goes to church whenever she can and it is the only place where she wears pants. Commenting on her choice of clothes for church, she said, 'I respect God'. She further asserted, 'The Bible tells us about the condemnation of sodomites to Hell, but as long as we are not sodomites, God will not punish us just because of our orientation as it is the way He created us.' She believes that as long as she does not engage in a sexual act with a person of the same gender, her sexual orientation alone is not going to bar her entry into Heaven.

A 22-year-old respondent who identifies as *tuai* mentioned being a regular church attendee prior to being a sex worker. On being asked about her expectations from the church, she said that she would like the church elders to be more welcoming and to care enough to ask her why she no longer attended church service. She remarked that people stare at her which makes it uncomfortable for her to be in the vicinity of the church. Another respondent too was an active member of the church before she began sex work. She now considers herself a 'problem' for the society, which is why she is no longer an active member. She said,

> Many people sneered at gay [persons] but I don't consider myself a sinner just because I am gay … the work I do—the sex work—is what I think is wrong … When I face trouble, I pray because [God] is the ultimate refuge I have.

There are other respondents who are forced to attend gospel retreats by their parents. Some comply to the rules and teachings in these retreats while others do not. The ones who comply often 'act heterosexual' for a short while but not in the long term. I often hear gay men joking about going to such retreats only to confirm that they are actually attracted to men after all.

These narratives clearly reveal the attributes of stigma attached to those in same-sex relationships. These respondents look at themselves through the eyes of others and analyse themselves as Cooley (1902) had described: 'Each to each a looking glass, reflects the other that doth pass'. The experiences and emotions shared by the respondents indicate how they feel alienated in a heteronormative world and how heterosexism has reduced them to 'problems' and 'deviants'.

ALTERNATIVE SEXUALITY AND CIVIL SOCIETY

Mizo society has well-established social organisations whose function is to preserve the culture and values of the Mizos. The most prominent civil society among these is the YMA. It was established with the help of Welsh missionaries on 15 June 1935 as the Young Lushai Association with an objective to uphold the culture and morality of the Mizo society. Its name was changed to Young Mizo Association on 7 October 1947. Its objectives include promoting productive use of leisure, development of the society and reverence towards Christian ethics. The YMA is the largest association in Mizoram, with other smaller associations as its members, and it has branches in other states of the Northeast as well. It also works in collaboration with the state government in dealing with the security of the villages and towns, keeping drug trafficking in check, dealing with refugees, environment and forest protection, helping the poor and needy, and providing assistance during calamities. Every year, 15 June is celebrated as YMA Day and it is a state holiday.

The YMA also has an anti-narcotics team known as Supply Reduction Service (SRS) that patrols the city and conducts raids, often confiscating narcotics from smugglers. It is necessary to point out here that since Mizoram shares an international border with Myanmar, drug-trafficking and smuggling is rampant in the region. The YMA thus plays an active part in safeguarding and protecting the state from social evils. In 2014, a Mizo minister in his speech at the YMA General Conference identified the government, the church and the YMA as the three important organisations who must work together for the benefit of the society. This comment of the state minister highlights the important place occupied by the church and the YMA in the life of the Mizos.

Another prominent organisation in Mizo society is the Mizo Hmeichhe Insuihkhawm Pawl (MHIP). This is an organisation of Mizo women established on 6 July 1974. The basic principle of MHIP is philanthropic, not-for-profit social work aimed at creating a state of welfare in which every individual is cared for irrespective of caste or creed. Being a women's organisation, most of their activities emphasise upliftment of women and children.

YMA AND MHIP'S ATTITUDE TOWARDS ALTERNATIVE SEXUALITY

Since organisations like YMA and MHIP work together to promote and safeguard the culture and traditions of the Mizos, their views on non-normative social behaviour and practices play a big role in shaping public opinion on those subjects. Over the years, especially after the 2009 verdict of the Delhi High Court, YMA and MHIP have raised their concerns regarding the practice of alternative sexualities. In 2009, when Section 377 of the IPC was scrapped by the Delhi High Court, the President of the Young Mizo Association made a statement saying, 'I do not see any positive part in scrapping Section 377. Personally speaking, I believe that the 1909 order is still a good order for the Mizo Christians' (Hmar 2009). An office-bearer of the YMA also remarked that instead of leniency, stricter actions would be more effective in correcting the 'deviants', thus emphasising the need to control the behaviour of individuals with non-normative sexual orientations and identities.

On 14 September 2015, the MHIP Executive Committee in their meeting remarked that there are many *tuai* and *patil* individuals in Mizoram. The MHIP expressed their concern that this could have a negative effect on the society and the church. They passed a resolution to consult other associations such as YMA, Mizo Upa Pawl (MUP),[9] Mizo Zirlai Pawl (MZP) and Mizo Students' Union (MSU). A meeting was held on 22 December 2015, attended by the office-bearers of all the aforementioned associations, in which it was proclaimed that the *tuai*s and *patil*s were becoming bolder and more audacious, and that therefore measures should be taken to restrain these individuals. This reveals the patriarchal and heterosexist structure of the Mizo community, which demands that everyone conform to heteronormative gender norms and conduct themselves in ways deemed moral and acceptable by that dominant social structure.

THE ORDEALS FACED BY THE SEXUAL 'NON-CONFORMISTS' IN A HETEROSEXIST WORLD

Individuals who do not conform to the societal expectations with regards to behaving in accordance with their perceived gender often encounter violence. As Menon (2012) opines, 'There is zero tolerance for those who breach the carefully produced "natural" order of society by refusing to conform to norms of looks and behaviour'. People who are or appear to be gender non-conforming often face violence, estrangement from their families, and other forms of discrimination. This oppression of gender non-conforming individuals often results in them having poor physical and mental health (Willoughby et al. 2010). Butler (1990) asserts, 'Those bodily figures that do not fit into either gender fall outside the human, indeed, constitute the domain of the dehumanized and the abject against which the human itself is constituted'.

Chakrapani et al. (2007) expressed that in India same-sex sexuality has led to victimisation and an experience of physical and emotional violence from authorities and relatives. In their study conducted at Chandigarh, they found that the stigma attached to same-sex sexuality pushed their respondents to agree to marriage to avoid bringing shame to their family. Men who appear feminine, MSM sex workers and youth who are attracted to the same sex are highlighted as those who are more prone to abuse in multiple forms. In Mizo society, since Christianity influences all aspects of life, sexuality that is non-normative is labelled as deviant and is therefore stigmatised. Interviews conducted among the MSM sex workers in Aizawl city reveal the extent of this stigma. The sex workers claim that their lifestyles call for occasional or frequent intake of drugs and alcohol as a coping mechanism against the stigma they face because of their sexual identity and alienation from their family. The alcohol and substance abuse result in further stigma. Thus within Christian purview, they are doubly stigmatised.

These individuals—especially the sex workers—come under the watchful eyes of the YMA and the MHIP because of their 'deviant' behaviour. While the MHIP is not very involved in vigilantism, the members of the YMA are considered the 'secondary guardians of the Mizo society' as they assist the work of the police in multiple ways.[10] After the reformation of the SRS, one of my respondents, who is a trainee beautician and a sex worker, informed me in an interview that soliciting clients and cross-dressing on the streets have become more dangerous as the level of vigilantism has been increased. She said that she used to wear stilettos and cross-dress openly but now it makes her a target. She has to dress differently now to keep her identity hidden from the vigilantes. But the need to find clients, drugs and alcohol still pushes her to be on the street. She recounted an incident where she was caught by the YMA in the heart of the city at night. When asked what they did to her, she said, 'They shaved off my hair'. When I asked why she did not approach human rights activists for help when such things happened, she responded, 'It is not advisable to do something against the YMA. What if they suddenly turn their backs on us?' Overhearing our conversation, one of the social workers added:

> The problem is that even when we try and help these victims, most of them [*referring to MSM sex workers*] always have drugs in their possession which is illegal. If the violence is only induced towards their sexuality, there could be something we can do, but not when they are found possessing illegal drugs.

I prompted my interviewee to narrate the incident involving the YMA in detail. She obliged and said,

> I was passing by the Excise Department office in Aizawl when they caught me. This was night time. One of them told the others, 'The Rehabilitation Homes do not entertain tuai, so let us cut her hair to ensure that she wouldn't come out again'. I didn't want them to cut my hair because, you know, it takes a long time to grow. Then they struck a blow with a stick while one of them pulled my hair and said, 'I'm going to cut it', and they did. They set me free the next morning. I know that I can't do sex work forever but I find it difficult to save money.

Majority of the sex workers I have come across so far in my research have had an encounter with the YMA. One of my respondents, C, was once caught while she was with a friend. She was not a cross-dresser when they had caught her. The friend she was accompanying that day however was a sex worker. She says,

> The YMA [members on duty] accused me of being a pimp for the call girls. I told them that I'm not a pimp. I come from a village and to earn my living I searched for customers for my friends, and when I found clients for them, the clients used to give me a small amount of money. After I told them my story they let me go but they sent my friend to a rehabilitation centre. Since she was my main source of income I had no other choice but to turn to sex work to earn my livelihood. I could not go back home to my family because I'm hiding my identity from them. But after [I started doing] sex work, the YMA caught me again for the second time. This time they did not let me go easily. They cut my hair, they beat me up and handed me over to the police. The police never laid hands on me; they escorted me to a court trial the next day. I was asked to pay a fine and then I was released.

Another 19-year-old cross-dresser and sex worker, whom I often met in an FXB drop-in-centre, told me in an interview that she was questioned by the YMA [members on duty] while she was waiting for a friend at a taxi stand. She said that at the time she did not possess alcohol or drugs, nor was she found soliciting clients, despite which she was scolded and beaten, and sent by the YMA members to a rehabilitation home, where she stayed for ten months.

My key informant added:

> Upon hearing that MSM sex workers often endure violence and retribution from the YMA members on duty, the authorities of FXB decided to have a meeting with the key players. The YMA and the police department were requested to send representatives for the meeting. In that meeting, requests were made to not harass or catch our clients [the sex workers] unless they are caught in the act of soliciting clients or possessing and using illegal substances.

It is true that vigilantism on the part of the YMA has made the city more peaceful and reduced drug trade and other illegal activities. The SRS has been working voluntarily to eradicate the presence of 'No. 4' (the local name for heroin) in Mizoram. They conduct raids in the city mostly between 5 p.m. and 2 a.m. and this vigilance has considerably curbed the activities of drug dealers and sex workers in the city.

When questioned about the physical violence that the vigilants use, one of the YMA leaders said, 'Our vices are made more prominent than our good deeds', thus admitting some flaws in their methods. Regarding violence against sex workers, their justification is that the YMA's main objective is to eradicate drugs and in the process, they catch sex workers because they are drug abusers. The YMA is not as concerned about sex work. Unfortunately, in most cases, these individuals are involved in sex work because they need money to buy drugs. One of the SRS members commented, 'Heroin is an expensive drug… if they do sex work they could earn Rs 8500 per night'. In his opinion, sex work and drug abuse are intertwined. He further explained how they would take the sex workers found with drugs to the central YMA office for questioning and documenting their personal details. This would be followed by counselling, after which they would either be released, or in some occasions, sent to the police. If they are caught a second time, they are sent to rehabilitation homes. The SRS member claimed that it was the workers of the rehabilitation homes who cut the hair of the tuai interviewed earlier. Here, other SRS members intervened to say that most queer sex workers usually answered queries willingly, so the use of physical force was not required. However, not all were willing to cooperate, and then a little 'shoving around is necessary', they admitted, and said that this was often misrepresented as physical harassment in media and news reports, thus giving YMA a bad name.

The YMA members further added that there are times when the individuals caught are transferred to police custody. But the state government does not have proper laws to deal with sexual non-conformists. Moreover, it is an extra burden for the government to provide food to the people in police custody and so they are released after a day or two.

CONCLUSION

Woggon (1981) opines, 'When homosexual persons come out of the shadows and into the mainstream of life, there is in the majority of the population a fear of the unknown, revulsion at the supposed practices, and a dislike for the outrageous and hostile behaviour of some'. Unlike in other states where there are LGBTQ communities which are strong enough to organise social movements, Mizoram has barely any LGBTQ groups, and awareness on alternative sexuality is minimal. Most families are not ready to deal with the topic nor is the larger society open to accepting non-normative sexualities yet. If there existed a platform for open dialogue among the representatives of the civil society, the churches, the government and the members of the LGBTQ community, many of the problems could be solved. In the absence of such a space, those who do not follow stereotypical gender norms may continue to be subjected to discrimination and violence. Lack of awareness and misconceptions lead to stigmatisation and makes it difficult for LGBTQ individuals to have access to healthcare and other kinds of social support. This enables the spread of sexually transmitted diseases like HIV as many get discouraged from getting tested or treated for fear of harassment. Mizoram has a high HIV infection rate and if we continue sweeping these issues under the carpet, the situation will only become worse.

On 6 September 2018, an outstanding judgement was made by the Supreme Court of India in Navtej Singh Johar v. Union of India which struck down Section 377 of the Indian Penal Code and decriminalised homosexuality. As Parthasarathy (2018) writes, 'Not only has the Court struck down the wretchedly wicked Section 377 of the Indian Penal Code, insofar as it criminalises homosexuality, but it has also recognised the Constitution's enormous and extraordinary transformative power'. The Supreme Court upheld constitutional morality over public morality in this landmark judgment, thus protecting members of the LGBTQ community by law. In recent years, the LGBTQ community has gained some visibility. Mainstream media such as Bollywood cinema have produced several films that capture the transition of society towards awareness and acceptance of alternate sexualities. Central and state governments too are taking measures to aid the upliftment of the community. However, progress is yet to be witnessed with regard to legalisation of same-sex marriage, right to inheritance, right to adoption and other privileges which are accessible for cisgender subjects. As we continue to see progress and increasing inclusivity alongside the fight to overcome challenges in other parts of India, LGBTQ activists in Mizoram are still looking forward to the day when community members will gain the courage to step out with pride under the rainbow flag.

NOTES

1. As on 1 April 2017, as per *Statistical Abstract of Mizoram: 2017* published by Directorate of Economics and Statistics, Government of Mizoram.

2. Blogs visited include:

(i) http://mizolgbt.blogspot.com

(ii) http://thehtm.blogspot.com201001tuai-leh-patil-homosexuality.html

(iii) https://www.bible.combible10481ti.1.mizo

(iv) http://pclalnghinglova.blogspot.com2011_07_01_archive.html?view=classic

(v) http://vairengtebranchktp.blogspot.com201201homosexuality-dr-c-lalhrekima.html

(vi) http://kakhawvel.blogspot.com200907tuai.html

(vii) http://zcariboulh.blogspot.com201011klinefelters-syndrome.html

3. Books published by the superintendents of the Lushai Hills while Mizoram was a British colony.

4. From an interview with C. Chhuanvawra, Padma Shree awardee for their contribution to literature and education, in May 2015.

5. J. H. Lorrain's *Dictionary of the Lushai Language* describes 'tuai' as 'a man who practices sodomy and dresses and works like a woman; a sodomite who masquerades as a woman' (p. 518).

6. See *Dictionary of the Lushai Language* by Lorrain.

7. Reported in several national newspapers and magazines including *Pink Pages* (a popular LGBT magazine).

8. Pseudonyms have been used to protect the identities of the respondents. I interviewed A in July 2014 at a drop-in-centre run by FXB, an NGO.

9. Mizoram Upa Pawl is an association where the members must be at least 50 years of age or older.

10. YMA members voluntarily guard each locality by turn, especially during festive seasons such as Christmas and New Year's Eve, to ensure that there are no disturbances. They also check the use of alcohol and drugs by banning people in their localities from selling them. Sometimes they force people selling drugs and alcohol to leave the locality and find residence elsewhere. Heavy drinkers and alcoholics are given warnings if they disrupt the peace and harmony of the locality and resident families.

REFERENCES

Adams, Bert N., and R. A. Sydie. 2011. *Sociological Theory.* New Delhi: Vistaar Publications.

Andrew, Y. K. T. 1997. 'Attacking the Attacker: Gay Christians Talk Back'. *The British Journal of Sociology* 48(1): 113–127.

Boswell, J. 1980. *Christianity, Social Tolerance and Homosexuality: Gay People in Western Europe from the Beginning of the Christian Era to the Fourteenth Century*. Chicago and London: The University of Chicago Press.

Butler, Judith. 1990. *Gender Trouble: Feminism and the Subversion of Identity*. New York: Routledge.

Chakrapani, V., Peter A. Newman, Murali Shunmugam, Alan McLuckie, and Fredrick Melwin. 2007. 'Structural Violence against Kothi-identified Men who Have Sex with Men in Chennai, India: A Qualitative Investigation'. *AIDS Education and Prevention* 19(4): 346–64. Available at https://guilfordjournals.com/doi/10.1521/aeap.2007.19.4.346 (accessed May 2023).

Chakrapani, V., M. Kaur, P. A. Newman, S. Mittal and R. Kumar. 2019. 'Syndemics and HIV-related Sexual Risk Among Men who Have Sex with Men in India: Influences of Stigma and Resilience'. *Cult Health Sex* 21(4): 416–431. Available at doi: 10.1080/13691058.2018.1486458 (accessed April 2023).

Cooley, C. H. 1902. *Human Nature and the Social Order.* New York: Charles Scribner's Sons.

Crompton, L. 2003. *Homosexuality and Civilization.* London: The Belknap Press of Harvard University Press.

Dandona, L., Rakhi Dandona et al. 2005. 'Sex Behaviour of Men Who Have Sex with Men and Risk of HIV in Andhra Pradesh, India', study. Available at https://www.ncbi.nlm.nih.govpubmed15802980 (accessed on 20 May 2015).

Dillon, P. J., and Ambar Basu. 2014. 'HIV/AIDS and Minority Men Who Have Sex With Men: A Meta-ethnographic Synthesis of Qualitative Research'. *Health Communication* 29(2): 182–192.

Directorate of Economics & Statistics. 2018. *Statistical Abstract of Mizoram.* Government of Mizoram.

DNA India. 2009. 'Mizoram Church Frowns on Transvestites', 28 July. Available at https://www.dnaindia.com/india/report-mizoram-church-frowns-on-transvestites-1277856 (accessed on 5 May 2013).

Dooley, J. 2009. 'Negotiating Stigma: Lessons from the Life Stories of Gay Men'. *Journal of Gay and Lesbian Social Services* 21(1): 13–29.

Elouard, Y., and B. Essen. 2013. 'Psychological Violence Experienced by Men Who Have Sex with Men in Puducherry, India: A Qualitative Study'. *Journal of Homosexuality* 60(11): 1581–1601.

Gandhi, J., and Smriti K. Ramachandran. 2015. 'RS Passes Bill on Transgender Rights'. *The Hindu*, 24 April. Available at http://www.thehindu.com/ (accessed on 15 September 2015).

Goffman, E. 1963. *Stigma: Notes on the Management of Spoiled Identity*. New Jersey: Prentice Hall Inc.

Hennessy, R. 2000. *Profit and Pleasure: Sexual Identities in Late Capitalism*. London/Great Britain: Routledge.

Hmar, B. 2009. 'Now, Mizos Fall Back on 1909 Order to Ban Gay Sex'. *The Times of India*, 13 July. Available at https://timesofindia.indiatimes.com/city/guwahati/now-mizos-fall-back-on-1909-order-to-ban-gay-sex/articleshow/4773615.cms (accessed on 12 August 2014).

Johnston, L. 1996. 'What is Vigilantism?'. *British Journal of Criminology* 36(2): 220–236. Available at https://doi.org/10.1093/oxfordjournals.bjc.a014083.

Joseph, S. 2005. *Social Work Practise and Men Who Have Sex With Men*. New Delhi: Sage Publications India.

Levy, Denise L., and Patricia Reeves. 2011. 'Resolving Identity Conflict: Gay, Lesbian and Queer Individuals with a Christian Upbringing'. *Journal of Gay and Lesbian Social Services* 23(1): 53–68.

Liangkhaia. 2011. *Mizo Chanchin*. Aizawl: LTL Publications.

Lorrain, J. H. 1940. *Dictionary of the Lushai Language*. Calcutta: Asiatic Society. Available at http://dsal.uchicago.edu/dictionaries/lorrain/ (accessed on 2 March 2018).

Manzo, J. F. 2004. 'On the Sociology and Social Organization of Stigma: Some Ethnomethodological Insights'. *Human Studies* 27(4): 401–416.

Menon, N. 2012. *Seeing Like a Feminist*. New Delhi: Zubaan and Penguin Books India.

Mizo Hmeichhe Insuihkhawm Pawl. Available at http://mizoram.nic.in/ (accessed on 25 March 2017).

Mizoram Population Census Data. 2011. Available at http://webcache.googleusercontent.com/search?q=cache:http://www.census2011.co.i/ (accessed on 25 March 2017).

NDTV. 2015. 'Shashi Tharoor Fails to Introduce Gay Sex Ban Bill in Lok Sabha', December 18. Available at http://www.ndtv.com/india-news/shashi-tharoor-fails-to-introduce-gay-sex-ban-bill-in-lok-sabha-1256604 (accessed on 19 December 2015).

Parry, N. E. 2009. *A Monograph on Lushai Customs & Ceremonies*. Aizawl: Tribal Research Institute.

Parthasarathy, Suhrith. 2018. 'Section 377: Drawing a Curtain on the Past'. *The Hindu*. Available at https://www.thehindu.com (accessed on 1 October 2018).

Pattanaik, D. 2000. 'Did Homosexuality Exist in Ancient India?'. *Debonair Magazine*. Available at https://devdutt.com/articles/did-homosexuality-exist-in-ancient-india/ (accessed on 16 September 2016).

Rajagopal, K. 2016. 'Five-judge Constitution Bench to Take a Call on Section 377'. *The Hindu*, 2 February. Available at http://www.thehindu.com/ (accessed on 2 February 2016).

Remkunga. 2008. *Zirlaite Dictionary English-Mizo*. Aizawl: Remkunga & Sons, Aizawl.

Seidman, S. 1997. *Difference Troubles: Queering Social Theory and Sexual Politics*. UK: Cambridge University Press.

Sitlhou, M. 2013. 'Let He Who Is without Sin: The Mizoram Church and Homosexuality'. *The Sunday Guardian*, 12 October. Available at http://www.sunday-guardian.com/ (accessed on 1 October 2018).

Subhi, N., and D. Geelan. 2012. 'When Christianity and Homosexuality Collide: Understanding the Potential Intrapersonal Conflict'. *Journal of Homosexuality* 59(10): 1382–1402.

Supreme Court Observer. 2021. 'Constitutionality of Section 377 IPC: Navtej Singh Johar v. Union of India; Akkai Padmashali v. Union of India', 24 December. Available at https://www.scobserver.in/cases/navtej-singh-johar-v-union-of-india-constitutionality-of-section-377-ipc-background/ (accessed April 2023).

UNAIDS. 2006. *HIV and Men who Have Sex with Men in Asia and the Pacific*, UNAIDS Best Practice Collection. Geneva: UNAIDS. Available at https://data.unaids.org/publications/irc-pub07/jc901-msm-asiapacific_en.pdf (accessed April 2023).

Vanglaini. 2015. 'MHIP day sawrkar chawlha puan zel duh'. September 15. Available at http://www.vanglaini.org/ (accessed on 30 October 2015).

Vanita, R. 2005. *Love's Rite: Same Sex Marriage in India and the West*. New Delhi: Penguin Books.

Vanita, R., and Saleem Kidwai. 2008. *Same-Sex Love in India: A Literary History.* New Delhi: Penguin Books.

Varghese, R. 2009. 'Mizoram's Largest Church Decries Gay Ruling, Says Homosexual Only 0.3%'. *Christian Today.* Available at https://www.christiantoday.co.in/news/mizorams-largest-church-decries-gay-ruling-says-homosexuals-only-03.html (accessed on 3 October 2018).

Willoughby, B. L. B., N. D. Doty and N. M. Malik. 2010. 'Victimization, Family Rejection, and Outcomes of Gay, Lesbian, and Bisexual Young People: The Role of Negative GLB Identity'. *Journal of GLBT Family Studies* 6: 403–424. Available at https://doi.org/10.1080/1550428X.2010.511085 (accessed May 2023).

Woggon, H. A. 1981. 'A Biblical and Historical Study of Homosexuality'. *Journal of Religion and Health* 20(2): 156–163.

Yip, AKT. 1997. 'Attacking the Attacker: Gay Christians Talk Back'. *The British Journal of Sociology* 48(1): 113–127. Available at https://doi.org/10.2307/591913 (accessed May 2023).

Young Mizo Association. 'Dan Bu'. Available at http://cyma.co.in/yma-dan-bu/ (accessed on 30 November 2015).

Zee News. 2009. 'Mizo Churches Pray for retention of section 377 IPC', 16 August. Available at http://zeenews.india.com/home/mizo-churches-pray-for-retention-of-section-377-ipc_555800.html (link discontinued).

Zoram Today. 2015. 'Tuai leh Patil chungchang hi'. Available at http://zoram2day.blogspot.in/2015/10/tuai-leh-patil-chungchang-hi.htm (accessed on 14 November 2015).

8

Women in Conflict Situations

Experiences of Marginalisation of Displaced Kuki Women in Manipur*

Ruth Nengneilhing

Conflict is a universal phenomenon which affects the lives of people in many ways, leaving in its aftermath significant humanitarian challenges. The 1990s in Manipur was one such historical point which witnessed conflict between two ethnic communities, namely the Kukis and the Nagas. Both sides experienced massive violent killings, mass displacements, and physical and psychological injuries. Villages in various parts of the state were affected differently and post-conflict rehabilitation too was different among the various segments. Studies conducted on the impact of ethnic conflict show negative public health consequences mediated by population displacement, disruption of economic activities, food scarcity and the collapse of basic healthcare.

The Kuki–Naga clash led to large-scale displacement, which included spontaneous fleeing from life-threatening situations as well as organised and planned population transfer and relocation involving the use of force and other human rights abuses. Those displaced were exposed to a multitude of problems.

*I would like to acknowledge and thank my supervisor, Ritu Priya Mehrotra, faculty at Centre for Social Medicine and Community Health, Jawaharlal Nehru University, New Delhi, for her guidance in conducting this study. I am also grateful to the anonymous reviewer for their valuable feedback.

Many conflict-displaced people are still rebuilding their lives in resettlement colonies.

Even after almost two decades since the conflict sparked off, residues of the ethnic clash, and its widespread impact on the social, political and economic life of the people of Manipur are still evident. Kidnappings and killings are common even to this day. Bandhs and agitations have become a way of life. The conflict has crippled the economy as well as social and institutional structures across the state.

A REVIEW OF THE CAUSES OF THE CONFLICT

The Kuki–Naga clash which occurred in 1992 had its genesis in a much earlier period. The British during the colonial period exploited the ethnic diversity of Manipur as a part of their colonial policy. As Dena (1999) states, in a way, the Kuki–Naga animosity is a colonial legacy because numerous land disputes between the two groups at the village level were left unresolved by the colonial administrators and these likely contributed to the aggravation of the conflict between the two ethnic groups.

Shimray (2001) has listed the following factors as responsible for the emergence of distinct ethnicities in Manipur: (i) distinctive social and cultural identities manifested by all social groups in the state; (ii) limited social and cultural interaction between the different ethnic groups despite their physical and linguistic affinities; and (iii) a heightened importance of historical and religious differences in political struggles against the dominance of larger and more powerful ethnic groups. Phanjoubam (2005) has written on the ethnic cleansing between the Kukis and the Nagas. In his words, 'attempt to divide Manipur along ethnic lines was considered the main reason of the decade-old Kuki-Naga clash which broke out in the early 1990s and involved large-scale violence of mass killings, execution, forced expulsion, etc.'. T. T. Haokip (2002) also examines the Kuki–Naga question in the context of issues of identity and ownership of land, which resulted in the uprooting of hundreds of villagers, the loss of more than a thousand lives and enormous internal displacement.

Singh (2008) too records the causes of the Kuki-Naga clash, its extent and its ramifications. According to him, the Kuki-Naga conflict is an extension of the dispute due to the claim over a territory as one's own exclusive homeland—a claim made by the ethnic armies—and the resistance to it. He assumes that the complacency and perplexity of the state-machinery and its failure to contain the clashes in its initial phase are the reasons why the conflict escalated to such mammoth proportions. Singh further observes that the conflict was the result of both historical as well as contemporary factors and cannot be attributed to any one single factor. Traditional rivalries, unresolved inter-village disputes, sporadic as well as systematic violence committed by one group against another, fight for control over homelands, lack of political will on the part of the state government, inefficient administration and ineffective agencies for enforcing law and order have all contributed to the outbreak of the clash (Singh 2008). Similarly, Kipgen mentions three issues behind the ethnic conflict between Kukis and Nagas, namely, identity formation, land disputes and responses of the state (Kipgen 2013).

The Kuki-Naga conflict is also referred to as 'ethnic cleansing' by many scholars and civil bodies such as the Kuki People's Forum for Human Rights (Singh 2008). Tohring (2010) highlights some terms used by various segments of people in explaining the Kuki-Naga conflict of the 1990s, such as 'ethnic cleansing', 'genocide', 'communal clash' and 'ethnic conflict'. In documents such as 'Does Violence Get Mandate', the Government of India used the term 'ethnic cleansing' (ibid.). Similarly, Kuki Inpi Manipur (KIM), which is the apex body of the Kukis, also rejected the use of the term 'communal or ethnic clash' to describe the violence between the Kukis and the Nagas and instead considered the events as ethnic cleansing of the Kukis. Kamaroopi (1993) too states that 'a process of ethnic cleansing of Kukis from areas claimed to be "historically" Naga areas is now going on in Manipur'. Tohring on the other hand considers the term 'ethnic cleansing' inappropriate to describe the conflict and rather referred to it as the Naga-Kuki violent ethnic conflict. However, her analysis has been refuted as reproducing 'certain ethnic politics in academic work'.

EFFECTS OF THE CONFLICT

A literature review shows that studies on ethnic conflicts in Northeast India mostly focus on ethnicity and identity and ignore other dimensions of the conflict. There are however some studies that have looked at the dimension of gender in the context of conflict or war around the world. Thomas Plumper and Neumayer (2006) have studied the unequal burden of war and they argue that women are likely to suffer most from the indirect consequences of armed conflict. No doubt that armed conflict kills, injures and harms more men than women as combatants are predominantly male and it is the men who are also singled out for massacres and killed as civilians, yet women are overall more negatively affected than men, thereby suggesting that the indirect consequences are stronger than the direct effects (ibid.).

Another study by L. Kelly (2000) observes the effects of war which can be felt by women in two extreme ways. Firstly, during the war, there is extra pressure placed on women to put themselves in danger as they shelter, feed and clothe soldiers, courier messages secretly at the risk of getting caught, and this is often overlooked. Secondly, Kelly observes how, contrastingly, women can be empowered during wartime as the traditional 'feminine' role is challenged, allowing them to be heads of households, and to display qualities and skills which are often reserved for men or regarded as 'masculine'. However, there are cases where women's responsibilities diminish as soon as the men return home and the skills they had erstwhile displayed are ignored or overshadowed, although some women do retain or benefit from the rights and responsibilities (ibid.). In the present study of displaced Kuki women, I observed that there were cases where a woman headed the household and she was left with no choice but to shoulder the entire responsibility of supporting the family. Women often became the primary breadwinners in their families due to forced displacement, and/or death of their husbands or other male members of the family, which forced them to take up new economic roles and encounter the challenges of livelihoods.

The underlying focus of this chapter is thus to explain the differential impacts of armed conflict on men and women by tracing the different vulnerabilities that derive from the social roles men and women assume, and the differential access to resources (Moser 2001). In fact, most often, less attention is paid to the gender-specific aspects of the negative impact of ethnic conflict. The present study is an effort to bring out the experiences of women affected by the conflict and their marginalisation. It captures the much neglected but important dimension of conflict: the experiences of the displaced population, particularly the women, and the impact on their livelihood and health.

REHABILITATION OF THE DISPLACED POPULATION AND PROBLEMS FACED BY THEM

Kukis are one of the three major ethnic groups in Manipur. The other two major groups are the Meiteis and the Nagas. Manipur with a population of 27,21,756 (Census of India 2011) has an area of 22,327 sq km. The geography of Manipur is such that the valley—which constitutes about one-tenth of the total area of the state, and is mainly inhabited by the Meiteis—is surrounded on all sides by hill areas that are inhabited mainly by the Kukis and the Nagas. The state is surrounded by Nagaland in the north, North-Cachar districts of Assam in the west, Mizoram in the south and the Kabow Valley and the Chin Hills of Burma in the east. Manipur lies between latitudes 23°83'N–25°68'N and longitudes 93°03'E–94°78'E.

Like in other instances of large-scale post-conflict displacement around the world, the displacement that took place subsequent to the Kuki-Naga clash too included both spontaneous fleeing from life-threatening situations as well as organised and planned population transfers and relocations involving the use of force and other human rights abuses. M. J. Toole and R. J. Waldman (1993) in their article 'Refugees and Displaced Persons: War, Hunger and Public Health' state that populations affected by conflict often experience severe public health consequences mediated by population displacement, food scarcity and the collapse of basic health services, and this has given rise to the term 'complex humanitarian emergencies'.

A similar study by Bradarić et al. (1996) notes how in addition to the experience of loss and trauma, displaced populations have to routinely endure limited or no access to public health, medical care, social security, paid work and food aid, as well as face indifference, rejection or even hostility from their new neighbours. Indeed, since the status of being 'local' is given importance, the displaced population is invariably discriminated against and faces widespread resentment from the already resident populace, with whom they must compete for space, scarce resources and jobs, and hence are looked upon as interlopers by the latter. The trauma of war and displacement is intertwined with the political issue of who gets what and under which conditions (ibid.).

The present study deals with similar cases in which residents of the newly established villages, after getting evicted from their ancestral site, were stigmatised and discriminated against by the neighbouring villages. Usually, this happened if they were not consanguineal or did not belong to the same clan as the chiefs of surrounding villages, or in some cases the host villages.

According to Goodhand (2001), conflict and war represent the systemic and deliberate violation of individual and group rights to produce and secure an adequate livelihood. Wars and conflicts have a range of effects on poor people's entitlements. Prolonged wars devastate rural livelihoods by destroying crops, killing livestock, damaging irrigation networks, dislocating markets and forcing farmers to abandon farms either due to insecurity or land-mines (Luckham et al. 2001). This is clearly evident in the case of the Kukis as well, who previously lived on subsistence farming, but had to abandon their farms and become wage labourers after their displacement.

K. T. Silva, Anuji Upekshika Gamage and V. Chitravale, who studied the civil war in Sri Lanka, talk about the resulting disruption of livelihood and the war's impact on the health sector. The bombing and artillery attacks during the war destroyed the health infrastructure. The unstable situation led to health personnel fleeing from the conflict areas which hampered the process of sending medical supplies. There is a higher level of malnutrition in conflict areas because of the disruption of food production and food supply, higher food prices, low purchasing power of those living in conflict areas, inadequacy of supply of food relief and nutritional supplements, higher infection rate, and inadequacy of services (Silva et al. 2002).

Jaspars and O'Callaghan (2010) have described how livelihood strategies in active conflict zones become severely restricted, and were often limited to subsistence agriculture and marginal economic activities. Their studies show that most camp residents made a meagre living from ill-paid and dangerous work and faced long periods of malnutrition despite receiving humanitarian assistance. Internally displaced persons (IDPs) in Darfur and Sri Lanka relied on brick-making, collecting firewood and working as domestic labour and farm labour.

Numerous studies have also been made on conflict- and health-related issues in Northeast India, which have shown how armed conflict and public health interact. Those directly impacted by conflict include those who are killed, injured, disabled, abused or traumatised due to armed strife. Agriculture, healthcare, architecture and infrastructure are damaged because of bombing, shelling and other types of destruction and violence. This leads to food shortage and breakdown of healthcare and sanitation services, in turn increasing starvation, malnutrition and incidence of infectious diseases (Guha-Sapir and van Panhuis 2002).

NEED FOR AN INTERSECTIONAL ANALYSIS

This study looks at the varied dissimilar experiences of conflict-affected women to understand the intersectionality across the displaced women in Manipur. Intersectionality is a strategy for linking the grounds of discrimination (e.g., race, gender, class) to the social, economic, political and legal environment that contributes to discrimination and structures experiences of oppression and privilege. It studies the intersecting effects of race, class, gender, and other marginalising characteristics that contribute to social identity and affect health. Adverse health effects are thought to occur via social processes including discrimination and structural inequalities (Symington 2004). In an intersectional analysis, identity, equality and power need to be seen differently by focusing on points of intersection, complexity and the structures that define access to rights and opportunities (ibid.). Symington further argues that using intersectionality as a tool entails valuing a 'bottom-up' approach to research, analysis and planning. Accordingly, collection of information should begin with questions about how women and men actually live their lives. The picture can then be built 'upwards', accounting for the various influences that shape women's lives while specific inquiries need to be made about the experiences of women living at the margins, the poorest of the poor, and women suffering from different types of oppression (ibid.). The present study aims at identifying the most marginalised and vulnerable among the conflict-affected population in Manipur.

It also becomes necessary here to understand what 'gender' means in order to determine whether the effects of conflict are gendered. Gender can be defined as the 'socially constructed differences between men and women', that is, the social construction of masculinity and femininity (El-Bushra 2000). Euan Hague claims that 'society constructs masculinity as a bearer of power and subjugates femininity to maintain the dominance of that power through patriarchy' (Hague 1997). There are some universal gender stereotypes which associate with masculinity qualities of being rational, dominant, active, powerful and strong, of being an economic provider and a protector, and the general ideas of the public sphere, mind and culture; and with femininity irrationality, qualities of being submissive, caring, passive, a nurturer, of existence in the domestic and private sphere, and the ideas of body and nature.

Symington however stresses that a gender-specific approach alone would not be adequate for designing programmes for refugee camp residents displaced by war or conflict. The needs, vulnerabilities and priorities of the many identities—the young and the old, persecuted ethnic groups, families with multiple dependents, and those who have experienced personal or psychological trauma—all need to be understood and taken into account. It is essential to understand how gender intersects with these other identities and structures the experiences of the residents of a conflict zone in order to design effective programmes for them (Symington 2004). Such a perspective is often found to be lacking while describing the conflict-affected, displaced population of the Kuki-Naga conflict. This study takes these various aspects into consideration and attempts an intersectional analysis of the experiences of displaced Kuki women.

THE AFFECTED SITES

While the displaced population faces conflict firsthand as they flee from their homes and land, the repercussion of the conflict is also indirectly felt by many who live under constant threat of violence. Of those who have been displaced, rehabilitation has occurred in various ways—some have gone back to resettle in their own villages while others have made the refugee camps their 'permanent' home. In this regard, three sites have been selected for the study: one resettlement camp housing those affected in the ethnic clash of the 1990s, one village whose population had gone back to its previous settlement after displacement, and one village whose population was not displaced but which faced the indirect effects of the conflict.

The first site is a resettlement colony named Chavangphai which is located in the periphery of Moreh town, a commercial town bordering India and Myanmar. The grouping centre has now developed into a permanent locality and is considered part of Moreh town in Chandel district. The second site is Gelnal village where the houses had been attacked and burnt but the settlement was rebuilt. Gelnal is located in the Sadar Hills West sub-division of Senapati district. These two villages are the settlement sites which have been severely affected by the conflict. The third study area is Tujang Vaichong village, also in the Sadar Hills West sub-division of Senapati district, which, although never evacuated or directly affected by the conflict, was under constant threat during the conflict and thereby not spared from its ramifications.

THE METHOD USED IN THE STUDY

Social mapping of the three selected villages was initiated in the early phase of the field study. Household survey was conducted by selecting fifty households from each village using systematic random sampling, which amounted to 150 households in total. The household survey of these selected households recorded the age-wise distribution and educational level of its members; the nature of family—whether nuclear, joint or extended; the size of the family; the number of its earning members and their occupations; total monthly income and assets; and attitude towards health and treatment. Interviews focused on the changes in the livelihood pattern and attitude towards health and treatment prior to and after the conflict. The methods used for conducting the study included a semi-structured interview assisted by a schedule, a focus group discussion with elderly persons and collection of oral history from key informants. Anthropometric measurements (BMI, height and weight) were noted for selected age groups to determine the nutritional status in the three study sites.

To identify and understand any existing differences or transition, temporal markers were determined: In the case of Chavangphai, 1992 was the year the displaced people moved into the area and so it was marked as the transitional year connecting the periods before and after the conflict, whereas in the cases of the other two villages, Gelnal and Tujang Vaichong, it was the year 1993, in which Gelnal was attacked and devastated and the then chief of Tujang Vaichong, Khothang Kipgen, was killed.

EXPERIENCES OF MARGINALISATION OF KUKI WOMEN

While conflict inflicts suffering on everyone, women are particularly affected in the short as well as long term. Often, sexual assault and exploitation are employed as tools of war. The long-term effects can be seen especially where the victims face isolation, alienation and prolonged trauma. As culturally designated caregivers, women struggle to support their families and hold their households together while the men are fighting and keeping vigil during a conflict.

My study shows that three-fourths of the Kuki families of erstwhile Joupi village under Tamei sub-division of Tamenglong district became female-headed households when the majority of men were killed and their wives widowed. The women had to shoulder the responsibility of being the sole bread-earners for their respective families as there were no male earning members left to support them. Similar cases were also found in the other study sites and many other conflict-affected villages such as Chavangphai and Gelnal.

As accounted in a study by USAID (2007) on women and conflict, this new role of the women as primary providers expose them to further abuse. Although in some ways gender relations may improve in the aftermath of conflict due to the shift in gender roles, by and large, the impact of conflict is always negative. Both women and girls are adversely affected when they are exposed to conflict and they become vulnerable as the social support they had once depended upon is no longer available.

Gender-based Violence

Women are among the most vulnerable and marginalised groups during conflict as they are subjected to more than just physical violence. Gender-based violence is common in conflict zones and conflict-affected communities. Reports from human rights advocacy groups document many examples of the exploitation and abuse of women and children during conflict. Women in refugee and IDP camps face sexual exploitation and a lack of physical security (USAID 2007). This is especially common in case of families without adult male members, and as observed in my study, female-headed households are more vulnerable. Such households are also at a greater risk of facing marginalisation during rehabilitation and migration. A study by Cahill (2003) narrates the plight of women in conflict owing to their lack of documentation to prove their entitlement to food, health services and shelter. Consequently, they may be forced to endure sexual abuse in exchange for basic necessities which further puts their health at risk. The absence of a patriarch in the family thus causes further marginalisation of women in the larger social structure.

Effects on Livelihood

Traditionally, land has been considered the basis of political power and social status in most tribal societies. Likewise, for the Kukis, land is their most valued wealth, as it provides a sense of identity and rootedness within the village, and unlike other assets, is often associated with durability and permanence. Even to this day, it is the most important among all forms of immovable property (Sitlhou 2015). As Sitlhou notes:

> Broadly categorized, individual household-owned land falls under two types: ancestral land and acquired land. Ancestral land, as the name suggests, is passed down the male line from generation to generation. Acquired land, on the other hand, is land obtained on purchase by an individual. In the process, land can be reclassified as ancestral land when it is passed down to the children of the one who has acquired it. (Sitlhou 2015)

Land, especially ancestral land, is a highly valued and sacred entity for all the Kukis in general as agriculture is their basic means of livelihood. However, the conflict between the two ethnic groups which erupted in the 1990s created an unfavourable situation leading to the alienation of land from both the parties, and especially from the displaced population. Singh (2008) writes about how after getting displaced, many previous landowners became landless wage labourers, which is similar to the findings of the research for the present study.

Although the main source of livelihood among the Kukis is agriculture, a negligible proportion of the population does engage in other non-agricultural occupations. Agricultural landowners own at least a plot of land either for wet rice cultivation known as '*phailei*' or for jhum cultivation (slash-and-burn) called '*thinglhang lei*'. Landless agricultural labourers are those who work in fields which do not belong to them, but who obtain a share from the total agricultural produce. Daily wage labourers earn their livelihood by engaging themselves in work that pays on a daily basis. There are also those who are engaged in private jobs working for NGOs, or as school teachers in private educational institutions. Skilled labourers—such as craftsmen, blacksmiths, weavers, carpenters—earn their income by selling their handmade finished products. Those in small-scale businesses are engaged in profit-making activities such as buying and selling of market products, or running shops or tea-stalls. There are also government employees and people who take up more than one occupation.

There is a noticeable shift in the nature of occupation before and after the conflict in the study areas. In the sample group from Chavangphai, which is inhabited by a fully displaced population, the majority work as manual contractual labourers, while a few are skilled in handicrafts. The National Rural Employment Guarantee Scheme (NREGS) provides some days of employment to the people. In comparison, in Gelnal village, which was burnt down but where villagers later resettled, the majority of the villagers are engaged in agricultural labour, jobs provided by the NREGS, and government jobs. This data shows the transition of occupation from agricultural labour to daily wage labour among the displaced population. They have no choice but to adopt the available means of livelihood to sustain their new life in the resettlement colony.

In many cases, women affected by conflict are unable to earn enough for their own subsistence and those of their families. Often, due to lack of education and because of being overburdened with household responsibilities, women are unable to obtain meaningful paid jobs. The study shows how womenfolk in the resettlement colony are also often engaged in small, informal businesses such as sale of fruits and vegetables at the border market. Unlike other local businesswomen who open registered shops and sell household or dress items, the displaced women run their businesses in the open enduring cold, heat and rain.

Poor Household Assets and Housing Facilities

With regard to household assets, majority of the households in Chavangphai own only a plot of land on which they have constructed their houses, whereas in Gelnal and Tujang Vaichong, the majority of the households own agricultural land and livestock, besides the house they live in. While the villagers in the latter villages are able to depend on their agricultural land for livelihood, the displaced population is in a more vulnerable position with respect to their livelihood.

Most of the housing facilities in the resettlement colony are in a deplorable condition with thatched roofs and mud walls, while a few better-off households have wooden or cemented flooring and tin roofs. The average number of rooms in these houses is three. Households with many family members have to share space in these limited number of rooms and the notion of privacy or the space to relax, especially for the womenfolk, after a tiring, long day remains out of question. It is the women who take care of the household and ensure the premises are clean and tidy and the limited space of the house well-arranged to accommodate all the members. The housing facilities are comparatively better in Gelnal and Tujang Vaichong with more spacious rooms and open space in the vicinity of the house.

Lack of Proper Formal Education

Education is a determining factor in empowering women which further influences their participation in the social and political arena. The level of education received by women in Chavangphai resettlement colony is lower as compared to the other two villages. Conflict had disrupted the entire education system in the state of Manipur. Academic activities came to a complete halt in many parts of the state for at least four to five years during the conflict. The poor education of the displaced women also reduced their opportunities for earning a decent livelihood. Even before the outbreak of the conflict, girls and women were already facing a number of hurdles in pursuing education. Majority of the rural girls did not receive formal education as education was not considered necessary and the girls were required to take up household work or work in the agricultural fields. Other reasons include the high cost of education, the responsibility of looking after younger siblings and lack of proper school facilities. Also in some cases, women were not encouraged to pursue education and instead, were married off at a young age (Nengneilhing 2014). Lack of education and awareness is also related to the poor health of women as it often leads them to make poor decisions about their health and results in further marginalisation.

Effects on Health

Women continue to face a variety of conflict-related health issues even after the violence has ceased. Some of the persisting health issues are malnutrition, post-traumatic stress or other injuries. The risk of contracting communicable diseases also rises due to widespread poverty, lack of awareness, congested living and the absence of adequate healthcare services. The impact of conflict on the health of the conflict-affected population can be analysed by studying the health indicators such as height, weight and body mass index.

BMI Cut-off Points to Determine the Nutritional Status of Adults

The body mass index [=weight in kilograms/square of height in metres] is used as an indicator of nutritional status of adults. For many Asian populations, the trigger points for public health action are identified as 23 kg/m^2 or higher, representing increased risk, and 27.5 kg/m^2 or higher, representing high risk. The suggested categories are as follows: less than 18.5 kg/m^2 represents underweight; 18.5–23 kg/m^2 represents acceptable risk; 23–27.5 kg/m^2 represents increased risk; and 27.5 kg/m^2 or higher represents high risk (James et al. 1988).

Important differences exist in the form of higher/lower body fat content for a given BMI in Southeast Asians, Polynesians and Asian Indians. With this in mind, the International Diabetes Federation has accepted a BMI value of >25 kg/m^2 and 23 kg/m^2 as the cut-off for obesity for Asian men and women, respectively (Eckel, Grundy and Zimmet 2005).

Table 8.1: Nutritional Status of Adults Aged 36 to 43 Years Based on South Asian BMI Cut-off Points

Study Area	*% of Adults Who Are Obese*			*% of Adults Who Are Overweight*			*% of Adults Who Are of Recommended Weight*			*% of Adults Who Are Underweight*		
	F	*M*	*T*	*F*	*M*	*T*	*F*	*M*	*T*	*F*	*M*	*T*
Chavangphai	5.0	2.5	7.5	2.5	5.0	7.5	25.0	30.0	55.0	20.0	10.0	30.0
Gelnal	2.5	5.0	7.5	5.0	10.0	15.0	25.0	32.5	57.5	12.5	7.5	20.0
Tujang Vaichong	5.0	5.0	10.0	12.5	7.5	20.0	30.0	25.0	55.0	10.0	5.0	15.0

Source: Primary data.

Table 8.1 shows the nutritional status of adults aged between 36 to 43 years based on South Asian BMI cut-off points. Chavangphai has the highest percentage of underweight adults (30 per cent), followed by Gelnal (20 per cent) and Tujang Vaichong (15 per cent). The table also shows that the percentage of overweight adults is highest in Tujang Vaichong (20 per cent), followed by Gelnal (15 per cent) and Chavangphai (7.5 per cent).

Table 8.2: Heights (in cm) of Two Adult Age Groups at the Three Study Sites

Study Sites	*19 to 23 Years*			*37 to 43 Years*		
	Mean Height (Male & Female)	*Mean Height (Male)*	*Mean Height (Female)*	*Mean Height (Male & Female)*	*Mean Height (Male)*	*Mean Height (Female)*
Chavangphai	153.0	158.8	147.8	153.9	159.9	148.6
Gelnal	154.5	159.0	149.6	155.3	159.3	150.4
Tujang Vaichong	154.6	159.1	150.9	155.1	160.1	151.4

Source: Primary data.

Table 8.2 shows that there is not much difference in height of males across the three sites whereas the height of women increases with the ascending socio-economic status of the settlements. It also shows the change in height over two generations: who were 19–23 years old at the time of the conflict (37–43 years now) and who were 19–23 years at the time of the survey. There is an overall decline in height from the older generation to the newer across all the three sites. The decline is in descending order of socio-economic status, i.e., the greatest decline is found among those with the poorest standard of living: the youth of Chavangphai are the shortest, followed by Gelnal and Tujang Vaichong. The decline follows a consistent pattern in the case of women but does not in the case of men. Since these differences are small, and the study was conducted with small sample sizes, the need was felt for a T-test to be conducted to see the statistical significance of the differences. The test indicated that the differences were not statistically significant. However, they do conform to the trend that is seen with other health indicators and therefore, have a corroborative value.

CONCLUSION

The issues of conflict-affected women need to be understood with an intersectional approach, taking into consideration the importance of women's rights and gender equality. An analysis of poverty would not stop at finding that women are disproportionately poor in a given region, but would explore which groups of women are poorest, which policies and practices contribute to their poverty, how the historical and political situation contributes to their condition, and whether development projects and policy initiatives are addressing the specific problems faced by different groups of women in a particular setting. The study also calls for a more gender-sensitive approach in understanding the conflict-affected population and addressing its issues.

Prioritising the most marginalised by analysing intersecting discriminations, empowering those who lack access to rights and resources and focusing on ameliorating processes that lead to poverty and exclusion may facilitate tangible advances in terms of women's rights and gender equality. This chapter emphasises the need to ensure that the marginalised can claim their human rights and have access to basic healthcare, educational opportunities, livelihood security, and other essential needs. The study shows how some women benefit from occupying comparatively more privileged positions while some are pushed to the extreme margins and experience severe discrimination, such as the conflict-displaced Kuki women in Manipur.

REFERENCES

Bradarić, Nikola, et al. 1996. 'Two Outbreaks of Typhoid Fever Related to the War in Bosnia and Herzegovina'. *European Journal of Epidemiology* 12(4): 409–412.

Cahill, Kevin M. 2003. 'Issues of Power and Gender in Complex Emergencies'. In Kevin M. Cahill (ed.), *Emergency Relief Operations.* New York: Fordham University Press.

Dena, Lal. 1999. 'The Kuki-Naga Conflict: Juxtaposed in the Colonial Context'. In Kailash S. Aggarwal (ed.), *Dynamics of Identity and Intergroup Relations in North-East India.* Shimla: Indian Institute of Advanced Study.

Eckel, R. H., Scott M. Grundy and Paul Z. Zimmet. 2005. 'The Metabolic Syndrome'. *The Lancet* 365: 1415–28.

El-Bushra, J. 2000. 'Transforming Conflict: Some Thoughts on a Gendered Understanding of Conflict Processes.' In S. Jacobs, R. Jacobson, and J. Marchbank (eds), *States of Conflict: Gender, Violence and Resistance.* London: Zed Books.

Goldstein, Joshua S. 2003. *War and Gender: How Gender Shapes the War System and Vice Versa.* New York: Cambridge University Press.

Goodhand, Jonathan. 2001. *Aid, Conflict and Peace-building in Afghanistan: What Lessons Can Be Learned?* London: International Alert.

Guha-Sapir, D., and W. van Panhuis. 2002. *Armed Conflict and Public Health.* Brussels: Centre for Research on Epidemiology of Disaster (CRED).

Hague, Euan. 1997. 'Rape, Power, and Masculinity: The Construction of Gender and the National Identities in the War in Bosnia-Herzegovina.' In Ronit Lentin (ed.), *Gender and Catastrophe*. London: Zed Books.

Haokip, T. T. 2002. 'Ethnic Conflicts and Internal Displacement in Manipur'. In C. J. Thomas (ed.), *Dimensions of Displaced People in North East India*. New Delhi: Regency Publications.

Haokip, Thongkholal. 2013. 'Essays on the Kuki-Naga Conflict: A Review'. *Strategic Analysis* 37(March).

James, W. P. T., et al. 1988. 'Definitions of Chronic Energy Deficiency in Adults'. *European Journal of Clinical Nutrition* 42: 969–989.

Jaspars, Susanne, and Sorcha O'Callaghan. 2010. *Challenging Choices: Protection and Livelihoods in Conflict - Case Studies from Darfur, Chechnya, Sri Lanka and the Occupied Palestinian Territories.* London: Humanitarian Policy Group, Overseas Development Institute. Available at https://odi.org/en/publications/challenging-choices-protection-and-livelihoods-in-conflict-case-studies-from-darfur-chechnya-sri-lanka-and-the-occupied-palestinian-territories/ (accessed May 2023).

Kamaroopi. 1993. 'Ethnic Cleansing'. *Economic and Political Weekly* 28(41): 2172–2173.

Kelly, L. 2000. 'Wars against Women: Sexual Violence, Sexual Politics and the Militarised State'. In S. Jacobs, R. Jacobson and J. Marchbank (eds), *States of Conflict: Gender, Violence and Resistance*. London: Zed Books, 45–66.

Kipgen, Nehginpao. 2013. 'Politics of Ethnic Conflict in Manipur'. *South Asia Research* 33(1): 21–38.

Luckham, R., et al. 2001. 'Conflicts and Poverty in Sub-Saharan Africa: An Assessment of the Issues and Evidence'. IDS Working Paper 128. Brighton: IDS.

Moser, Caroline O. N. 2001. 'The Gendered Continuum of Violence and Conflict.' In Caroline O. N. Moser and Fiona C. Clark (eds), *Victims, Perpetrators or Actors?* London: Zed Books, 30–51.

Nengneilhing, Ruth. 2014. 'Women's Health and Healthcare Accessibility: A Case Study of Kuki Women in Gelnel Village of West Sadar Hills in Manipur'. In Hoineilhing Sitlhou (ed.), *Kuki Women*. New Delhi: Bookwell Publishers.

Phanjoubam, Pradip. 2005. 'Manipur: Fractured Land.' *India International Centre Quarterly* 32(2/3): 275–287.

Plumper, Thomas, and Neumayer, Eric. 2006. 'The Unequal Burden of War: The Effect of Armed Conflict on the Gender Gap of Life Expectancy'. *International Organisation* 60: 723–754.

Shimray, U. A. 2001. 'Ethnicity and Socio-Political Assertion: The Manipur Experience'. *Economic and Political Weekly* 36(39): 3674–78.

Silva, K. T., et al. 2002. 'Sri Lanka: Civil War and the Health Sector, in Surviving Crisis, How Systems Cope with Instability, Insecurity and Infection'. Workshop at The International Conference Centre, Manila, Philippines.

Singh, Aheibam Koireng. 2008. *Ethnicity and Inter-Community Conflicts: A Case of Kuki-Naga in Manipur.* New Delhi: Akansha Publishing House.

Sitlhou, Hoineilhing. 2015. 'Patriarchal Bargains and Paradoxical Emancipation: Issues in the Politics of Land Rights of the Kuki Women'. *Indian Journal of Gender Studies* 22(1): 92–115.

Symington, Alison. 2004. 'Intersectionality: A Tool for Gender and Economic Justice.' *Women's Rights and Economic Change* 9, August. Available at https://www.awid.org/sites/default/files/atoms/files/intersectionality_a_tool_for_gender_and_economic_justice.pdf (accessed April 2023).

Tohring S. R. 2010. *Violence and Identity in North East India: Naga-Kuki Conflict.* Delhi: Mittal Publications.

Toole, M. J., and R. J. Waldman. 1993. 'Refugees and Displaced Persons: War, Hunger and Public Health'. *JAMA* 270(5): 600–5.

USAID. 2007. 'Women and Conflict'. Available at https://2012-2017.usaid.gov/sites/default/files/documents/1865/toolkit_women_and_conflict_an_introductory_guide_for_programming.pdf (accessed May 2023).

Christianity and Gender

A Study of Protestant Mizo Women

V. Sawmveli

It is difficult to make a conclusive statement on the status of women in terms of the degree of liberation they are afforded or the oppression they are subjugated to in the context of Mizoram. It is essential that we question the 'status of women' and even problematise the very category 'women', as many feminist historians and thinkers like Joan Scott, Denise Riley and Judith Butler have done. Studying the socio-cultural history and religious lives of women has always been a challenge due to the diversity of language, ethnicity and geography that Mizo women occupy. But nevertheless, it is crucial that we analyse the contradictions in the status of women—whose lives are liberated in certain ways and oppressed in other ways—by exploring the various realms of cultural, religious and social life where women either take an active role or remain invisible or inactive. This chapter reflects on this conflicting status of women in Mizoram with special reference to the church life. Keeping in mind that the accessibility of women to religious spheres differs from church to church, my study will focus on Protestants in the Mizoram Presbyterian Church Synod (the largest denomination in Mizoram), the Baptist Church of Mizoram (BCM) and the Evangelical Church of Maraland (ECM).

There is a popular idea that the status of women in Mizoram is better than that of women in other parts of India and that this is because of Christian influence. Interestingly, a state which boasts of a female literacy rate of 89.27 per cent (Government of India 2011) is void of a woman representative in the state assembly.[1]

It is also surprising that despite the high literacy rate, only few women are able to occupy high positions in the society. Mizo women are also denied influential positions in the church. The high status of women in Mizo society thus is highly contested. Lalrinawmi Ralte argues that 'women in Mizoram do not enjoy freedom just because of the absence of dowry. Their freedom is only at the surface level, but not a reality.'[2] Chatterji argues that the status of women in Mizoram is far better than that of women in other parts of India. She speaks of women's place in the family, their role during courtship and marriage and offers detailed descriptions to prove how Mizo women have greater freedom and a higher status in the society. She writes, 'A woman in Mizo society enjoys a distinctively high status with a lot of freedom for the satisfaction of her natural impulses without being tied down' (Chatterji 1975: 5). But this view is contradictory to what two British officials, Chapman and Clark, who had visited Mizoram in 1940s observed. According to them,

> The worst feature in the life of the South Mizo district at that time was the treatment women received from men. A woman had no rights at all. Body, mind and spirit, she belonged from birth to death to her father, her brother, her husband. Her menfolk could treat her as they liked, and a man who did not beat his wife was scorned by his friends as a coward … She was responsible for all the work—the menfolk just helped [in] building the house. She could not go out without their permission. It was she who carried all the burdens up and down the hills—wood, water, rice and anything else. Daily we watched the women with their heavy loads staggering uphill, and should men be with them they would often be empty-handed. (Chapman and Clark 1968: 13–14)

Traditionally, Mizo society excluded women from religious rites and ceremonies. The patriarchal structure of Mizo society acknowledged men as the sole providers for a household and honoured them with the responsibility of administrative functions of the village. Women could become neither priests nor exorcists. In certain ceremonial functions and sacrificial rites, women were excluded from eating the meat of the animal killed or from the feast altogether. Christianity paved the way for women to participate in activities from which they were earlier barred. The introduction of Western education by the Christian missionaries resulted in the opening up of new opportunities for Mizo women.

At present, research on gender is relatively scarce in Mizoram. The most notable works are those of the Mizo feminist theologians like T. Vanlaltlani's 'The Experience of Pathian (High God) and Other Deities in Mizo Religion and Its Influence on Mizo Christians' (1990), R. L. Hnuni's 'Women in the Context of Bible and North East India' (1990) and Lalrinawmi Ralte's 'Crab Theology: A Critique of Patriarchy, Cultural Degradation and Empowerment of Mizo Women' (1993). All these works are unpublished. They argue that a strong patriarchal system exists within the church as well. The patriarchal character of Christianity complements the existing patriarchal character of Mizo society. In fact, Lalrinawmi Ralte argues that traditional Mizo society was both 'patriarchal and liberating' and then Christianity penetrated into the social structure and dangerously strengthened the patriarchal elements. This has led to women being more suppressed than ever before (Ralte 1993: 64). She noted the existence of women deities like Khuannu in traditional Mizo religious beliefs ('Khua' means 'village' and 'Nu' refers to a feminine adjective or the noun 'mother'). Khuannu is believed to be a benevolent protector and guardian of the whole village. This woman deity has now been replaced by the Christian male version of God, Pathian.

Some other feminist work on the region does exist. Bonita Aleaz's *Emergent Women: Mizo Women's Perspective* (2005), and more recently, Anup Shekhar Chakraborty's essay 'The Emergence of Women from "Private" to "Public": A Narrative of Power Politics from Mizoram' (2008) are notable ones. Aleaz (2005: 19) is of the opinion that 'the current journey of Mizo women from the realm of the private to the public, started within, and through the channels of religion'. Chakraborty notes that Mizo women are not seen as active political agents with voices of their own in Mizo culture; they are 'repressed and directed'. Chakraborty shows that one cannot place the blame for the patriarchal nature of Mizo society on the introduction of Christianity. Christianity with its own clearly patriarchal genealogy merely fitted Mizo society quite well and made the transition from a traditional society to a Christian one relatively smooth.

MOTIVE, METHOD AND MATERIALS OF THE STUDY

This chapter explores the ways in which different stereotypical gender roles are perpetuated by religious and cultural norms which create inequalities between men and women. I discuss how the gender dynamics within the church administration relegates women to a secondary status. Through a study of the middle-classes in the Mizo society who are believed to have benefitted most from Christianity and are highly influenced by Western education, I argue that gender inequality is maintained and perpetuated by the Protestant Christian community in Mizoram, in particular among those belonging to the Mizoram Presbyterian Church Synod (MPC), the Baptist Church of Mizoram (BCM) and the Evangelical Church of Maraland (ECM).

The material presented here is based on a study conducted in 2005 in Aizawl, Lunglei and Siaha in Mizoram. Data collection and analysis were carried out through an intensive scrutiny of secondary sources. Questionnaires, in-depth interviews and participant observation were the methods used for collecting primary data. Population samples were selected from three denominations, namely, Presbyterian (MPC), Baptist (BCM) and Evangelical (ECM), across a wide geographical area to provide a broader perspective to the study. These three denominations believe in the Holy Trinity—God the Father, Jesus the Son and the Holy Spirit, uphold the same religious principles and their motives and actions with regards to the society are the same.[3]

There are ten respondents from MPC, seven from BCM and 36 from ECM. Respondents were selected on the basis of their active involvement and participation in the church. This makes a total of 53 respondents, of which 26 were male and 27 female. Most of the respondents had at least a Bachelor's degree, and some of them were doctors, engineers, pastors and teachers by profession. Most of them belong to middle-class and lower-middle-class families while a few are from upper-middle class households in Mizoram. The respondents' names have been withheld and letters have been used in place of names.

GENDER DYNAMICS WITHIN THE CHURCH STRUCTURE

Within the three denominations one can see a clear division of gender roles. The societal pattern of gendering functions smoothly alongside the church's notion of gender. There are always limitations imposed on women and both the society and the church dictate what women can do or should do. Women are permitted to occupy positions only at the lower levels of church administration while men are put in the higher positions. Women's roles are recognised only when it comes to participation in women-oriented activities and not beyond that. For example, preaching from the pulpit is seen as highly inappropriate for women. Women are not encouraged to deliver sermons, solemnise marriage ceremonies, minister burial ceremonies, or be ordained as pastors. The common 'explanation' given for this is that the two genders have different proficiencies. These differences are often justified as differences in biological sex and probing further to discuss the idea of 'gender' would only create hostility and uneasiness among the members. Restrictions on women's appointment in church administration are most visible in the matter of women's ordination. Ordination is denied to women by members of the Christian community, especially the leaders of the church, who misinterpret the scriptures to justify their bias.

Moreover, the traditional patriarchal attitude of Mizo society, which considers men to be more suitable for the job, and the ingrained feeling of inferiority among the female members of the church fail to challenge this form of sexism and gender inequality.

Interestingly, a large section of the respondents (98 per cent) feel that of all the religions, Christianity is where women enjoy the most freedom. One of the respondents, who is also an active member of BCM, remarked that 'Christian women are given the right to become completely free women in the Holy Spirit which no other religion can give to women.'[4] Christianity gives equal spiritual dignity, which means that all those who believe in Jesus can attain salvation irrespective of one's sex. Another respondent says that, 'Christianity being the most influential religion has not only developed the remote areas, but has also given more freedom to women who were once bound in their [traditional] belief systems.'[5] Majority of the respondents believe that since women can freely participate in church activities and other religious events, unlike in other religions, they enjoy more freedom.

One of the reasons why this idea is very common among Mizo Christians is because Christian women can read the Holy Bible at any time and anywhere they please. This seems liberating when juxtaposed against the fact that among Orthodox Jews, only males are given the privilege to read the Torah. One female respondent, drawing comparison with other religions, said, 'Hindu or Muslim women are restricted and dominated in their lives by purdah and sati.'[6] While the validity of such views is highly debatable and making comparisons between different religious practices is not always logical, in the minds of partly Westernised, educated, middle-class Mizo Christian women, only Hinduism and Islam are patriarchal, and not Christianity.

WOMEN'S CONTRIBUTION TO THE CHURCH

Mizo women engage themselves with various activities and work within their limited space at the church. Although their financial contributions are crucial to the survival of the church and they are even called the 'backbone of the church', they are assigned secondary roles in the institution as 'support groups'. The Mizoram Presbyterian *Kohhran Hmeichhia* (the women's wing) collected as much as Rs 4,05,22,441 between April 2002 and March 2003 through the *Buhfai Tham* scheme, which may be translated in English as 'a handful of rice' (*Synod Dan Bu* 2003). According to this practice, every family would keep aside a handful of rice twice a day from the amount measured out for daily cooking and consumption. The church would later collect this amount as donation. From Buhfai Tham, the Baptist Church's women's wing collected as much as Rs 82,72,654 in the year 2003. Every year they are given a target to raise. In the year 2000–2001, they collected Rs 10,94,083, and in 2001–2002 Rs 7,31,648. In 2002–2003 they raised Rs 5,97,455 (Vanlaltlani 2005: 96). The women's wings use these funds to organise support for missionary charities, hospitals and orphanages and participate in other initiatives. It is also observed that women's attendance at church is more regular than their male counterparts.

My respondents are of the opinion that women's organisations and their contributions are as crucial to society as they are to the church. Their dedication towards church activities, outreach works such as visiting inmates in jails and juvenile homes, and prayer support to the needy are some of their important social contributions. A few of the respondents are of the view that such activities and outreach work help to broaden the mental and social horizons of the participating women, who are otherwise confined within the church.

RELIGIOUS LEGITIMISATION OF GENDER INEQUALITY

In most of the churches in Mizoram, even though the participation of women is considered crucial, ecclesiastical leadership roles and activities are considered the prerogative of men and are assigned to them. In the oft-criticised patriarchal structure of religion, androcentric religious texts often deem women to be inferior to men. Majority of the respondents seemed to agree with and accept this idea of inequality, which can be summarised as:

> Man is the head of the woman, as the Holy Bible tells us, and the Lord made woman to serve man. A woman can never become the head of men. And this is how our traditions as well as the Bible want us to live.

This is how gender inequality, prevailing both in religious as well as social spheres, is often justified using religious texts and institutional arrangements. Scriptural interpretation thus plays a tremendous role in legitimising subordination and subjugation by reinforcing the role and position of women in society as inferior to that of men. In the Old Testament, women are rarely seen as leaders whereas men are seen to hold both political and religious leadership (Clark and Richardson 1977). Women are asked to cover their heads and be subservient to their husbands. Their secondary status is justified by the creation theory in the Bible which states that woman was born from a man's rib. Mr T, one of the respondents, said,

> Being a Christian and a believer, I strongly believe that all religions are fundamentally sexist, and this is how it should be. God created Adam out of the soil, and breathed life through his nostril and he became alive. But Eve was formed out of Adam's rib.[7]

Another respondent said, 'Women and men play different roles and women are to follow men, but that does not mean they are inferior.' This is presently the more common view among the Mizo Christian community which justifies women's subjugation by stating that women are biologically different and therefore they cannot be treated as equal. Some are of the opinion that men are allowed more privilege because they are the bearers of religion. This idea finds its origin in traditional patriarchal Mizo society where men are considered the bearers of religion while women do not have a religion of their own. Women are supposed to follow and accept their husband's or father's (the men's) religion.

Christian women are also expected to be patient, humble, and submissive to men and to act as their emotional support. Gender roles assigned to men and women are complementary. Karl Barth, the famous theologian, believed that God created humans in two kinds, wanting us to understand sexual differentiation as the most basic of all human distinctions (Frykberg 1993). He further said that it is part of our 'vocation' to preserve the differences of masculinity and femininity. He criticised all attempts to overcome these differences and said that man is the 'initiator' while woman is the 'follower'. He quoted from the book of Ephesians (5: 22–24), which states that wives should submit to their husband as man is the 'head of the family, and the head of man is Christ'. According to him, to try to disregard one's accorded gender role would only mean challenging 'nature's order', and the sexes ought to be viewed as complementary.

ORDINATION OF WOMEN PASTORS

Women are often not allowed to fully participate in church, and especially not allowed to occupy higher positions in the ecclesiastical hierarchy. Feminist theologians have raised their voice against the denial of ordination of women. Ordination is a process in which, through praying and laying on of hands, a person is set apart in the name of God for leadership as priest or pastor. Some churches hold on to the tradition of apostolic succession in which the priestly ministry is believed to be direct successors of Christ's Apostles. Some theologians have even considered ordination to be the ultimate goal. Ordination bestows certain privileges and powers which makes one eligible to conduct ministerial services in the church (Lungsanla et al. 2005). Being ordained means the recognition of being capable of looking after church members—a position that commands respect and trust. When women are denied these rights, it is because they are deemed inferior. In the early past, women could serve as church leaders, but gradually ordination became the monopoly of men (ibid.).

The Protestant Reformation challenged the hierarchical structure of priesthood and the criterion of celibacy in the Roman Catholic Church, but women's position in church remained unchanged. Even after the Reformed Church was established, ordination remained a special calling only for men. The evolution of attitudes in the course of time apropos of the priesthood of all believers led to the question of the ordination of women. In India, the question of women's ordination was first brought up in 1970 in the Synod of the Church of South India by the ministerial committee on behalf of the Diocese of Madras, and the decision was taken to accept women's ordination. On 6 May 1976, the first female deacon was ordained. After a long gap, in 1982, the ordination of women as presbyters was accepted. In the Northeast of India, the issue was raised only in 1980, and at present there are only five Baptist women ordained in the whole region. In the Baptist Church of Nagaland, only single, celibate women are ordained.

In Mizoram, women's ordination is often denied as the patriarchal clergy interprets the scriptures to their own advantage and the religio-cultural traditions view women as inferior. In Mizoram, no Protestant Christian denomination has yet ordained women as pastors. In the Presbyterian Church of Mizoram too, ordination of women is still denied, even though the issue has been raised for discussion. The general perception is that women should not ask for ordination, but prove their commitment through their actions in church.

In the year 1978, Pi Saptawni was elected as *Kohhran Upa* (church elder) at the Mission Veng Presbyterian Church, but she was refused ordination as the church was not yet ready to have women as church elders. After this, the issue of women's ordination was again brought up for deliberation in the Presbyterian Synod thrice: in 1989, 2000 and 2002, and each time the decision was in favour of maintaining the status quo. In spite of their crucial contribution and hard work, women have been consistently rejected for certain posts and denied certain rights. Unlike the Presbyterian Church, in the Baptist Church, women are ordained as church elders (*Upas*). There are 18 church elders at present belonging to various local churches. They even have a female Assistant Pastor, though there are no female pastors (Vanlaltlani 2005: 100). The ECM, while I am writing this, has a *Tual Upa* (deacon) but no *Kohhran Upas*.

Data from my research shows that the majority of male respondents cannot accept women's ordination, and 87 per cent of male respondents feel that women are unsuitable for higher positions in the Christian ministry. One of them candidly said, 'No woman should hold the post of priest or pastor'. This study thus shows that since traditional patriarchal attitudes are deeply rooted in society, women's ordination is seen as something strange and inappropriate. The majority of women among the respondents themselves feel that at present, women's ordination is not acceptable. A senior pastor[8] told me that the ordination of women is for the present 'out of question'. Women's roles are limited to being teachers at the Sunday schools, members of the women's wing, or missionary nurses.

CHRISTIANITY ON SEXUAL RELATIONS AND MARRIAGE

Many religions have rules and regulations in relation to sexuality and marriage, and Christianity is one which places a strong emphasis on these. The Holy Bible prescribes that human beings should control their sexual desires and live a holy, pure life. Sex before marriage is regarded as a sin. In the early days of Christianity, celibacy was regarded as the highest form of purity that humans could attain. After the Protestant Reformation, views on marriage were reformed so that married women could have an equal sacred significance as Catholic nuns if they demonstrated Christian virtues (Clark and Richardson 1977).

Religious consciousness is deeply rooted among members of the church and it orients their lives towards certain social norms and cultural practices. Among the Protestant community in Mizoram, marriage is a respected institution, in which a couple is united by God and only then is sexual activity permitted for them. Majority of the respondents stated that 'sex before marriage is sin, because it is sin in the eyes of God as well as our fellow human beings'. Majority of them feel that as 'good Christians' they should obey and follow whatever the Bible says. Only a few respondents opined that sex is a matter of personal choice and one cannot be constrained by the dictates of religious texts.

Marriage is viewed as a religious sacrament in which a man and a woman are bound in a permanent lifelong relationship, physically, socially and spiritually, with the aim of procreation and perpetuating the human race. However, even among Christian leaders and pastors, there are divergent views on marriage. Some say that marriage is necessary because God advocates perpetuation of the human race (Gen 1:28; 9:7), while others champion celibacy. Majority of the respondents said that they would marry only the person they love, considering love as the dominant reason for entering the institution of marriage. One female respondent remarked that it is necessary for a woman to be married because marriage offers certain privileges and a coveted social status. In many cases, the decision to marry arises out of social expectations and the need for security, and in many others, it may be an obligation or an aspiration.

Storkey (2000) has pointed out the nineteenth-century problems of 'superfluous women' in British society, where an unmarried middle-class woman was considered a liability. Working-class women could join domestic or factory work, but elite and high-bred women were always dependent on a man. So the solution was often to marry them off, or ship them out to the colonies as governesses, companions to elderly widows, and wives of English officers. Like in many other societies, in Mizoram too women are largely dependent on men and encouraged to get married, and a good marriage becomes a major determinant of their future social status. Women have always been expected to achieve fulfillment in marriage and motherhood and this tradition continues, even as they succeed in careers and opportunities outside their homes.

GENDERED DIVISION OF LABOUR

According to Kamla Bhasin (2000: 32), gendered division of labour refers to

> the allocation of different roles, responsibilities, and tasks to women and men based on societal ideas of what men and women should do and are capable of doing. Different responsibilities and tasks are divided and assigned to boys and girls, women and men, according to their sex-gender role, not necessarily according to their individual preference or capabilities.

Gendered division of labour associates space as male and female. Women are confined within the private sphere whereas men occupy the public sphere. The public sphere is the government, the job market, and places that are accessible to a large number of people. The private, on the other hand, is associated with the ideas of family or home (Keohane 1992). Gendered division of labour is often justified citing biological difference between the two sexes.

There can be gendered division of labour along three lines—production, reproduction and community work/activities. Production refers to work and activities which produce goods and services for consumption and trade, such as work in factories and companies, and this kind of work is considered to be productive labour that contributes to the economy and the Gross National Product of countries. This kind of 'skilled' work is mostly done by men and is better paid whereas women's work is confined within the household and is often undermined, and they are expected to work out of 'love'. Bhasin talks of two kinds of reproduction, biological and social, and both are processes which only women can perform though they are often underpaid and undermined (Bhasin 2000). Parsons (1951) conceptualised basic roles in the family as 'instrumental and expressive', and dichotomised them as male and female roles respectively. He says that division of labour in the family is based on sex and is functional for the integration of the family (see Rayaprol 1997: 87). Women's subjugation is necessary for the performance of their crucial roles in the family: as a helper, as a caregiver, and as an obedient aide to her husband.

Some people view gendered division of labour as inevitable necessary roles assigned to men and women. A few of the respondents supported this viewpoint and considered the gendered division of labour as divine ordinance. For instance, one respondent, Miss T, is of the view that 'This is how God has planned it and it has nothing to do with inequality; it is natural.'[9] According to another respondent, a male theologian, the purpose of God's creation of women was to assign different roles to men and women. He further states that 'God's intention of creating woman is to help and assist man. Therefore, women should behave in a very submissive manner.'[10]

The Mizo traditional worldview sees the 'ideal woman' as a woman who is a good homemaker and a dutiful wife. The Mizo women I interviewed were all involved in raising children and played a critical role in the process of children's socialisation. While some may interpret this as an indicator of the significance of women in Mizo society, others may argue that it is an excuse to curtail the movement of women and confine them within home.

CONTROL OF ECONOMIC RESOURCES

All over the world women have less leisure than men because their labour is more likely to be unpaid or underpaid, and they have less economic power. Unpaid labour such as child care, nursing and household chores are considered as women's jobs. Their lack of economic power results in their being subjected to social oppression.

Kramer (2001: 115) says that 'an individual's links to the economy have crucial influences on many aspects of the quality of that person's life: political power, material well being, access to educational opportunities, and even length of life are closely tied to one's position in the stratification system'. Women have historically had restricted access to economic resources and power. Men's control of the economy thus influences their political power, social status, privileges and decision-making at the macro as well as micro levels.

Marxist feminists view women's economic dependence on men as the primary basis of patriarchy—it often results in the husband's complete control over his wife and the household, and this economic inequality further justifies men's absolute authority over property. As Blumberg (1989: 163) says 'Relative male/female economic power is the most important of the major independent "power variables", affecting overall gender stratification'. Now the question that arises is if women have greater economic power, will it ensure gender equality? Women's economic power could grant her a better life and more power over the household even if there is no change at the societal level. Blumberg (ibid.: 165) says that, 'the greater women's relative economic power, the greater their control over their own lives in a variety of dimensions with broader economic implications'.

However, in the context of Mizoram, most of my respondents are of the view that increase in women's economic power does not necessarily bring in a corresponding change in the structure of society. She may be able to control her life, but she does not have absolute control over the household. To some extent, economic empowerment may result in women's emancipation from male subjugation, but not always. Women's economic independence offers them more choices at the personal level, such as better clothing, better nutrition, etc., but it is not sufficient to change women's position in the society. My informant Miss T said,

'I think women are economically more and more secure but not powerful.'[11] This shows that while the economic condition of women has improved, gender inequality still persists in the patriarchal social system.

The study has revealed that even when women are aware of societal restrictions and the lack of privilege, they often cannot bring themselves to question the system that subjugates them. Many accept it as their fate without questioning. And since the gendered division of roles is seen as the design and will of God, any transgression is considered sinful and thus avoided. Majority of the female respondents said that the subservient role they are assigned is 'natural' and it is their religious duty to embody it. The common responses are, 'God wants me to take care of my husband and my family, to be a blessing for them, to help and serve my husband—that is my duty.'[12] Here, to be a 'blessing' for the family means to be a good mother, an obedient daughter and a faithful, loving and dutiful wife. Women's personal religious experiences often lead them to believe that their religions are not fundamentally sexist (Burn 2000: 171).

CONCLUSION

The study revealed the gender inequality within the Protestant community in Mizoram, particularly among the three denominations—the Presbyterian Church of Mizoram, Baptist Church of Mizoram and Evangelical Church of Maraland. The study was conducted in the three towns of Aizawl, Lunglei, and Siaha. The chapter discussed the issues and challenges involved in the processes of women's ordination. I found, interestingly, that the main opposition to the elevation of women in the church precinct comes from the women themselves who do not want their fellow women as church leaders or pastors and thus play a part in the transmission and continuation of patriarchal ideology. While examining the claim that Christianity brought gender equality in Mizoram, we discussed how various forms of inequality and oppression are intertwined and explored the links between economic status of Mizo women and their lack of agency.

In conclusion, we may say that Mizo Christian women enjoy a certain amount of autonomy in specific aspects of their life, as compared to women elsewhere in the country, but that it does not necessarily result in gender equality. Esther Breitenbach makes a distinction between autonomy and equality: equality refers to women's access to opportunities and resources as compared to men's, whereas, autonomy is the individual woman's relative freedom within personal relationships (see Lovenduski and Randall 1993: 24). Although Mizo women enjoy individual autonomy in their restricted private spheres, when it comes to major decision-making or actions in the public sphere, there is continued male dominance. The question remains: Will she ever be considered equal to men?

NOTES

1. At the time of data collection during this research, there was no female representative in the state legislative assembly. In May 2014, Miss Vanlalawmpuii Chawngthu, a Congress candidate, became the state's first female MLA since the 1987 state election by winning the Hrangturzo by-poll election. See *The Indian Express* 2014.

2. Interview with Dr Lalrinawmi Ralte, Associate Professor, Department of Women's Studies at the United Theological College, Bangalore on 16 February 2009.

3. One may argue that all three denominations do not follow the same pattern of lay management setup. As Wood has pointed out, 'there is a great variation from denomination to denomination on the authority of lay boards and within denomination, there is a great variation from Church to Church [of] informal power' (2000: 2377). Therefore, the way in which the Presbyterian Church of Mizoram organises their local church administration may be different from how the Baptist Church organises theirs. However, in Mizoram, the variations from denomination to denomination are neither too complex nor diverse especially among the three main denominations.

4. Interview at Lunglei in June 2005.

5. Interview with Miss Y in June 2005 at Siaha.

6. Interview with an active male member of MPC at Aizawl in May 2005.

7. Interview with Mr T, a theologian at Siaha, Mizoram in May 2005.

8. Interview with a senior pastor of the Presbyterian Church of Mizoram (name withheld on request) in July 2005.

9. Interview with Miss T at Aizawl in June 2005.

10. Interview with Mr V at Siaha in May 2005.

11. Interview at Aizawl in June 2005.

12. Interview with Miss L at Lunglei in May 2005.

REFERENCES

Aleaz, Bonita. 2005. *Emergent Women: Mizo Women's Perspective*. New Delhi: Mittal Publications.

Bhasin, Kamla. 1986. *Feminism and Its Relevance in South Asia*. New Delhi: Kali for Women.

———. 2000. *Understanding Gender*. New Delhi: Kali for Women.

Blumberg, R. L. 1989. 'Toward a Feminist Theory of Development.' In Ruth A. Wallace (ed.), *Feminism and Sociological Theory*, 161–191. London: Sage Publication.

Burn, S. M. 2000. *Women across Cultures*. Mayfield Publishing Company.

Chapman, E., and M. Clark. 1968. In Marjorie Sykes (ed.), *Mizo Miracle*. Madras: The Christian Literature Society.

Chakraborty, Anup Shekhar. 2008. 'Emergence of Women from "Private" to "Public". A Narrative of Power Politics from Mizoram'. *Journal of International Women's Studies* 9(3): 27–45.

Chatterji, N. 1975. *Status of Women in the the Earlier Mizo Society*. Aizawl: Tribal Research Institute.

Clark, Elizabeth, and Herbert Richardson. 1977. *Women and Religion: A Feminist Sourcebook of Christian Thought*. Harper & Row.

Frykberg, Elizabeth. 1993. *Karl Barth's Theological Anthropology: An Analogical Critique Regarding Gender Relations (Studies in Reformed Theology and History)*. Princeton: Princeton Theological Seminary.

Government of India. 2011. *Census of India 2011*. Available at www.censusindia.gov.in. (accessed May 2023)

Hnuni, R. L. 1990. *Women in the Context of Bible and North East India.* Unpublished thesis. Aizawl Theological College Archives.

Keohane, Nannerl O. 1992. 'Preface'. In Dorothy O. Helly and Susan M. Reverby (eds), *Gendered Domains: Rethinking Public and Private in Women's History.* Ithaca and London: Cornell University Press.

Kramer, Laura. 2001. *The Sociology of Gender.* Los Angeles, California: Roxbury Publishing Company.

Lovenduski, Joni, and Vicky Randall. 1993. *Contemporary Feminist Politics.* New York: Oxford Press.

Lungsanla et al. 2005. 'Women in Religion and Society'. Paper presented at a seminar at Eastern Theological College, 28 February.

Parsons, Talcott. 1951. *The Social System.* Glencoe: Free Press.

Ralte, Lalrinawmi. 1993. 'Crab Theology: A Critique of Patriarchy, Cultural Degradation and Empowerment of Mizo Women', PhD thesis submitted to Episcopal Divinity School. Michigan, USA: A. Bell and Howell Company.

Rayaprol, Aparna. 1997. *Negotiating Identities: Women in the Indian Diaspora.* Delhi: Oxford University Press.

Storkey, Elaine. 2000. *Created or Constructed: The Great Gender Debate.* Om Books.

Synod Dan Bu [Law book of the Synod]. 2003. Vawi 79th Na [the 79th] Mizoram Presbyterian Kohhran (Presbyterian Church of India). Aizawl: Synod Press.

The Indian Express. 2014. 'V Chawngthu Becomes Mizoram's First Woman MLA since the 1987 State Elections', 16 May. Available at https://indianexpress.com/article/political-pulse/v-chawngthu-becomes-mizorams-first-woman-mla-since-the-1987-state-elections/ (accessed on 4 May 2023).

Vanlaltlani. 1990. *The Experience of Pathian (High God) and Other Deities in Mizo Religion and Its Influence on Mizo Christians.* Unpublished thesis submitted to the Senate of Serampore College.

_____. 2005. *Mizo Hmechhiate Kawngzawh.* Aizawl: Mizoram Publication Board.

Wood, James R. 2000. 'Religious Organizations'. In Edgar F. Borgatta and Rhonda J. V. Montgomery (eds), *Encyclopedia of Sociology, Vol. 4*, 2376–2382. USA: Macmillan.

V

Indigeneity, Land and Identity

10

Megalithic Culture of the Chakhesang Nagas

Reinterpreting the Self

Venusa Tinyi

Stones have always played an important part in the history of human civilisation. They are so fundamental to human civilisations that even civilisational orders in the past are named in relation to stones.[1] The relationship between humans and stones in the past went beyond utilitarian and aesthetic functions; it was symbolic and spiritual as well. Spiritual beliefs in the past assumed that a stone has a life of its own. J. H. Hutton, an eminent colonial anthropologist, while writing on the use of stones in the context of the Nagas, classified the study of stones as utilitarian, ceremonial, and magical (Hutton 1926: 71). He admits that it is, however, impossible to be consistent while dealing with the subject matter in question. He was probably the first to attempt a theorisation of the Naga's use of stones. The central focus of this chapter is directed towards exploring and examining Hutton's views.

Before Christianisation, like all other tribes in Nagaland, the Chakhesangs[2] too practised a form of animism. The modern concept of 'subject' and 'object' to demarcate the world of existence was unheard of. Instead, different worlds of conscious beings were recognised. The animists established all kinds of relationship with nature, both with natural entities and the forces of nature. One such natural entity with which the Chakhesang people shared a unique relationship was stone. Stone was not just a common object for building structures or making tools and implements. Some stones were considered to be spirited beings.

According to the beliefs of our ancestors, it was also possible to establish communication with these spirits. The objective of such communication was to make them a part of the human world and to transform them into symbols of identity and markers of historic achievements, and this was done through the Feast of Merit. Stones thus constituted an integral part of social life, of history, culture and identity. It would be incomplete and unilateral trying to understand the history and society of the people in question without considering how these histories were made. This chapter attempts to show how history represented the megalithic culture of the Chakhesang Nagas through a study of relevant colonial discourses.

FROM THE PERSPECTIVE OF AN OUTSIDER

H. H. Godwin-Austen, who is known for his works on Khasi monuments, noticed the tradition of erecting monoliths by the Nagas, and the Angami tribe in particular (the Chakhesangs were formerly known as the Eastern Angamis). He writes,

> On visiting the Naga Hills District last cold weather, 1872–73, I was very much surprised and interested to find that some of the tribes, Angami and others, erect upright cenotaphs, similar to those to be seen in the Khasi Hills, … The custom is here in full force, [and] not, as is the case among the Khasis, undoubtedly fast dying out. (Godwin-Austen 1875: 144)

According to his records, these stones, some 12 feet in height, were erected by individuals during their lifetime to commemorate the feast organised by them. This is in contrast to the stones erected by the Khasis in memory of their dead, which are as tall as 24 feet. The details of the feast and the rituals involving the erection of the monoliths were left unexplained in his writing. Stephen Dewar, on the other hand, provides a vivid first-hand account of stone-erecting by the Angamis in the following words:

> They stalked around the stone, tapping it with their wands while another party was pulling down from the trees the strongest and

> best creeper-ropes they could find. These were twisted into thick cables and fastened to the sledge. The megalith was levered and man-handled onto the sledge, and bound there securely with smaller ties … The warriors ranged themselves along the creeper-ropes, and next to them the younger men, and then the youths, followed by smaller boys in order of age and height. At the very end of the ropes were two tiny little boys, so small that with their mothers' aid they could only just touch the rope ends with their fingers. There one could see the whole chain of tribal and clan life, from age behind the stone to babyhood right in front, most convincingly symbolical as it appeared to us. (Dewar 1966: 266)

He calculated that for performing such a feast, five tons of rice, twelve bulls and eight pigs were needed (Dewar 1966: 265). The descriptions provided by the colonial writers based on their experiences and observations were more or less accurate. In the following section, I will present some of their important observations and theories.

As noted by most colonial writers, those who performed the feast acquired a higher social status, subsequently represented by special decorations of their houses and distinctive clothes in addition to having a monolith erected in their honour. Some writers have analysed the symbolic meaning behind the erection of the monolith beyond its social function to something deeper and more complex. They connected it to fertility rites and belief in afterlife. Hutton, for instance, thinks that the custom of erecting stones among the Nagas, like those in the Pacific and in Madagascar, was connected 'with the worship of the dead' (Hutton 1926: 82). Their observation was perhaps not incorrect, but the manner in which these connections have been emphasised and exaggerated requires a more critical appraisal and will be discussed later in this chapter.

Stephen Dewar, like Hutton, explains that the idea behind the practice of the feast-cum-stone erection was to make the whole community fruitful, including the crops and cattle. He somewhat summarily observes, 'Fertility of people and crops, bringing wealth and success in the social scale was the idea behind all the ceremonies that led up to stone-pulling, and they had all to be completed' (Dewar 1966: 265). The strongest proponent of the fertility hypothesis is arguably Hutton. He associates the belief in afterlife and fertility cults with the culture of erecting stones. He argues, 'The use of a stone as a receptacle for the soul of a dead man is but a step to its magical use as a means of promoting the fertility of the earth' (Hutton 1926: 78). He found these two beliefs to be intricately related. He bases his argument on the observation that the stones erected as memorials were erected, as a general rule, in the rice-fields. He furthers his argument and says that

> the stones that are put up by the giver of a feast of merit seem to be very definitely *phallic* (emphasis mine) and to be intended to communicate to the soil, and to the participants in the feast, the prosperity, the *mana*, so to speak, of which anyone rich enough to perform the requisite ceremonies must necessarily be the possessor in a high degree. (Hutton 1926: 78)

Hutton thus generalises that the stones were used as a phallic symbol, or as vehicles of fertility (Hutton 1926: 82). Interestingly, he remarks that 'the Angami himself has forgotten what the stones actually represent' (Hutton 1922: 242), but maintains that considerable evidence was available to support the assumption that Naga monoliths are phallic in origin. He points out that the Angami people of Kohima village erect a pair of monoliths, representing the male and the female, instead of a single stone. He justifies his point by saying that, for the natives, anything else is abhorrent to nature (Hutton 1922: 243). He further notes that when the Lothas, a neighbouring Naga tribe of the Angamis, performed the ceremony of erecting monoliths, only one was erected in the first stage and then subsequent stages would involve erecting a pair of stones. For him, this 'merely emphasizes in a different way the importance of making a pair' (Hutton 1922: 243), a pair symbolising a male principle and its counterpart. He admits seeing single erect stones in other tribes but then he undermines this observation by saying that they were probably 'informal erections of the vaguest significance only' (Hutton 1922: 243). There are others who emphasised the social meaning and significance of the stones, a view which is closer to mine. In the following section, I critically analyse Hutton's position.

IN THE EYES OF A NATIVE

The feast was considered the most important cultural practice of the Chakhesang people. In a sense, the life of the people revolved around this culture of feasts. It was not just another celebration, but an activity which involved years of planning, effort and discipline that would culminate in a month-long celebration. In Chokri language—spoken by the sub-group of Chakhesang tribe to which I belong—this feast was called Zhotho-ni and the performers of this feast were called Zhothomi. Literally, 'zho' means big or great, 'tho' means deed or work and 'ni' means feast or festival. A loose translation of the term is thus 'the feast of great achievement' or more simply, 'the Feast of Merit'. Although the erection of the stone was only a part of the feast, it was undoubtedly the most eventful and significant part of the feast as it would involve the whole village community. The process of pulling and erecting a monolith was to welcome it into the human world. A stone that once belonged to a different world order would be made to become a part of the human society. It would bear the name of the one who performed the feast and dwell among humankind who would treat it with great respect and reverence.

The feast, which is no longer performed today since the tribes performing this event have converted to Christianity, was performed only by married couples. In other words, it could not be performed by an unmarried individual no matter how rich and powerful he or she was. The use of the term 'perform' instead of the usual term 'host' in this context is deliberate (though I will use them interchangeably) because there is more of performances and activities than merely hosting a one-time feast for the people. This feast was normally performed in winter, after the harvest was done, between November and January. The specific time and duration of the feast varied from village to village and the feasting season of a village would normally extend up to a month. During the feasting season, more than one could host the feast. For instance, at Zamai village, twelve couples had performed the feast at the same time. The performance of this feast may be broadly divided into two stages:

Pre–stone-pulling Stage

Once a couple decided to perform the feast, they would declare their decision to the community. Following their declaration, sacred animals would be butchered and the meat would be distributed among the households. Here, households were counted in terms of the number of kitchens or fire places that a family had, and in case the married children jointly shared a house (and a kitchen) with their parents, they would be considered a single household. The practice varied from village to village. The common practice was that the performers of the feast would give pig meat though meat of oxen and buffaloes was equally acceptable. Usually, the quantity of meat would be between 250 grams to 4 kilograms. Although there was no strict norm regarding the quantity of meat, a higher quantity certainly reflected the wealth and generosity of the feast performers.

Rice beer would be prepared in special log drums and served at the house of the hosts. Rice beer would be available in plenty, as much as the guests could drink. There would be no fixed time for the guests to come and leave. Guests would not be served by women-folk but by men-folk fully dressed in their best traditional attires. The women however would assist in all kinds of household chores indoors. During the feast, rice, cooked meat or vegetable was normally not provided, but meat-porridge or meat-chutney might be served along with the rice beer. It was usual for the guests to bring their own mugs and some chutneys. The guests would spend their time singing and merry-making and would shower praise and offer gratitude to the host couple for their generosity and wish them success. Eulogy constituted an important part of this festival, and it was offered either in plain words or through songs. Elders would invoke divine blessings upon the feast-givers. As per the custom, different guests would be invited on different days. For instance, a day would be earmarked for relatives from the same village and other villages; another day would be reserved only for those who had previously performed the feast, the elite group in the village; still another day would be chosen for those who helped with the arrangement of the feast; a day was kept separate for close friends and peers, and so on. Thus, a couple would have to provide feasts two, three or even four times in some cases, before moving on to the next stage of erecting a monolith.

Stone-pulling Stage

After a year of completing the first stage, the couple would have to distribute raw meat to each household in the entire village again, just like in the first stage. Only after this would the couple be ready to perform the main event of the feast—the stone-pulling ceremony. The pulling of stone constituted the main attraction of the feast wherein the whole village community would have to participate in one way or another. The stone to be pulled would be identified and chosen well in advance either by the couple or by some of their close and honourable relatives. Once identified, the couple would seek the consent of the stone in a dream before pulling it. During the day, they would go and talk to the stone, saying:

> Don't be in the wild; come and live with us in the village. Don't hide here; come to the place of fame where your name will be called.

After talking to the stone, the couple would wait to hear back from the stone in their dream that night. Traditional belief had it that the spirit of the stone would reveal his or her decision in their dream. It was not necessarily revealed to both of them, revelation to either was sufficient. And if the stone agreed and accepted their request, it would reveal its name to the couple too.[3] But if there was no response, they would consult another stone and so on till they received the consent of a stone. Stones were normally pulled from the jungle to a selected site near a village. The stone would be tied to a wooden frame using a special kind of creeper found in the jungles. Two very long creeper-ropes would be used simultaneously to pull the stone, one on the right and the other on the left. For the pulling, all the able-bodied men were required to take part. No woman could participate in the pulling ceremony of the stone; they could touch neither the stone nor the creepers used to pull the stone. At the time of pulling, one of the warriors, usually the most well-known one from the village, would stand on top of the stone. The couple would walk before the stone, calling the stone by its name and saying,

> Let's go home, home where you belong. Let's go home smoothly and quickly before it gets dark.

A strikingly similar expression was recorded by Hutton in this context:

> Your place is not here. We have made another for you. You must go to that which we have made for you. Go lightly and go quickly! (Hutton 1922: 246)

Site for the Erection of the Stone

The couple would choose a prominent site to erect the monolith. Usually, the stone was erected outside the village at a site where it would be clearly visible to the people. The common location was therefore beside the village paths which lead to the fields. It could also be on a hillock or a prominent view-point near the village. The reason for choosing such a visible site was to ensure that people called the names of the performers of the feast as often as possible. The site of the monolith would become a landmark in the village. If the couple had no plot at a suitable location, they could request someone to give them just enough space to erect their stone. Normally, the land owners would be obliged to give their consent to such an honourable request.

Before these two main stages, there is also a preparatory stage, which consists of a set of things to do before performing the feast. First, the prospective couple intending to perform the feast would have to consult the chief priest in the village before declaring the feast. Consulting the priest was necessary in order to obtain the needed blessings from him. Besides, this step was necessary to maintain order in case many couples expressed their desire to perform the feast in the same year. Next, the couple would have to abstain from having sexual relations for one whole year once they have made the declaration to perform the feast. Apart from the ceremonial reason of keeping themselves pure, practising chastity had a pragmatic purpose as well: it would keep away complications related to pregnancy and childbirth which could otherwise create hurdles in the path of performing the feast.

The Cycle of Feasting and Erecting Monoliths

A couple could perform the feast a number of times. In Kikruma village (my native village), the maximum number of stones a couple could erect by performing the feast was nine. Only three persons from my village had succeeded in pulling nine stones. Most could not perform the feast even once in their lifetime though it was everyone's wish to perform it. It is said that the sacrifice required for performing even a single feast was so costly that it was equivalent to the loss of a child. To achieve the highest feat of erecting nine stones would require life-long commitment and dedication. After erecting nine stones, a couple would have to start from the beginning all over again if they so desire to perform the feast again. It may be noted that for many villages, the couple would have to provide the feast at least once or sometimes twice (depending on the customs of their villages) before they could erect a monolith. In most Chakhesang villages where a couple could pull only one stone at a time, it was the name of the husband that was associated with the stone. However, in some villages, two stones could be pulled at a time, one for the wife and the other for the husband. One such village is Chozuba and the maximum number of stones pulled by a couple in this village was 28. The pattern for pulling the stones was as follows:

First time: 2 stones
Second time: 2 stones
Third time: 4 stones
Fourth time: 4 stones
Fifth time: 4 stones
Sixth time: 8 stones

While the stones erected in the first and the second times were associated with the names of the husband and the wife, the other stones in the subsequent times were erected to symbolise the achievements and the generosity of the couple. In addition to having monoliths erected in their honour, the couple would be entitled to wear a certain type of shawl each—*thipiku* shawl for the husband and *murhikhu* for the wife. They would also be entitled to decorate their house with a horn-shaped wooden structure called *chikka* which was usually placed just above the entrance. These material symbols would signify their status in the society.

SIGNIFICANCE OF THE STONE-CULTURE

Through the collective performance of the entire village community at the time of the feast, a natural stone was baptised or reborn into the cultural world of the humans, a world of values and meanings. The stone would become a living and symbolic embodiment of the core values and beliefs of the community. One of the important values was honour or respect and it was earned by sacrifice and hard work coupled with discipline and planning.

Performers of the feast would need to consume less and work more in order to save enough to provide for the entire village. Not many would own big cultivable lands because labourers required to cultivate the land were scarce. Normally people used to cultivate just enough to provide for their own family. The supply of food for the community feast was thus primarily the result of the virtues possessed by the feast givers—the virtues of hard work and sacrifice. In this sense, honour was not directly related to power or wealth. It could be gained instead by disposing of wealth for the happiness of the community. On the other hand, if a person succeeded in accumulating wealth but refused to use their wealth for the benefit of the community, the person would be looked down upon. A miser could not occupy a seat of honour in the community no matter how rich. For instance, a couple with a good terrace field would become an object of ridicule if they were unable to provide the feast for the community. It would reflect the lack of virtues mentioned above. It was considered shameful if one had the resources but did not utilise them for the good and happiness of the community. Those who performed the feast would be given a lot of respect and special privileges since they had succeeded in performing and preserving the culture and values of the people. They were considered more knowledgeable and experienced since performing the feast involved a lot of rituals and discipline. Thus the performers of the feast would themselves become a living embodiment of the knowledge of their cultures and traditions and a living symbol of their communities' values and norms.

There was a natural tendency among the feast givers to try and outdo each other in terms of their generosity for the simple reason that whoever could provide more meat and rice beer would receive more adulation from the people. Having observed this competitiveness even in such a noble pursuit, Wouters remarks,

> Seen as a historical social institution, the Feast thus seemingly invoked contradictory principles, combining tendencies of economic redistribution and social differentiation, of both

> socialism and snobbery, but crucially it vested social eminence in a person's ability to act as a provider, not, say, in mere accruing. (Wouters 2015: 27)

He further notes that '[e]ven if the feast-giver himself had long deceased, the monolith continued to commemorate and venerate his deeds, and was a continuing source of esteem for his progeny and the wider clan he had belonged to' (Wouters 2015: 27). The stone is thus irreplaceable and indispensable as a part of a social institution. The highest recognition that was given to an individual in a society could not be gained without the pulling of stones.

The stone-pulling ceremony in relation to the feast was a customary practice that was essentially performative—a performance that required the involvement of the whole community and not just some individuals or groups of individuals.[4] From this perspective, the erected monolith was not just a monument of celebration and commemoration of successful persons or events of the community; it was also an embodiment of religious, socio-economic and political practices and beliefs of the community. The performative and public culture of erecting a monolith thus played an important role, both in the imagination and memory of the community, to weave together a very strong sense of belongingness. Every monolith served to remind the villagers how their ancestors were part of the history-making. Each would tell a story that could be claimed by everyone. Its location—usually prominent viewpoints or the sides of the common paths that lead to fields—serves to reinforce the values and beliefs vis-à-vis the memory and history of the community.

A CRITICAL REFLECTION

Hutton posited that the erection of a monolith in the context of the Nagas, especially the Chakhesang/Angami tribe, was connected with fertility rites and that a monolith was a phallic symbol. Of course, his view was not without basis since he drew insights from his knowledge of people other than the Nagas as well (Hutton 1922, 1926). What however was lacking in his works was the native perspective that would have helped to further develop his theory. In his inference, he had overlooked or ignored the narrative of the native Chakhesangs and in doing so, he committed a fallacy of accident. Moreover, being influenced probably by the methodological concerns of his time, he tried to interpret and explain the actions and activities of the people 'objectively' from direct observation as though the subjects of his study were mere inanimate 'objects'. Or perhaps he tried but failed to elicit a response that fit his assumption and so he conveniently reasoned that the natives themselves had forgotten the meaning and origin of the culture of erecting stones. He infers from analogical observation that

> the erect stone has first come to be regarded as the memorial to a feast, *the original meaning being forgotten* (emphasis mine), and thence as a suitable memorial to a giver of feasts. Indeed, there is perhaps no reason why these two ideas should not have been combined, and it is possible that a parallel for the second suggested explanation is to be found in the Khasia Hills. (Hutton 1922: 244)

When there was a mismatch between his theoretical framework and the observational data, he tried to undermine the latter. For instance, as pointed out above, he admits that there were other Naga tribes who used to erect a single monolith in relation to the feast. However, he brushes this fact aside by saying that they were 'informal erections' without any cognisable significance. This point is highly contentious. The Chakhesang tribe, with the exception of a few villages, used to erect only a single stone. On being asked why, unlike other Chakhesang villages, the ancestors of those exceptional villages pulled two stones,[5] one each for the husband and the wife, they replied that it was because both worked equally hard to provide a feast for the whole community. They mentioned nothing about fertility rites though I was told that they pulled a female stone for the wife and a male stone for the husband. This had more to do with equality. They explained to me that originally they also used to pull only one stone at a time. These villages with the exceptional rituals—my native village Kikruma, some old Angami villages, Kohima village (that Hutton observed), and others—were relatively young compared to other Chakhesang villages. Most of the older Chakhesang villages still had the tradition of pulling only one stone at a time. This observation is certainly not consistent with Hutton's hypothesis. Moreover, interpreting the erected monoliths as phallic symbols is rather odd as the shape of the stones do not resemble the female reproductive organ in any manner, considering his hypothesis which states that one of the two stones represents the female principle. Though he refers to dolmens as a female principle (Hutton 1922: 243), these stone structures have hardly anything to do with the feast.

Contrary to the magical and mythological symbolisms found in the account of Hutton, I found socio-political reasons behind stone-pulling when I went around the Chakhesang villages in 2016[6] asking about this ceremony. Some common reasons are as follows:

(1) A couple could decide to perform the ceremony of their own volition with the desire to gain the social status that performers of the feast enjoy.
(2) The informal practice of shaming a wealthy couple for not performing the feast and bestowing honour on those who performed the feast often influenced the decision to perform the ceremony.
(3) Clan members or relatives used to pressure a prospective couple to perform it.
(4) The elite group of the previous performers of the feast could directly throw an open challenge to any promising couple to perform it.
(5) Feelings of rivalry among the villagers, either between clans or between the original settlers (*thuvomi*) and the migrant settlers (*sohemi*), could lead to the decision to perform it.[7]

To this list I would like to add a couple of points to further strengthen and elucidate my argument that the erection of a stone in connection to the feast primarily served a social purpose and not a spiritual one, and neither was the stone a phallic symbol.

First, as a rule, the site for the erection of the stones was selected based on its visibility or accessibility. As mentioned earlier, the stones were usually erected at a prominent view point or beside the paths commonly used by the villagers. This suggests that the erected stones had hardly any direct phallic symbolism or association with fertility of the soil as argued by Hutton. The reason for choosing a visible site was to create a landmark which would be known by the feast-performers' names. It was thus the desire to be immortalised that encouraged a couple to perform the feast. In the context of Chakhesang culture, stone and wood typically connote durability or permanence and hardness.

Second, the desire of the couple to earn a higher social status was another primary reason that drove them to perform the feast. Other possible reasons were pressure from elders and relatives and to avoid being ridiculed as misers or lazy or bad cultivators. Unlike the first reason of ensuring immortality, this reason is relevant to one's lifetime and their present social standing: the performers of the feast enjoyed special privileges like the right to decorate their house with *chikka* and to wear special shawls of dignity, as mentioned earlier. The performers of the feast would invite a village priest to perform the rites and bestow blessings upon them, and guests would eulogise the couple's great deed, express gratitude and invoke the spirit's blessings of prosperity upon them—traditions that were not just followed for the Feast of Merit but all feasts in general. Hence, the spiritual role of the priest to pronounce blessings upon the couple was not unique to the Feast of Merit. Moreover, if we pay close attention to the role of the feast-goers, especially their eulogy to the feast-givers, we will see that the feast in question was valued more for its social significance than its spiritual importance. The couple would be praised for their sacrifice, hard work and discipline which the preparation for the feast must have required. They were praised because they deserved to be praised, because they were the embodiment of the values and virtues that governed the Chakhesang society.

Third, Hutton's idea that a couple would decide to perform the feast to be rich and healthy is debatable. As some colonial writers correctly noted, it required a huge expenditure to perform such a lavish feast. Thus by performing the feast, a couple would actually be exhausting their wealth. One might argue in his defence that although it was expensive, by performing a feast, a couple might have desired to get more wealth and good health in their future. But this too is refutable since a wealthy couple was expected to perform more and more feasts which would once again deplete their wealth and health. If we look at this argument critically, we realise that health and wealth were therefore not the end-goal of the feast.

In this context of the megalithic culture of the Chakhesang Nagas, something else which merits our attention is the fact that the practice of erecting stones continues even though the actual animistic beliefs and rituals relating to the feast had come to an end with the coming of Christianity and modernity. A stone is now erected to mark almost every important occasion and achievement. So the practice of erecting stones is no longer associated with the feast but is a marker of any great success of the community. For instance, a jubilee celebration of a church or a significant anniversary celebration of a tribal organisation is marked by erecting a monolith with an inscription. At times, stones are also erected to mark important governmental events and achievements. In this sense, the literal meaning of the 'Feast of Merit' or 'Feast of Great Achievement' is being retained because of the connection of the stone-erecting ceremony with socio-cultural values and practices. A stone erected to mark an important milestone stands to tell that the organisation that erected it has reached a certain age and is now worthy of respect and honour for the service it has rendered to the people. If the erection of monoliths, which Hutton viewed as phallic symbols, was indeed a wish for fertility and wealth, then we will fail to account as to why the Chakhesang people, 99.27 per cent of whom are Christians,[8] erect stones to mark important occasions even to this date. The basic doctrines of Christianity are incompatible with the beliefs and practices of such a phallic culture, that is, the norms and values associated with erecting monoliths for fertility.

Hutton's theories about the megalithic culture of the Chakhesang Nagas are thus in many ways fallacious and his observational data seems to have been conveniently selected to yield an inference that fits his theoretical framework. In doing so, he made the beliefs and practices of the Chakhesang people vis-à-vis the Nagas appear strange and unreasonable, even though his intention may have been honest—an intention to document and share the culture of the Nagas with the world. It is however probable that he was more keen to amuse his Western readers with these 'exotic' narratives than to really understand the culture of the Chakhesang people or the Nagas in general. It is difficult for a Chakhesang person such as myself to look at the past through the colonial-ethnographic lens of Hutton and the like who have forced their biased interpretations upon our indigenous traditions and cultures.[9] In contrast, when I look at our colonial history from other perspectives found in local oral and performative cultures, I can with great ease connect to and appreciate my culture with all its flaws and peculiarities. The values of the contemporary Chakhesang people are shaped and informed by our past traditions. The social values and norms that were intertwined with the practices of the past such as the Feast of Merit are some of the things that define the communitarian fabric and structure of the contemporary Chakhesang society even today.

CONCLUSION

By and large, the descriptive accounts of the colonial writers were an accurate study of the Nagas. However, while trying to make sense of the customs, beliefs and practices of the Nagas, they often employed their own Western lens instead of trying to let the Nagas speak for themselves. The colonial narratives are often inconsistent and so it is difficult to obtain a holistic, comprehensive view from them. This appears to be the case for Hutton especially. Today when we, the contemporary Naga researchers, try to understand our cultures from both the records of the colonial writers and from the oral narratives of our elders, we encounter problems: they seem to tell two different stories from the same set of descriptions. To highlight this issue is one of my main objectives. There were certain Naga beliefs which were mythical in nature, but it does not mean that every practice and custom of the community can be reduced to myths in order to explain or interpret them. To do so would be to assume that the natives did not pursue socio-political interests or goals for their own sake. Though every socio-cultural occasion in the past involved some spiritual elements, it is incorrect to assume that spirituality was the reason behind the performance and observation of those occasions. I have argued, as a native and an insider, against this assumption in order to understand better our socio-cultural values and beliefs behind the practices of our people, with special reference to the culture of erecting monoliths in the context of the Feast of Merit.

NOTES

1. According to recent classification of ages in the geologic timescale, the latest age has been named the Meghalayan Age. This age is named after the state of Meghalaya in Northeast India which was the location of the sandstone cave formation and its sediments, the study of which helped to define and classify this age. The cave, locally known as Mawmluh cave, is the longest cave in the world. The onset of this Age, which began some 4,200 years ago and whose effects lasted two centuries, was marked by a mega-drought that crushed a number of civilisations worldwide. It is believed that the destructive drought severely disrupted civilisations in Egypt, Greece, Syria, Palestine, Mesopotamia, the Indus Valley, and the Yangtze River Valley. See Amos (2018).

2. The Chakhesang tribe is one of the seventeen recognised tribes in Nagaland. The term 'Cha-khe-sang' is an acronym for three dominant linguistic groups within the tribe, namely, Chokri, Kheza/Khuzha and Sangtam. This acronym has become a subject of debate today among the Chakhesang people as the people referred to here as Sangtam are actually the Pochuris, a separate tribe recognised by the Government of Nagaland. Sangtam is altogether a separate tribe which has no role in the identity formation of the Chakhesang tribe. Formerly the Chakhesang people were known as the Eastern Angamis.

3. The stone could be either male or female. On inquiring if anyone could recall any name of a stone, I could gather only one—Dani, which is a male name. Interestingly, this name is a Mao name (Mao is another Naga tribe), though the stone was found in the Chakhesang village at Zapami (in Phek district of Nagaland).

4. Because of this reason, when people started converting to Christianity, it became increasingly difficult to perform the feast since Christians cannot take part in the ceremony and the ceremony remains incomplete unless the whole village participates. The performance of the feast was finally brought to an end during the Naga struggle for independence. People were not allowed to cultivate properly for years and villages, including granaries, were burnt rampantly. Out of the sixty-two Chakhesang villages in the 1960s and 1970s, only two were not torched. Porba village was burnt fourteen times.

5. I visited and interviewed some prominent leaders and elders of two Chakhesang villages—Chozuba and Yoruba in Phek district of Nagaland—which had the tradition of pulling two stones.

6. In relation to one of my projects on the custom of erecting monoliths amongst the Chakhesang tribe (funded by the UPE-Phase II of the University of Hyderabad), my field assistant and I visited and studied about ten villages.

7. These reasons were cited during a discussion on who held the records of pulling the highest number of monoliths in Kikruma and Zapami villages in Phek district of Nagaland.

8. See https://joshuaproject.net/people_groups/16562/IN (accessed on 30 August 2018).

9. Since I have not experienced this megalithic culture vis à vis the feast and have only heard the narratives from elders who either performed the feast or witnessed its performance, I am also an 'outsider', in a way, to the cultural practices of my own community.

REFERENCES

Amos, Jonathan. 2018. 'Welcome to the Meghalayan Age - A New Phase in History'. *BBC*, 18 July. Available at https://www.bbc.com/news/science-environment-44868527 (accessed May 2023).

Dewar, Stephen. 1966. 'The Ceremony of Erecting a Megalith among the Angami Nagas'. *Folklore* 77(4): 264–269.

Godwin-Austen, H. H. 1875. 'On the Rude Stone Monuments of Certain Naga Tribes, with Some Remarks on Their Customs, etc.'. *The Journal of the Anthropological Institute of Great Britain and Ireland* 4: 144–147.

Hutton, J. H. 1922. 'The Meaning and Method of the Erection of Monoliths by the Naga Tribes'. *The Journal of the Royal Anthropological Institute of Great Britain and Ireland* 52: 242–249.

———. 1926. 'The Use of Stone in the Naga Hills'. *The Journal of the Royal Anthropological Institute of Great Britain and Ireland* 56: 71–82.

Wouters, Jelle J. P. 2015. 'The Social Lives of Stones: Studying the Past in the Chakhesang Naga Village of Phugwumi'. *Anthropology Today: An International Peer Reviewed Neira Journal* 1(1): 21–41.

11

Livelihood Interventions and Marginalisation in Land and Forest Rights of Rural Khasi Women*

Rekha M. Shangpliang

Livelihood needs are gender-specific and not always the same for men and women, due to their differential roles, responsibilities and resources. The impacts of different livelihood interventions thus also vary according to gender. That women are biologically different from men is often emphasised with reference to their child-bearing and nurturing capacities. What is generally ignored is the fact that gendering of tasks is based on many different socio-cultural factors and processes of socialisation, and not on natural, biological differences between men and women alone (Krishna 2003). Gendered division of work in all societies around the world is based on the naive argument that women's tasks are less physically arduous than that of men, which is why when it comes to livelihood patterns, women tend to undertake roles that suit their supposedly lower physical strength, unlike men who undertake the more labour-intensive tasks. Thus, a comparison of the quantum and intensity of work done by the two genders reinforces the notion that women only supplement the family income and are not engaged in productive labour. This notion tends to undermine the significant role of women in economic pursuits such as the collection, processing, consumption and trade of forest products which have traditionally supplemented

*Previously published as 'Livelihood and Gender: Marginalisation of Khasi Rural Women in Land and Forest Rights' in *The NEHU Journal* 16(2): 86–100.

the income of rural families. It must be understood that their expertise in dealing with forest products is not merely a gift of 'green fingers' but a result of their traditional, social and familial roles over generations.

Women's centrality to resource management can hardly be underestimated. The traditionally demarcated roles that women perform in the domestic domain such as washing clothes, collecting firewood, farming, tending animals, growing vegetables and collecting non-timber forest products (NTFP) contribute greatly to resource conservation. The conserving and sustaining roles that women perform have been glorified to the extent that women are valourised as 'resource managers'. No one can forget the historic Chipko Movement that took place in 1973 in Mandal, a small hamlet in Chamoli district of Garhwal, where village women staged protests against felling by literally hugging the trees, their only means of livelihood ('chipko' in Hindi means to 'cling to' or 'hug'). That was the starting point of a conservation endeavour that was pro-poor and more importantly, women-centred. The Chipko Movement, with its slogan 'Our lives before our trees' was an important event in environmental conservation and studies in eco-feminism.

The Chipko Movement may have been a landmark and well-fought battle, and a women-centred movement for natural resource conservation, but today, about five decades after its inception, a few questions remain: What role do women have in natural resource management today? What are the challenges that restrict their accessibility to forest resource? Let us start by understanding the close link between natural resources and rural livelihoods, in particular the increasing role of tribal women as household providers in declining rural economies. Tribal economy is inextricably linked with forests since a major part of their income is derived from forest-related activities. Poverty has since long been one of the most serious problems plaguing the country and the tribal communities living on the margins are hit the hardest. Studies conducted by the World Bank (2005) have revealed that dependency on forests and common property resources increases when a tribal household becomes economically weaker. There is no denying the fact that as the rate of poverty increases, women's roles become more prominent in ensuring the survival of households by assuming greater responsibility to collect resources from forests and common lands. The importance of women in collection of forest produce is evident in data from almost every country in Asia, Africa and Latin America. For instance, a study in the North-West Frontier Province of Pakistan showed that 78 per cent of morel mushrooms collected are by women and children, and these wild mushrooms supplement their daily requirements of food and their sale pays for other basic necessities (Iqbal 1993: 65). Similarly in West Bengal, tribal women gather sal (*Shorea robusta*) leaves for six months a year and earn about 72 rupees per month under the best circumstances. Like most other tribal women in India, Naga women too depend on the forest and its resources for their livelihood, spending most of their labour and time tending their agricultural field and foraging the forest to meet the subsistence needs of their families and for some additional income. They have a very close relationship with the environment they live in and can be called the 'guardians of biodiversity' as they are the caretakers of most agricultural resources and livestock (NEPED).[1]

THE ROLE OF WOMEN IN KHASI SOCIETY

The main focus of the chapter is on the Khasis, who are a matrilineal tribe inhabiting the Khasi Hills in the Northeastern state of Meghalaya. While there are many interpretations of the origin of the Khasi race, the term 'Khasi' is believed to have been derived from the terms 'kha' meaning 'born of' and 'si' meaning 'ancient mother', thus meaning 'born of the mother'. The term portrays the matrilineal character of the Khasis who trace their descent from their mothers: ancestral property is passed from the mother to the daughter, preferably to the youngest daughter or the 'khadduh'. The matrilineal Khasis of Meghalaya believe in the ideology '*long jait naka kynthei*', which means 'from the woman sprang the clan' and this ideology is deeply rooted in the Khasi ethos. The line of descent in a Khasi family is reckoned only from the mother's clan or 'kur', as a result of which children belong to the clan of the mother by descent. Therefore it is customary for them to speak of a family of brothers and sisters who are great-grandchildren of one great-grandmother, and identify themselves as 'shi-kpoh' which literally means 'of one womb'. It is important to note that the Khasi ideology of human reproduction describes the father as the provider of stature and form (*u kpa u ba ai ka long rynnieng*), while the mother contributes the flesh and blood (*ka kmie ka ba ai ia ka doh ka snam*) to the child. This filial bond between the mother and the child is strongly reflected even in familial relations and kinship ties where the *parakur* ('mother's kin') is given greater importance than the *bakha* ('father's kin').

A woman is central to the family in Khasi ideology. She has the responsibility continuing the matrilineal line of descent through reproduction. The Khasi woman has numerous familial and kinship roles to perform. Besides being the custodian of the family property, the khadduh or youngest daughter has to take up many other important tasks. She has to look after the aged members of the family and other members of the matrikin, and as she inherits the family property, she has to continue the tradition of carrying out the religious rites and ceremonies from time to time with the help of her mother's male relatives. The Khasis believe in the saying 'Ka kynthei ka bat ia ka niam', meaning, 'It is the woman who holds the religion', and this signifies her responsibilities in the religious domain. However, it must be noted that Khasi women are excluded from having any say in village durbars and meetings. They are not even allowed to speak aloud in public meetings such as village council meetings.

Even though Khasi women are not allowed to voice their opinion in public matters, they have always been free to participate in economic activities outside home. They frequent market places, participate in trade and business, and take part in festivals, dances and the like. Khasi society is free from social evils such as bride price, *stridhan*, child marriage, etc. Khasi women are usually very industrious. On this topic, P. R. T. Gurdon writes 'Khasis carry very heavy burdens ... women carry almost as heavy loads as men ... They are certainly more industrious than the Assamese ... Khasis are devoted to their offspring, and the women make excellent nurses for European children.'

The Khasis have a deep-rooted affinity with nature. The Earth which is symbolised as the 'mother' or 'meiramew' is looked upon as the caretaker of all natural resources. The forest holds an important place in the social, economic and religious life of the Khasis. It is looked upon as a well-loved home, a game sanctuary and an abode of worship all rolled into one, around which their social, cultural and religious activities revolve. It is a familiar sight to see women and children setting off into the woods to collect edible fruits and roots. A typical day out for an average Khasi village woman would be best described as follows:

> She carries her baby on her back, climbing the hills she sets off for the woods with a *ja-song* (cooked rice packed in a leaf), salt and some dry fish (*ktung*). Going to the forest virtually takes her the whole day. So besides collecting twigs and fuelwood and other forest products, she also spends the day washing clothes on the riverside in the foothills. (Shangpliang 2012: 26)

As nurturers of the family line, Khasi women have always had a significant role to play in the domestic sphere (Uberoi 1994: 180). A Khasi woman's familial roles are well defined and her 'glorifying status' as a mother means she has added responsibilities of meeting the immediate needs of the family. These include some burdensome duties and household chores such as carrying water, fetching firewood, washing clothes, collecting twigs and edible plants and roots—all of these activities are carried out in the jungle skirting the village. This is partly the reason why women have had a closer interaction with nature and this in turn has enhanced the emotional bond these women share with nature, which has helped them cope with a number of economic hardships.

RURAL KHASI WOMEN AND INDIGENOUS ECOLOGICAL WISDOM

Women's indigenous knowledge of ecosystems has contributed considerably to ecological sustainability, and is illustrative of the strength of their ecosystem-based learning and commitment to non-violative uses of nature (Krishna 2003). A cursory glance over the Khasi rural ecosystem reveals how intimate the relationship between women and ecological sustainability is. Their wisdom and knowledge about certain species of edible and non-edible plants, food culture and the regenerative process of soil fertility has been instrumental in their judicious use of the ecological resources. As part of her doctoral research, the author had the chance to interact with the residents of Lawbyrwa village of Ri-Bhoi District of Khasi Hills who revealed that 80 per cent of the time spent by the women of this village in a day was mainly to fulfill the subsistence needs of their family and these activities included collecting fuelwood, water, edible roots and tubers, broom shrubs and other NTFPs.[2] Most villages located in the forested regions and fringe forest areas have properly defined gendered work patterns and responsibilities. While men are actively involved in agriculture, daily wage labour and farming activities, women spend more time in the woods and are the main providers of basic needs such as fuelwood, food, medicinal herbs and other NTFPs.

There are many Khasi folktales and legends (*khanatang bad puriskam*) that focus on the close relationship between women and nature. These folklores are mostly woven around the various forces of nature such as the hills and vales, rocks and caves, and the flora and the fauna. These elements of nature are personified in the legends as mother and son, husband and wife, and friend and foe and the stories project their natural behaviours—the love, hate, jealousy, pride and vanity—with the sole purpose of teaching moral and spiritual values.

The ecological wisdom of the Khasis is solidly based on experience and they depend on this knowledge to fulfil most of their day-to-day needs. They sustain themselves through agriculture, hunting, fishing and gathering a huge range of forest foods and materials with which they make their houses and most of their articles of daily use, such as ploughs, baskets and leaf-plates. The majority of Khasi houses have thatched roofs, plank flooring, bamboo or stone walls and all of these materials are obtained from the forest. A fire is always kept lit in a stone hearth in the centre of the house, which means that a considerable amount of firewood is burnt by each family on a regular basis. They possess knowledge of herbal medicine as well as many other aspects of nature and human life. Much of this ancient wisdom has been passed down through generations as an oral tradition. Indigenous wisdom and knowledge of the forest have enabled the Khasis to live in harmony with nature.

It is also interesting to note their use of simple natural objects in day-to-day activities which reflect the importance of nature in their cultural and religious life. Let us take for instance the naming ceremony of a newborn infant, Ka Jer Ka Thoh, which is an important occasion for the whole family. As is the tradition, pounded rice flour is placed on a bamboo winnower called *ka prah*. When the expectant mother delivers her baby, a sharp splinter of bamboo is used to cut the umbilical cord. No metal objects such as a knife can be used on this occasion. When the umbilical cord falls off a ritual is performed by offering prayers to certain water deities or Ka Blei Sam Um.

Singing and dancing form an important component of Khasi culture. There are many Khasi traditional dances that are of ecological significance, such as dances that are performed during a harvest. A well-known dance is Ka Shad Kynthei in which only women take part and which involves invoking God and thanking him for a good harvest. There are also fertility dances exclusively for women. One such dance is Ka Shad Noh Sakyriat which is performed by the women who spin around a traditional pole to symbolise their strength, femininity and motherhood.

FOREST-LINKED LIVELIHOOD AND RURAL KHASI WOMEN

Like most tribal communities, land and forest are the two most important natural resources to the Khasi. However, land and forest have to be dealt as separate entities. Land—locally known as *ri* by the Khasis—is closely linked to the community's social organisation and permeates every aspect of their socio-economic life. Land to the Khasis is a gift of nature that belongs to the community, and therefore access to land not only ensures economic security for the individual, but control over it symbolises territorial integrity for the community as a whole (Nongbri 2003).

One of the most important sources of livelihood for the Khasis is the forest, which is their well-loved home, a place of worship and a storehouse of their daily necessities such as food, water, fodder and firewood. The Khasis hold a deep sense of awe and reverence for the different elements of the forest. This symbiotic relation between the Khasis and nature has been appropriately defined by H. O. Mawrie, a Khasi author, in the following words: '*U Khasi u im bad ka mariang, bad ka mariang ka im bad u*' (Mawrie 1981: 78), which means 'A Khasi lives with nature and nature lives with him'. Every day, rural Khasi women venture out into the forests and engage themselves in cutting fuelwood; collecting fruits, vegetables, broom grass, and other necessities; drying and processing the collected items; and at the end of the day, return home with heavy bundles on their heads. Throughout the year, one can find on the hill slopes and in the deep gorges wild banana trees, bamboo, innumerable varieties of edible and non-edible mushrooms, and different kinds of tubers and corms. Tender bamboo shoot is a common tribal delicacy consumed either pickled or in a curry. Every Khasi stall located along the Shillong–Guwahati National Highway sell bamboo shoots and other wild fruits and vegetables gathered from the forests. The forests of the Khasi Hills are home to many plants and herbs of great medicinal value with which Khasis have developed an indigenous system of medicine that is widely used as an alternative to the costlier, and often inaccessible, allopathic medicines. Wild broom grass collected by the Khasi women and children are bound into bundles to make broomsticks which are then sold locally or exported out of the state. The broomsticks fetch Rs 20 to 50 each depending on the market and the quality of workmanship. Some of the other NTFPs gathered from the forests of Khasi Hills such as cinnamon, sandalwood, pepper, fruits and herbs are of very high economic and medicinal value in urban markets.

Of late, the Government of India has introduced a number of schemes through which degraded forests are to be rejuvenated and regenerated for augmentation of forest resources and development of the environment. It is imperative that the institutions responsible for forest management and for creating livelihood opportunities in the area must work closely with women, since it is the womenfolk in Meghalaya who are the major players in this aspect. Among the Khasis, the strength of the village community is their social capital, where all members of the family are actively involved in contributing to the subsistence economy, and in this, the women play a singular role as gatherers of NTFPs. Thus the policy framework in question must put an emphatic thrust on the involvement of women in planning, implementation, monitoring and review of any activity (Darlong 2002). However, the fact of the matter remains that during the past five decades of planning and policy-making in India, women have been thoroughly marginalised in matters of development, implementation and reorientation. Needless to say, the constraints faced by the women in controlling and managing land and forest resources have to a certain extent deprived them of their claims on sustainable livelihood. The scenario with respect to women in Khasi society, which is matrilineal, is no better. Though in principle the matrilineal rules of inheritance and descent are followed, the customary practices are certainly not gender egalitarian. The power of administration and superintendence of all domestic matters is vested in the mother's brother. Khasi women inherit property but lack the power to manage it. The woman might be the central figure in the organisation of the household but when it comes to allocation of rights over land, a sharp distinction is maintained between ownership and control. While ownership of land remains with women, control invariably lies with men (Nongbri 2003).

In the case of community forests (*khlaw raid* and *khlaw adong*), the management and control lie with the traditional institutions, clans and a few authorised individuals. In matters such as the upkeep of the forest and related decision-making, the Khasi women have no right whatsoever. The village council (*durbar shnong*), which is traditionally responsible for the overall development of the village, does not recognise a woman as its member nor does it entertain her views or opinions. Problems faced by women are mostly voiced by the adult male members of their households.

The following table (Table 11.1) throws some light on the quantum and type of work done by Khasi women as opposed to Khasi men.

Table 11.1: Distribution of Work between Men and Women in Khasi Society

S. No.	*Activities*	*Sex*	*Number of Persons Engaged*	*Percentage of Total*	
1.	Cultivation and labour	Male	41	22.78	45%
2.	Making charcoal	Male	40	22.22	
3.	Collecting firewood	Female	37	20.50	55%
4.	Collecting NTFP	Female	31	17.25	
5.	Selling vegetables/fruits	Female	31	17.25	
	Total		180	100.00	

Source: Author's doctoral research, 2007.

The above data shows that approximately 55 per cent of rural Khasi women are engaged in forest-related activities while

45 per cent of men are engaged in activities not related to the forest. This reveals the preponderance of Khasi women engaged in activities related to the forest, their primary source of livelihood.

INTERVENTIONS IN FOREST RIGHTS AND MANAGEMENT

As we have seen, in matrilineal Khasi society, although women are given importance in theory, they are more often than not marginalised in reality. Even though their contribution through labour is higher, they do not have any power or agency. Making the plight of women worse is the system of forest management in the Khasi Hills. Here, the management of forest lands falls under three agencies:

(1) Autonomous District Council, in charge of green blocks, protected forests, unclassed forests, private forests owned by clans, domestic groups, individuals and organisations
(2) State government, in charge of reserved forests or national parks
(3) Community, in charge of *khlaw raid* or community forests, and *khlaw adong* or community-protected forests.

This shared form of control and management of forests in Meghalaya by the State Forest Department and the Autonomous District Councils has contributed to dual forest policies, lack of co-ordination and division of accountability. The two authorities formulate their own forest policies and follow separate sets of forest rules and regulations in their respective areas of operation. The main reason for such a diarchy is that while the State Forest Department maintains a well-qualified team of skilled technical staff, it has a comparatively meagre forest area of 1127.23 sq km of under its jurisdiction. The District Council on the other hand has a large forest cover of 6250.68 sq km under its management and control but lacks adequate technical manpower which results in their inability to properly enforce rules. Since the forest is the principal source of revenue for the communities, the District Council cannot afford to stop forest operations owing to fund constraints. The private forest owners who own substantial areas of forest indulge freely in felling and sale of timber. This has led to a reduction of forest cover and has had a serious impact on the Khasi people's livelihoods. This can be considered an infringement on their traditional rights over forest resources.

As per custom, only the permanent residents of the villages have the right to access and use the resources of community forests and other common property resources. They can collect fuelwood, cut trees for construction of houses, collect wild vegetables, orchids and medicinal herbs, and quarry sand and stones from permitted sites (Nongkynrih 2006: 55).

It is here that one finds an invisibility of women's role in forest management and decision-making. Although women shoulder heavy economic responsibilities, spend long and tedious hours toiling in the fields, trudge large distances through rugged forests in their struggle to meet the survival needs of the family, they have little say in village administration or in the management of forests. Women are often just silent observers of the changes around them with little or no involvement in decisions taken at the council meetings. Women have been further disadvantaged by gradual transformation of *ri-raid* (community land) to *ri-kynti* (private land). As large tracts of communal land and forest have been taken over by private owners, women have been increasingly marginalised as their access to common property resources have been significantly curtailed. It is not just the forest cover and land area that has seen a decline, but their quality has also suffered. Moreover, on 12 December 1996, the Supreme Court passed its historic judgment of the bans on felling of trees, removal of timber, and wood-based activities in the region. Although the judgment was made with a conservationist aim, it caused unexpected miseries to the tribal population who were totally dependent on the forest for their livelihood. The ban had a severe negative impact on women as it was now even more difficult for them to meet the economic needs of the family and their domestic chores increased manifold (Nongbri 2003: 1898).

Agriculture and sale of forest produce used to be the mainstay of the rural Khasi economy. Over the years, with the decline in forest cover, rural Khasi women have been forced into working as local and migrant labour. Livelihoods today depend on various factors such as availability of forest produce, land ownership and wage employment. Even though the forest cover has dwindled, women still depend upon the remaining areas for a supplementary source of livelihood, especially in the lean summer months. They have to walk longer distances to the forest for collection of resources and then carry back the produce on their head. For taking these products to the market, they have to depend on the bus service which is quite irregular and in poor condition. Often some villages are inaccessible by road which makes transport of goods even more difficult. Because of these reasons, the sale of produce is often relegated to the menfolk. This reduces the women's burden and saves their time, but the negative consequence is that they have lost control over the income they received from selling the firewood and NTFP that they collected. It is thus common for women to be primarily involved only in the lower stages of the value chain such as collection, cleaning, processing and sorting of forest produce but lack access to or control over the sale of the produce, which is mostly monopolised by men. Despite their important role in the value chain, women face marginalisation which leads to an increase in their economic hardships.

CONCLUSION

The conflict of interest between the government and the tribals over forest resources that begun during the colonial rule continued unabated long after India's Independence. The Government of India tightened its grip over the forests in Northeast India through the introduction of a new set of laws and rules, dismissing the traditional tribal rights of the Khasi community over land and forest. Customary laws with regard to land and forest and the working plan of the government have negatively impacted rural Khasi women in particular and indigenous people in general who have had to struggle for their right to use natural resources for their livelihoods.

Firstly, there has been a visible transition in Khasi society with regard to livelihood based on dependence on forest resources for food, fodder and shelter to wage employment. The depletion of land and natural forest cover, which was an important base for their primary economy, has resulted in a paucity of forestlands for livelihood and has subsequently affected the indigenous communities. The worst victims are the rural, tribal women who not only have had to bear the threats to their livelihood but also suffer subordination and the lack of agency because of their gender.

Secondly, women are allowed no role in forest management. This is largely due to prevailing Khasi customary laws according to which women have little say in village administration or resource management. Additionally, the gradual shift of *ri-raid* (community forest lands) to *ri-kynti* (private lands) have further diminished women's role with regard to the use of the CPRs or Common Property Resources.

Thirdly, there is a common perception that women are merely 'helpers' and not 'workers' in the flow of work within and outside the household. Activities like collection of NTFP, cleaning, sorting, and processing of forest products are often considered to be part of their 'household chores' and therefore not 'work'. In many remote villages women still lack access to the market and have no say in the sale of the produce, which is monopolised by men, thus losing control over the income from their labour.

The environment today is facing a crisis amidst stringent legislations of the government coupled with problems of development and conflict over resource base, which has had a massive impact on women as basic providers of subsistence needs. Issues of marginalisation of rural Khasi women and conflicts over their rights to NTFP will persist unless policy-level changes are introduced.

NOTES

1. The NEPED project aims to improve the income and welfare of farmers in Nagaland uplands through improved agro-forestry practices and more sustainable resource management. The Phase–I project of NEPED was called Nagaland Environment Protection and Economic Development through People's Action, but from the 2nd Phase onward NEPED came to be known as Nagaland Empowerment of People through Economic Development.

2. The PhD thesis is titled 'Forest in the Life of the Khasis: A Study in the Role of Forest in Khasi Socio-economic Structure'. The study focused on the divergent role of forest both as a socio-cultural necessity as well as an economic pursuit. The livelihood interventions of forest dwellers of two villages—Lawbyrwa in Ri-Bhoi district, which is a deeply forested village, and Mylliem village in E. Khasi Hills were studied with a view to understand the dynamics of the environment–development nexus.

REFERENCES

Darlong, V. T. 2002. 'An Overview of Forest Policies and Legislations vis-à-vis Forest Resource Management in North-East India'. In B. Datta Ray and K. Alam (ed.), *Forest Resources in North East India*. New Delhi: Omson Publications.

Gadgil, Madhav, and Ramachandra Guha. 1992. *This Fissured Land: An Ecological History of India*. Delhi: Oxford University Press.

Gurdon, P. R. T. 1975. *The Khasis*. Delhi: Cosmo Publications.

Iqbal, M. 1993. *International Trade in Non-wood Forest Products: An Overview*. Rome, Italy: Food and Agriculture Organization.

Khasi Hills Autonomous District Council. *The United Khasi Jaintia Hills Autonomous District (Management and Control of Forests) 1958 Act and The United Khasi-Jaintia Hills Autonomous District (Management and Control of Forests) 1960 Rules*. Available at https://khadc.nic.in/acts_rules_regulations_bills/Acts_Rules_arranged/19A_24A_Forest_Act_1958_Rules_1960.pdf (accessed May 2023).

Khongsit, S. 1999. *Kiba Ngi Khot Ja*. Shillong: Mrs. Sucila Khongngain, San Mer.

Krishna, Sumi. 2003. *Livelihood and Gender: Equity in Community Resource Management*. New Delhi: Sage Publications.

Kumar, N., N. C. Saxena, Y. Alagh and K. Mitra. 2000. *Poverty Alleviation through Forestry Development, Country Case Study, Operations Evaluation Department*. Washington DC: The World Bank.

Mawrie, H. O. 1981. *The Khasi Milieu*. New Delhi: Concept Publishing Company.

Mawrie, L. Barnes. 2001. *The Khasis and Their Natural Environment*. Shillong: Vendrame Institute Publication.

Nagaland Empowerment of People through Economic Development (NEPED). Available at https://nlsic.nagaland.gov.in/wp-content/uploads/2019/09/NEPEDori.pdf. (accessed on 16 February 2023).

Nongbri, Tiplut. May 2001. 'Timber Ban in North East India: Effects on Livelihood and Gender'. *Economic and Political Weekly* 36(21): 1893–1900.

———. 2003. *Development, Ethnicity and Gender: Select Essays on Tribes in India*. New Delhi: Rawat Publications.

Nongkynrih, A. K. 2006. 'Who Is in? Who Is out? Equity and Customary Community Forest Management in Meghalaya, India'. In Sango Mahanty, Jefferson Fox, et al. (eds), *Hanging in the Balance: Equity in Community-based Natural Resource Management in Asia*. Thailand: RECOFT.

Shangpliang, Rekha M. 2010. *Forest in the Life of the Khasis*. New Delhi: Concept Publishing Company Pvt. Ltd.

———. 2012. 'Forest Legislations and Livelihood Strategies: Khasi Women in Rural Meghalaya'. *Sociological Bulletin* 61(3): 479–493.

Sinha, A. C. 1993. *Beyond the Trees, Tigers and Tribes: Historical Sociology of the Eastern Himalaya Forest*. New Delhi: Har-Anand Publication.

Tucker, Richard P. 1988. 'The Depletion of India's Forest under British Imperialism: Planters, Foresters and Peasants in Assam and Kerala'. In Donald Worster (ed.), *The Ends of the Earth*. USA: Cambridge University Press.

Uberoi, Patricia. 1994. *Family, Kinship and Marriage in India*. Delhi: Oxford University Press.

World Bank. 2005. *India: Unlocking Opportunities for Forest-Dependent People in India*, Volume 1, Main Report. Washington.

VI

Borders, States and Markets

12

Marginalisation

Everyday Life Activities at the Myanmar-Mizoram Borderland

N. William Singh

The advent of cable television network in Mizoram in 1996 led to a surge of television programmes representing various facets of Mizo society. Television programmes are broadcast twice a week on the vernacular cable television networks Zonet and LPS. Central themes of these TV shows are the culture and tradition of the contemporary Mizo societies scattered across Manipur, Assam, Meghalaya, Tripura and even trans-border Mizo societies of Chittagong Hill Tracts of Bangladesh and Chin Hills of Myanmar where these programmes are broadcast. Elders claim that all Mizo societies, including the ones outside Mizoram, are of one ethnic origin, but they have been divided by the fraught history of map-making and boundary delimitation. In the following pages, I would like to address this fragmentation of erstwhile unified Mizo societies, habitats, and homelands into different state subjects with unequal rights under different jurisdictions and discuss these 'postcolonial displacements'.

A popular weekly television programme, *Lamtluang* (travelogue), has been running since 1998 and its various episodes are based on Mizo cultures, lifestyles, religious institutions, educational institutions, public parks, markets, transport systems, and even some facets of non-Mizo cultures. The episode aired on 16 December 2013 had as its central theme the relationship between the Chins and Mizos.[1] In the episode, Chin elders mention that their region may have become a part of another country (Myanmar) but they are not different from Mizos in Mizoram in any significant way. They share a common culture and language and have kin living across the border, till date. On a sad note, they wished that Mizo society should be understanding of the fact that many of the Mizos inhabiting the Chin Hills of Myanmar cross the border to escape poverty and to seek a better livelihood.

This chapter explores the marginalisation of Chin migrants in Mizoram and aims to unearth how and on what grounds the Chin migrants remained at the fringes, why their voices are still unheard in media, why they continue to exist in the host society without any political emancipation and why they are being looked down upon in the host society?

Based on ethnographic fieldwork and published reports by institutions and media, a main finding is that most of the Chin migrants struggle and face hardships in their everyday life in Mizoram. They are mostly engaged in the informal labour sector, working in sweatshops, running (unregistered) vendor stalls, selling Chinese goods as hawkers around the *vengs* (localities) of Aizawl. Many of the male Chin migrants earn their livelihood as bus drivers, taxi drivers while the women work as domestic workers. Some of them also engage in and are often convicted for smuggling and peddling illicit items such as drugs into Mizoram. They are hardly visible in the dominant churches of Mizoram; instead, they find community among smaller fellowships like the Methodist Church, which has a weak foothold in Mizoram. The common response of Chin elders during fieldwork was that most of the migrants are treated unfairly by the members of the host society.

The following sections study the available reports on Chin migrants gathered from daily newspapers and vernacular media outlets to make sense of the marginalisation which occurs in 'the practice of everyday life' (De Certeau 1984). These are supported by data gathered during my fieldwork in 2016–17 related to the social status of the migrants. The latter parts of the chapter study the connection between the Chins' exodus and the social and political reality in the Chin Hills of Myanmar.

EVERYDAY LIFE ACTIVITIES AT THE BORDERLAND: A STUDY OF MARGINALISATION

Marginalisation is an ongoing phenomenon experienced by the Chins in Mizoram in their everyday life. They live in a poorer condition than the other members of the host society due to the former's officially non-recognised status. This marginalisation is further aggravated due to instances of drug peddling and liquor brewing among the Chins as well as the absence of mediating institutions and emancipatory policies for them. The media, while reporting on the extent of marginalisation, omits the history behind the present-day issues such as cross-border migration, shortage of food, forced labour and unemployment. Ethnographic fieldwork on borders and borderlands becomes an essential tool that helps to bring out the reasons behind these ongoing issues. It is due to the fieldwork conducted at the border townships and provinces around the Mizoram-Myanmar border that the issue of marginalisation of the migrants in the host society has received attention.

Borderlands studies is a relatively new field of research that looks at a whole range of social issues. Ethnographic studies of borders and borderlands are needed, Dean (2012) argues, since it is the only way to research borderlands as 'lived spaces challenged and inspired' by international boundaries. Unfortunately, ethnographic studies of borders have so far been scarce. Gupta and Ferguson (1992) advise that anthropologists should become much more critical in their engagement with political borders, and not take these for granted. A critical historical engagement is also required to study the long-term impact that delimitation of borders have on people's lives. Border studies are gradually expanding from a geographical focus on the descriptive analysis of the location of the lines separating states in the international system to 'the study of the dynamics of the bordering process as it impacts society and space' (Newman 2012). Borders are man-made and continually produced by a variety of state actors, such as legislators, politicians and border guards, as well as by the people who legally or illegally cross them. Borders are not simply there; they are 'enacted' as van Houtum (2011) argues. Borders, he says, are the result of 'the interpretation and consequential (violent) power practices of those who construct and help to reproduce the border' (ibid.). The various manifestations of borders need to be researched in relation to the relevant actors. Border studies have shown that 'social relations, defined in part by the state, transcend the territorial limits of the state and, in so doing, transform the structure of the state at home and its relations to its neighbors' (Wilson and Donnan 2012).

Marginalised communities are excluded from the mainstream dominant narratives as they lack representation and mediating agencies such as public forums that would discuss the marginalised and their issues. Because they are at the centre of the exclusivity-inclusivity paradox,[2] although they have proper names, belongings, and an ethno-cultural history, they are voiceless. The marginalised life exists in pockets at the margin.

The Chins' marginalisation is evident in their everyday life practices. For instance, they do not have any established agencies or registered organisation which could voice their demands. There is also an absence of political engagement as many Chin names have been deleted from the electoral roll[3] beginning from 1998–99 till the present. There have been no proper policies adopted or planned for the migrant refugee Chins after the closure of the makeshift camps at the borderlands of Mizoram in 1998.

Everyday life practices of the Chin migrants involve finding any work that pays for survival by whatever means possible. They are often compelled to adopt illegal ways to earn their livelihood since the existing systems of commerce and politics in the host society do not favour the migrants. The larger social and political processes contribute to this difficulty faced by the Chins who have to deal with acute poverty and unemployment in the Chin province, which incidentally is the poorest province in Myanmar. The unequal development of regions and the harsh socio-political reality underlies the ongoing struggles of the Chins as the autonomous and subjective aspects of their everyday life are defined by marginalisation at the Mizoram borderland.

Data from the fieldwork reveals how the Chins are considered the 'other' because of their (illegal) migrant and undocumented status. Mizo elders commented that what makes it worse is that many of the migrants are involved in practices such as illicit brewing of liquor and peddling of drugs. In case of others, their everyday life practices are confined within the informal sector where they work as domestic workers, bus drivers, labourers in quarries, hawkers, and weavers. These jobs however are not only coveted by the migrant Chins but also by members of the host society. The Chins' linguistic closeness to the host community makes them not only eligible for these jobs, but in many cases more preferred.

The everyday life practices of the Chin migrants also defines their social status. Their low status can be seen as an indicator of marginalisation. The elders of the host society often view the Chin migrants as untrustworthy and as people who are not Christians in their heart and soul. According to them, the host society is totally against drug peddling and other illicit trades because the host society is 'God-fearing' and its members are staunch Christians. It must be noted here that Mizoram has a 93 per cent Christian population as per the 2011 Census of India.

During fieldwork, Mizo elders mentioned the following verse on many occasions. It is a popular lyric often sung in public forums. Given below is a rough English translation (AMPGSU 2013):

Unaute U In Dam Tlang Thin Alawm Maw

Unaute u, in dam tlang thin alawm maw,
Rinawmna chibai in dawng thei em?
Chhinlung chhungkhat Zoram chhehvel a mi te,
In suihkhawm leh zai i rel ang u.

Aw, thang leh thar te'n eng nge kan tih ang le?
Kan chanvo, kan bil neihna kawng chu;
Thawkchhuak turin eng nge kan tih tak ang le?
Insuihkhawm leh zai i rel ang u.

Unaute u, han dawn nawn leh teh u,
Khawvel unau hnamdang hriattir zelin;
Kan nih na chung Pathian lo ruat sa ang khan,
Insuihkhawm leh zai i rel ang u.

Unaute u, in dam tlang thin alawm maw,
Rinawmna chibai inbuk ang le;
Chhinlung chhungkhat Zofa kan nih hre rengin,
Insuihkhawm leh zai i rel ang u.

Brothers Hope You All Are Doing Fine

Brothers hope you all are doing fine
Can you receive a faithful salute?
We must remember and bear in mind that we all are Zofa who originated from Chhinlung[4]
Let us ignite together again.

What should the next generation do?
To get our share, what should we do?
Let us ignite together.

Brothers, think again
And tell the other races of the world
For what our Heavenly God had ordained for us
Let us ignite together.

Brothers hope you all are doing fine
Can you receive a faithful salute?
We must remember and bear in mind that we all are Zofa who originated from Chhinlung
Let us ignite together again.

SEEKING REFUGE CONTINUES

Cross-border migration across this part of the borderland is nothing new, and has been happening for decades, since the 1960s. There are various causes and factors of migration which are intrinsically linked to the prevailing social, economic and political conditions of the two nations. For instance, during *Rambuai* (the Mizo insurgency that lasted for twenty years from 1966 to 1986), many Mizos migrated to Myanmar to receive education at schools and universities there and seek a better life, rather than suffering in Mizoram.

The first influx of the Chin refugees into Mizoram was during 1962 due to the Burmanisation campaign launched by General Ne Win. The ethnic minorities suffered under Ne Win's regime (Son and Singh 2016). They began relying on economic opportunities across the borderland and took refuge in Mizoram to survive and support their livelihood. F. K. Lehman (1963) illustrates the various networks and linkages that the Chin community forms with other societies through trade, exchange of goods and migration. Later in 1988, there was a Chin exodus towards Mizoram, Vietnam, Thailand and Cambodia due to the establishment of the State Law and Order Restoration Council (SLORC) by the military junta. Mizo elders in interviews said that the refugees were initially welcomed into Mizoram, as the residents saw them as their own ethnic cousins. Thousands of Chins were given food, shelter and livelihood and the Mizoram authority made makeshift camps to shelter Chin migrants at the border town of Champhai. However, the members of the host society now look down on the migrants, failing to consider that these refugees are victims of the widespread ethnic, religious, and political persecution in Myanmar.

INDO-MYANMAR BORDER CROSSING

Cross-border movement between Mizoram and Myanmar is exempt from visa and passport requirements under Rule IV of Passport (Entry into India) Rules, 1950 due to the close cultural ties between the two nations. According to Part II of the *Gazette of India*, dated 1 July 1968, the central government exempts from the passport rules:

> … every member of the hill tribes, who is either a citizen of India or a Citizen of the Union of Burma and who is ordinarily resident in any area within forty kilometers on either side of the Indo-Burma frontier entering into India across the said frontier. (Government of Mizoram 2003)

On 21 July 2010, a newer notification by Ministry of Home Affairs, Government of India reduced the 40 km benchmark to 16 km. The *Gazette of India*, Part II mentioned the following changes:

> A permit issued by the Government of India or the State Government… may specify for the purpose, and he/she shall not, on the basis of that permit move into the area in India which is beyond sixteen kilometers from the aforesaid frontier. (Government of India 2010)

Data collected during fieldwork revealed that many of the Chins migrating to Mizoram did not (and do not) follow border-crossing rules. People from Mizoram crossing over to the other side of the border do not abide by the rules either. The total length of the border is 404 km. Aizawl, the capital of the state, is more than a hundred kilometers away from the stones marking the border. The Indo-Myanmar border being one of the most porous regions in South Asia, few follow the rules and obtain permits, pay permit fees, and deposit identification cards at the border checkpoints.

UNEQUAL ASSIMILATION OF CHIN REFUGEES IN MIZORAM

Assimilation and integration of Chins in Mizoram vary depending on the different social status of the migrants. Only the few well-to-do and educated Chin families, who migrated during 1970–80, were able to integrate themselves into the host community by changing their names. It is important to note that these assimilated few do not attend the marginalised Methodist Church but the dominant Presbyterian Church. Migration was relatively easier for these privileged few who were armed with economic and cultural capital, who often held degrees from institutes of higher studies in Myanmar such as Mandalay and Rangoon Universities, had bank accounts, had identification cards, electoral identity cards and had their names registered in the electoral roll. They mentioned that their shared language made it relatively easy for them to integrate and assimilate into the Mizo society while a majority of the not-so-well-fed and not-so-well-educated refugee families continued to live in the fringes without proper jobs, identity cards, bank accounts and proper papers.

One of the main observations from the study on Chins at the borderlands is that they lack legal recognition in the host society. As mentioned earlier in this chapter, the majority of them work in the informal sector, which does not require proper documentation. Men engage in manual labour, working in farms, quarries, or construction sites as contractual workers. They sometimes also work as bonded labour to repay loans they had to take from the farm and quarry owners. We interviewed workers in four quarries at the border town of Champhai who were all from Hakha (in Chin Hills of Mizoram) and working as bonded labour. When asked why they took the loan, they said that it was the only way out and they needed to feed their families, send their children for education, or tend to medical emergencies. All the quarry workers were not landless—some of them owned a few acres of land in their respective villages in Chin Hills. The migrant workers explained that the incomes from their own farmlands would never be sufficient to fulfill their daily needs. Women too work in the farms as farmhands and in quarries as stone-breakers. Chin men and women also work as loaders in markets, as attendants and service staff in hotels and restaurants and in weaving units run by private owners. The working conditions in these jobs are better than the exploitation of workers through bonded labour in mines and quarries.

These poorly paid workers suffer from a chronic economic insecurity that impacts all aspects of their lives on an everyday basis. They often live in overcrowded, inadequate housing from which they are frequently evicted. They are vulnerable to many serious ailments due to their inaccessibility to clean water, food, and healthcare. Many Chin children do not attend school because their families lack the necessary financial resources. Often, children below fifteen years of age have to work to support their families.

In the course of our survey, we found that Chin migrants often live in clusters, in cheap rentals, close to the Methodist Churches of Mizoram. Most of them would avoid going to the police or the courts for assistance because they are 'undocumented and fear arrest and deportation as undocumented foreigners'.[5] Among them, Chin women are the least likely to go to the authorities for help since they are often harassed, arrested or detained by the police for selling goods without permits.

Marginalisation manifests not only through discriminatory practices in terms of housing, employment and education, but also through stigmatisation. Chin migrant workers living in the outskirts of the town or city often seek out their livelihood by brewing alcohol. This is considered unacceptable by the dominant Presbyterian and Baptist Churches of Mizoram. In

2015, *Vanglaini*, a Mizoram daily, reported that up to 75 per cent of the families at Rangvamual and Phunchawng—regions in the outskirts of Aizawl—were engaged in brewing liquor. This mode of income has resulted in the Chin community being stigmatised. Brewing or consuming liquor is not found acceptable by the Young Mizo Association (YMA, the most influential civil organisation of Mizoram). It is considered neither Christian' nor a respectable practice. This results in the stigmatisation and marginalisation of the Chins (Chakma 2003a). Most of the migrants also often ignore the customary laws and regulations of the host society and behave as they see fit, engaging in illegal activities for survival. That is the main reason why the YMA[6] in Mizoram punishes and serves Quit Mizoram notices (Singh 2014) to Chins without government consent: they consider the migrants to be perpetrators of crime. Media reports too often label the migrants as law-breakers and problem-makers, which further emphasises the negative prejudice against the Chins.

Therefore, the general idea that Mizoram is a peaceful, developing state needs revision. Based on the information gathered during fieldwork, it was found that behind the semblance of civic order, there are different forms of marginalisation taking place between ethnic brethren. The minority at the fringe is rendered voiceless, deprived of basic necessities such as healthcare and education, and denied recognition by the host community. The civic order is further weakened when the host community refuses humanitarian help to the marginalised communities such as the Chin migrants—a fact widely reported in newspapers and local television networks. At present, there is not a single policy initiated by the state for the migrants. Civic order can be improved by adopting policies that address the issue of marginalisation and putting in place mechanisms that hold agencies accountable. The efforts to solve the migrant problem through institutional frameworks and policies and by redefining the role of civil societies are still nascent in Mizoram.

EXPULSION OF CHINS FROM MIZORAM

Mizo society is known for the strong solidarity among its members. So when an 'untoward act' is committed by an individual that threatens this solidarity, it is strongly resisted by the society which then unites against this 'outcast'. The result is that because of the few anti-social acts and crimes committed by a handful of Chin individuals, the whole community gets labelled as pathetic and obnoxious 'outsiders', and they are treated as an unwanted burden (Singh 2014). They are accused of polluting the civic order of Mizo society. They are then arrested and deported as undocumented foreigners, especially due to anti-foreigner campaigns initiated by the YMA. The association plays a central role in the expulsion of Chins in Mizoram. The YMA is occupied with the preservation of Mizo identity and culture, but excludes the plurality by ignoring the Mizo identities and cultures of the Chin Hills.

When the YMA vowed to clean up the foreigners (Chakma 2003b), the expulsion of the Chins was announced via dozens of loudspeakers on the streets of Aizawl. During 2003, some six hundred Chin migrants were repatriated to Myanmar, many of whom faced serious punitive actions by the Burmese government including imprisonment, payment of heavy fines and forced deportation.[7] Most of them had stayed longer than the permissible limit in Mizoram. Chins hardly ever renew their permit for an extended stay in Mizoram. The Myanmar junta punishes them on these grounds when they return home. In 2009, the Human Rights Watch issued a public report entitled *We Are Like Forgotten People* (Human Rights Watch 2009). The report detailed several cases of torture and execution of the Chins by the military regime in Myanmar. The YMA members however continued to drive the Chins back across the border into Myanmar, actively trying to limit migrant entry into Mizoram. Because of this, some Chins had moved out to New Delhi and Calcutta (McDuie-Ra 2012: 35). Chin non-governmental organisations (NGOs) including the Women's League for Chinland had to leave Mizoram as the alternative was to live in fear of the host society and its civil society groups.

In April 2013, YMA burned down forty houses in the borderland village of Saikhumphai at Champhai district of Mizoram. Mizo authorities (all of whom are YMA members[8]) reported that the houses were torched to control the increasing number of non-documented Chin migrants in the particular village. Earlier, the YMA had ordered the Chin to leave the area but the migrants did not comply, given the precarious circumstances in Myanmar (Khonumthung Chin News Group 2013). The YMA then proceeded to torch the village. The YMA members declared the Chins as illegal migrants, and Saikhumphai village as the main site of illicit drug trade. This declaration of the YMA was reported by *Vanglaini*, the largest circulated daily in Mizoram, on 26 April 2013.

In December 2011, Chin Baptist Churches USA, World Relief and Lutheran Immigration and Refugee Service and others published a report titled *Seeking Refuge: The Chin People in Mizoram State, India* (Wilch et al. 2011). The report revealed the refusal of aid, the condescending attitude of the YMA, and the impoverishment and marginalisation faced by the Chins in Mizoram.

THE REALITY OF CHINS IN MYANMAR

Myanmar has long been known for human rights violations. The military regime in Myanmar has persecuted people on the basis of their ethnicity, religion and political affiliation. The media is under the control of the junta and many journalists are imprisoned. The Chin exodus is an outcome of such institutional violence by the state of Myanmar.

During fieldwork at Aizawl in April 2011, we spoke to ZA, an eighteen-year-old who had fled from the Chin Hills in Myanmar to Mizoram, and they revealed,

> I fled to Mizoram due to the Burmese Army conscription. Even at my young age, the Burmese Army forced me into labour and I worked as a porter carrying Burmese Army supplies. Not wanting to be a part of the Burmese Army brutality I fled. My family does not even have food to eat, so I need to work to earn money.

A Chin man born in Tiddim in Myanmar, who later settled in the border town of Zokhawthar, a village in Champhai district, Mizoram, showed us a picture of a luxurious Buddhist pagoda that was built by the Chin labourers. In an interview in July 2013, he informed, 'This so-called pagoda was not built by the Buddhists of Burma. It was built by Christians of Chin townships who were forced into labour'.

Roughly, one million people have been internally displaced in Myanmar due to the brutality of the military regime, as reported by the Norwegian Refugee Council (2004). It notes, 'The Myanmar Junta has not taken any steps to stop this massive internal displacement of people which comprise mainly of minority ethnic groups—Karen, Rakhine, Chin, Shan, and Mon' (Norwegian Refugee Council 2004).

In November 2013, as part of my fieldwork I interviewed a journalist from Tahan, Myanmar, who revealed the poverty-stricken condition of Chin Hills,

> Every household in Chin Hills has at least one or two individuals (adults) who unwillingly left home looking for work elsewhere; sometimes in Thailand, mainland Burma, sometimes in Mizoram and sometimes in China or Malaysia. Outflow of Chin migrants is also due to the atrocities and disempowerment measures.

He further commented,

> Who wants to leave home, belongings and family? Chins are the largest minority ethnic unit in Myanmar who have been granted refugee status by the UNHCR. That is the reason why they are

everywhere, doing menial labour and taking up jobs to survive in First World nations.

According to a Physicians for Human Rights (2011) report, 92 per cent of Chin households suffer 'Crime against Humanity' across townships of Chin state. The report also mentioned that forced labour (conscription by the Myanmar Army) is very common. Although 90 per cent of the Chins in Myanmar are Christians, their Christian landmarks have often been replaced by Buddhist pagodas. Chin state is the most impoverished and underdeveloped state where 27 per cent of the population does not have access to primary schools, 70 per cent live below poverty line and 32 per cent lack access to proper healthcare.

A report published by Solidarités International (Win et al. 2012) mentioned that a market analysis of agricultural products in the southern Chin state exposed the lapse of cash crops in the agricultural sector. The popular crops harvested in Chin state are rice, maize and millets. When compared to other developing nations, the quantum of food production is abysmally low, which leads to low income, food insecurity and extreme poverty. The report suggested that the introduction of cash crops would empower and escalate income generation. In 2013, newspapers in Myanmar reported that ten thousand acres of farmland would be reclaimed in the Chin state by the Myanmar authority, which would then be used to set up industrial sites and military installments (Son and Singh 2016).

Democratic transition in Myanmar in 2015 witnessed the freeing of markets, but not of the people. Myanmar authorities prohibited the slash-and-burn technique of farming and denied management and control of land by regional or local authorities. The prohibition of swidden cultivation and exchange of goods with other provinces in Myanmar adversely affected the livelihood of Chins, as mentioned in F. K. Lehman's study (1963). Right to land, property and adequate housing are basic entitlements as per the Universal Declaration of Human Rights. We found out in the course of our fieldwork that most of the villagers in Chin Hills were not aware of their basic human rights. In 1948, the Land Nationalisation Act (LNA) was passed in Myanmar, then known as Burma. The LNA abolished lease, rental and sharecropping and brought all lands under the sole authority of the state, and not private or local authorities. In 1991, a central committee for management of cultivable land and wasteland was formed. This committee recommendation came into force without any public consultations. It further centralised land regulations on farmland, wasteland and cultivable land under the Myanmar authority. What can be observed from this series of land regulations is that the state of Myanmar audited and controlled land and legitimised this control without considering the impact of these authoritative decisions on common people. The Chin state thus became more impoverished.

The national average daily wage in Myanmar in 2011 was very low, the equivalent of three US Dollars (Government of India 2011). Sixty-two per cent of the population in Chin state is engaged in agriculture; 73 per cent lives in rural areas. Off-farm activities like mining are also widespread in Chin state (Hudson-Rodd 2004: 23). Fifty per cent of households have an average of three acres of land while the other 50 per cent is landless (ibid.). Forty per cent of households have a small quantum of livestock and 25 per cent own neither land nor livestock. There are 10.6 million hectares of cultivable land in Myanmar, but only 8.5 per cent of land is available for cultivation as the rest is under the rule of the military junta (Hudson-Rodd 2004: 22–36). As an outcome, the rate of poverty has increased manifold. Added to this, restricted access to land and unfriendly institutional mechanisms resulted in massive food insecurity and economic instability in the Chin state. Periodically, there are acute food shortages. In such times of grief, families would share basic supplies among themselves. Chin state remains the poorest and the most underdeveloped province of Myanmar. Migration for forest resources extraction and cultivation of unregistered fallow fields are also common. Since the concept of agriculture and foraging the forest are considered similar in this region, there are no separate jurisdictions demarcated or policies adopted by the authorities and these remain as loopholes of the State Land Regulations Department (SLRD).

Stripped of the right to private land ownership, as Myanmar authority leases only a few plots of farmland based on one's profession, the impoverished cultivators of the Chin Hills are further disadvantaged. United Nations Development Program (UNDP 2007) reported that 50 per cent of the households in Chin state suffer from poverty and food insecurity, while the national average of Myanmar food insecurity during 2005–06 is just 10 per cent.

LICIT AND ILLICIT TRADE

Trading of both licit and illicit goods, such as food items, medicine, clothing and auto parts, is common along the Indo-Myanmar border. Trading of selected items was legalised by the Indo-Myanmar Border Trade Agreement signed in 1994, one of many treaties signed between India and Myanmar promising cooperation in border trade.[9] The existing infrastructure for border trade at the Indo-Myanmar border town of Zokhawthar was funded by the DoNER Ministry, Government of India after the 1986 Mizoram Ceasefire Agreement (DoNER and RIS 2011: 50–54). There is also a subversive illicit economy that includes smuggling of jade, diamond, gold, silver and other precious stones and metals as well as illegal substances. The authorities turned the previously illicit border economy, which had relied on local networks and long-standing relationships between the borderland communities, into legal trade where the primary beneficiaries became the two governments. In 1986, Zokhawthar became a protected and official 'Special Economic Zone' following the peace agreement. It was a peace accord that had the express purpose of improving the lives of the people on both sides of the border as well as furnishing both governments with tax revenue (Rajagopalan 2008: 4–6).

CONCLUSION

To conclude, the future of Chins in Mizoram depends on their ability to earn their livelihood adequately, for which the host society needs to adopt policies that meet the needs of the Chins. The host society and the host state ought to coordinate and formulate a policy that ensures the migrants are hosted without discrimination and a policy to ensure safe return of the migrants to their homeland. There should be better policies to enable the Chins to support themselves so that the migrants too can contribute to Mizoram's economy. Proper documentation of the migrants is still absent and the necessity for documentation must be taken into consideration. The migrants could be enabled to build positive working relations with non-governmental organisations in Mizoram, including, for example, Mizo Hmeichhe Insuihkhawm Pawl (Mizo Women's Association or MHIP, a popular women's group), Mizo Zirlai Pawl (MZP), dominant churches and YMA. At the moment, the Chins' future in Mizoram looks sombre but one may hope that the Government of India and Mizoram authorities will find a creative way of addressing the Chins' humanitarian concerns, like they did for the Chins seeking refuge in Mizoram in 1988.

NOTES

1. The nomenclature of the communities as Chin and Mizo was proposed by the colonial authority and later adopted by the native elite of the region. It is commonly accepted by scholars that the umbrella term for both (as well as other groups) is *Zo*.

2. Exclusivity–inclusivity paradox in the context of Chin migrants can be understood using two parameters—their experience and their rights. First, Chin migrants in Mizoram experience feelings of being an outsider. Second, Chin migrants do not enjoy the same rights as the Mizo. They cannot avail of the same state facilities as members of the host society. For instance, they cannot apply for job card, ration card, health card and other provisions by the state.

3. Electoral rolls in Mizoram are still based on the National Citizenship Act, 1950. Refugee law does not exist in India and nor is India a signatory of the UNHCR. See UNHCR Global Appeal 2011 Update, available at https://www.unhcr.org/media/unhcr-global-appeal-2011-update-india (accessed on 5 May 2023).

4. Chhinlung is the name of a cave, located in the southern part of China, near present-day Kunming.

5. Comment by an elderly Chin migrant living in Aizawl (name withheld for anonymity), interviewed by the author on 5 August 2017 during fieldwork.

6. The association has been in existence since 1935. It was formed by Welsh Christian Missionaries along with the Mizo elite with three objectives: ensuing good use of leisure time, advocating a good Christian life, and preserving and fostering Mizo culture and society. It is the most influential civil society in Mizoram, with the largest number of members (over six lakhs as of 2023).

7. It is near impossible to determine the number of Chin refugees who were returned to Myanmar and what punishments they faced. There are a handful of verbal accounts we could record during fieldwork but the interviewees chose to remain anonymous for fear of reprisal.

8. It must be noted here that every Mizo is compulsorily a YMA member. When a Mizo attains the age of fourteen, they become a YMA member voluntarily or involuntarily.

9. These treaties include the Treaty of Friendship in 1951 and the later Border Trade Agreement of 1994. The 1994 agreement was designed to promote formal trade between the two countries and listed sixty-two items from agricultural products and clothing to hardware, as legal items of trade. The Government of India also implemented a schedule to provide Assistance to States for Developing Export Infrastructure and other Allied Activities (ASIDE) to foster trade.

REFERENCES

AMPGSU. 2013. *Hla Bu* (Song Book), Song Number 21. Shillong: All Mizo Post-Graduate Student's Union (AMPGSU).

Chakma, Suhas. 2003a. 'Complaint to Stop Forcible Eviction of the Myanmarese Chin Refugees from Lunglei Areas of Mizoram by a Private Organization, Mizo Joint Action Committee from 20 June 2003, Their

Arrest and Imminent Deportation to Myanmar'. In *Asian Centre for Human Rights*, 23 June. Available at http://www.achrweb.org/countries/india/mizoram/CR0103.htm. (accessed on 27 February 2014).

_____. 2003b. 'Complaint to Stop Forcible Repatriation of the Myanmarese Chin Refugees from Aizawl by Young Mizo Association and Peace Accord MNF Returnees Association (PAMRA)'. In *Asian Centre for Human Rights*, 28 July. Available at http://www.achrweb.org/countries/india/mizoram/CR0203.htm (accessed on 22 February 2013).

Dean, Karin. 2012. 'Spaces, Territorialities and Ethnography on the Thai-, Sino- and Indo-Myanmar Boundaries'. In Doris Wastl-Walter (ed.), *The Ashgate Research Companion to Border Studies*, 219–241. Farnham: Ashgate.

De Certeau, Michel. 1984. *The Practice of Everyday Life*. Berkeley: University of California Press.

DoNER and RIS. 2011. *Expansion of North East India's Trade and Investment with Bangladesh and Myanmar: An Assessment of the Opportunities and Constraints*, Report, 50–54. Shillong: Government of India.

Government of India. 2010. 'Extraordinary, Part II'. *The Gazette of India* XXIII, 1–3.

_____. 2011. *Census of India 2011*. Available at www.censusindia.gov.in.

Government of Mizoram. 2003. 'Extraordinary'. *Mizoram Gazette* XXXII, 1–2.

Gupta, Akhil, and James Ferguson. 1992. 'Beyond "Culture": Space, Identity and the Politics of Difference.' *Cultural Anthropology* 7(1): 6–23.

Hudson-Rodd, Nancy. 2004. *Housing, Land, and Property Rights in Burma*. Victoria: HRE Asia & Pacific Programme Publication.

Human Rights Watch. 2009. '*We Are Like Forgotten People': The Chin People of Burma: Unsafe in Burma, Unprotected in India*. New York: Human Rights Watch. Available at https://www.hrw.org/reports/burma0109_brochure_low.pdf (accessed April 2023).

Khonumthung Chin News Group. 2013. 'Mizoram Authorities Burn Down 40 Houses of Chin People'. http://www.khonumthung.org/?p=1435 (accessed on 10 October 2013).

Lehman, F. K. 1963. *The Structure of Chin Society*. Illinois: University of Illinois Press.

Levesque, Julien, and Mirza Zulfiqur Rahman. 2008. *Tension in the Rolling Hills: Burmese Population and Border Trade in Mizoram*. IPCS Research Papers 14. Available at https://www.files.ethz.ch/isn/55166/IPCS-ResearchPaper14.pdf (accessed on 5 May 2023).

Manchanda, Rita, and Tapan Bose. 1997. *States, Citizens and Outsiders: The Uprooted Peoples of South Asia*, 24–28. Kathmandu: South Asia Forum for Human Rights.

McDuie-Ra, Duncan. 2012. *Northeast Migrants in Delhi: Race, Refuge and Retail*, 35. Amsterdam: University of Amsterdam Press.

Newman, David. 2012. 'Contemporary Research Agendas in Border Studies: An Overview'. In Doris Wastl-Walter (ed.), *The Ashgate Research Companion to Border Studies*, 33–48. Farnham: Ashgate.

Norwegian Refugee Council. 2004. https://www.nrc.no/arch/img/9667049, (accessed on 15 February 2014).

Physicians for Human Rights. 2011. 'Life Under the Junta: Evidence of Crimes Against Humanity in Burma's Chin State', 1 January. Available at http://physiciansforhumanrights.org/library/reports/burma-chin-report-2011.html (accessed April 2023).

Rajagopalan, Swarna. 2008. *Peace Accords in Northeast India: Journey over Milestones*, Policy Studies 46. Washington DC: East-West Centre in Washington.

Sammadar, Ranabir. 2006. *Refugee and the State: Practice of Asylum and Care in India*. New Delhi: Sage Publications.

Singh, N. William. 2014. 'Quit Mizoram Notices: Fear of the Others'. *Economic and Political Weekly* XLIX(25): 5–9.

Son, Bianca. 2013. 'The Making of the Zo: The Chin of Burma and the Lushai and Kuki of India 1826–1988'. Unpublished PhD Thesis. London: School of Oriental and African Studies.

Son, Bianca, and N. William Singh. 2016. 'The Chin State-Mizoram Border: Institutionalized Xenophobia for State Control'. In Su-Ann Oh (ed.), *Myanmar's Mountain and Maritime Borderscapes: Local Practices, Boundary-Making and Figured Worlds*, 353–368. Singapore: ISEAS Press.

Thanga, Lal Biak. 1978. *The Mizos: A Study in Racial Personality*. Gauhati: United Publishers.

UNDP. 2007. *Myanmar Chin State: A Mountain of Trouble*. Available at https://www.thenewhumanitarian.org/report/87352/myanmar-chin-state-mountain-trouble (accessed May 2023).

U.S. Department of State. 2011. 'Background Note: Burma'. Bureau of East Asian and Pacific Affairs. Available at https://2009-2017.state.gov/outofdate/bgn/burma/189439.htm (accessed May 2023).

van Houtum, Henk. 2011. 'The Mask of the Border'. In Doris Wastl-Walter (ed.), *The Ashgate Research Companion to Border Studies*, 49–62. Farnham: Ashgate.

Vumson. 1986. *Zo History.* Aizawl: Author.

Wilch, Matthew, Zo Tum Hmung et al. (eds). 2011. *Seeking Refuge: The Chin People in Mizoram State, India.* Available at https://chinmd.org/wp-content/uploads/2021/11/Seeking-Refuge-The-Chin-People-in-Mizoram-State-India.pdf (accessed on 24 November 2022).

Wilson, Thomas M., and Hastings Donnan. 2012. 'Borders and Border Studies'. In Thomas Wilson and Hastings Donnan (ed.), *A Companion to Border Studies*, 1–26. Chichester: Blackwell Publishing.

Win, T. M., K. S. Lin, P. H. Aung and M. Thant. 2012. *Report on Market Analysis of Agricultural Products in Southern Chin State.* Yangon, Myanmar: Solidarités International (SI). Available at https://reliefweb.int/report/myanmar/market-analysis-southern-chin-state (accessed May 2023).

13

Global Markets, Local Risks and Social Marginality

A Study of Cancer-Affected People in Mizoram*

Lalhmangaihi Chhakchhuak

Sharing two international borders and surrounded by neighbouring states in Northeast India, Mizoram witnesses material and non-material transactions which contribute to the development of its economy. Historically, the Mizos have moved from one region to another, crossing borders, their main sources of livelihood being hunting and farming. The migrating tribes then settled in the then Lushai Hills, which is now Mizoram, and their livelihood changed as did their cultures of trade and consumption. Capitalist globalisation though colonisation reached every corner, bringing unpredicted and unwanted outcomes along with socio-political and economic developments. The socio-cultural scenario in Northeast Indian states further encountered significant changes because of the impact of the Christian missionaries. Although the Mizos practised a traditional system of exchanging goods with their neighbours even before the entry of the colonial rulers, the colonial rule completely disrupted the existing administrative structures, governance as well as the political economy of the state. In this chapter we will focus on the development of global markets in Mizoram and study how they are interrelated with the

*I wish to thank my supervisor, N. Purendra Prasad for his insightful comments, guidance and critical remarks on my draft essay. I am very grateful to Geraldine Forbes and Sajal Nag for the discussions on this chapter, and for giving me useful comments and suggestions.

social risk that marginal communities encounter, especially with regards to public health.

CONCEPTUAL FRAMEWORK

Giddens (1991) and Beck (1992) have described modernity as the introduction to capitalism and discusses how capitalism eventually pushed society beyond traditional norms, as cultural aspects and values practised for ages drifted apart. This resulted in various kinds of marginalisation and exclusion, and engendered a risk culture (Giddens 1991). Modernity significantly altered day-to-day life and radically changed lifestyles, perceptions, and rationality. This 'risk society' eventually affects human behaviour and the interpretation of disease, illness and health (ibid.).

This chapter raises the question that has Mizoram, having witnessed a shift in consumption culture, paved way for marginalisation of different ethnic groups? Mehretu et al. (2000) in defining the typology of marginalisation explains the theory of 'contingent marginalisation' in which an individual or communities get adversely affected by the free flow of the market. Contingent marginalised groups are those who are disadvantaged because of their ecological location and socio-cultural limitations in dealing with the market. The landlocked state of Mizoram shares international borders with two countries, Bangladesh to the west and Myanmar to the east, and domestic borders with its neighbouring states, Assam to the north, Tripura to the north-west and Manipur to the north-east. Its geographical location and ecological factors affect the trade and growth of markets in the state. In addition, Mizoram faces issues such as lack of social security and infiltration of illegal migrants from the neighbouring countries. It serves as a black market for a range of things, from consumer items such as household goods and food to drugs and other illegal substances. This chapter analyses how Mizoram's geographical location and the fact of it being a global market has led to the marginalisation of the local communities and ethnic tribes by deeply impacting their social lives.

This chapter has four sections: The first outlines the history of Mizoram, its colonial past, delving into the economic changes introduced by the British in Mizoram and their implications. The second section discusses the economic and political changes in Mizoram in the post-Independence (1947–1986) and post-statehood (1986–2018) periods, highlighting the important landmark of Mizoram entering global markets which engendered new forms of livelihood. The third section elaborates the concept of social marginality and discusses how risk is produced through border trade, state policies and changes in the consumption culture. The concluding section summarises the findings of the study.

METHODOLOGY

Data has been collected using both quantitative and qualitative methodology. Historical accounts of colonial rule have been collected from archival sources such as government records and documents as well as secondary literature. Primary data has been collected through in-depth interviews with one hundred respondents, who are patients at the Mizoram State Cancer Institute, Aizawl and Tata Memorial Hospital, Mumbai.

FROM CULTIVATORS TO TRADERS: A HISTORICAL ACCOUNT OF THE MIZOS

It is important to analyse how and when the Mizos entered global markets and embraced the big change in their consumption patterns. Traditionally, both women and men participated in farming for their livelihood, which was supplemented by hunting, which was mostly carried out by the men. Agricultural work holds a central position in Mizo culture: traditionally, farming not only yielded food crops, but served other socio-cultural purposes as well. Unmarried men and women would participate in *inlawm*,[1] a practice where young men and women helped their partners in agricultural work for a day or two, and then their partners would reciprocate the favour. This practice resulted in social bonding and interaction between families, individuals and different social groups (Nunthara 1996: 107). Thus, agricultural activities encouraged a sense of cooperation and 'we-feeling' among the Mizos. In contrast, activities such as outsourcing natural minerals or exporting local produce were not common practices among the indigenous people and these began only after they encountered traders from the neighbouring states. In traditional Mizo society where monetary economy did not exist, the possession of agricultural products like food grain would be considered a valuable asset that would indicate a person's affluence and relative prosperity. The measure of wealth was the quantity of paddy a person harvested by the end of the year. A ceremonial ritual performed at the end of an abundant harvest would indirectly upgrade the social status of a person (ibid.). Thus, agriculture was not just a source of livelihood but also a cultural practice which formed the centre of the social life of the Mizos.

The historical accounts of the Mizos reveal how they adopted trade and business strategies from their neighbours. One interesting result of this interaction and trade with the non-Mizo outsiders was the inclusion of new kinds of hunting weapons in their otherwise traditional arsenal. The traditional weapons include bamboo spears and *daos* (swords) for hunting, bamboo sticks and logs for trapping game, and ropes to make nooses. Gun, sulphur and flint glass were added to their hunting weaponry after their encounters with the outsiders, such as the Burmese and the Bengalis of Cachar and Chittagong. Mizos first came in contact with Bengali traders dealing in consumer goods such as rice, salt, sulphur, flint glass and tobacco around the year 1838. Silchar and Cachar districts in Assam, and Chittagong and Sylhet in East Pakistan (Bangladesh) gradually became popular trading markets. Wars with and raids on neighbouring tribes and other tribal chiefs were common and contributed to the development of the economy as well as helped the tribes attain new terrains (Kabra 2008; Lalrinmawia 1995; Shakespear 2008).

The shift from barter system to commercial trade that involved selling and buying for profit occurred with the advent of British colonial rule (Kabra 2008). John Shakespear, the first superintendent of the then Lushai Hills, mentioned that during his early years as a British official, there were no shopkeepers in the Lushai hills (Shakespear 2008). Mizos were not familiar with the idea of business for profit and money had very little meaning for them (Jackson 2016; McCall 2003). This also made them vulnerable to exploitation by foreign traders. Nevertheless, the Mizos quickly learnt the importance of money and became proficient in the art of money-making. Thousands of Mizos were hired as labour for clearing jungles and levelling mountains to lay roadways (Jackson 2016), and this significantly broadened the opportunity for trade between Mizoram and other neighbouring states. Now familiar with the value of money, the Mizos soon expanded their trade to the point where they even sold their rice stock that is used to produce *zu*,[2] which would earlier be preserved for the annual ceremonial festivals. This proliferation of business eventually led to the British colonial rulers controlling the market economy.

By 1871–72, the British government had set up more bazaars in the Lushai Hills. T. H. Lewin, the then lieutenant and administrator, knew very well that in order to maintain friendship with the Mizos, the British would need to cater to the requirements of the Mizos (Lewin 1978). The British set rules and regulations and even levied membership fees. The market centres at Tipaimukh, Sairang, Changsil, Demagiri, Kassalong and Barkhal sold a variety of commercial goods and not just the basic essentials like food items and ornaments. The popular items exported were beeswax, seeds of tea plants, rubber, bamboo and cane. Business was carried out on the Myanmar side too where salt, iron, beads, ornaments, and animals were imported (Chatterjee 1990; Kabra 2008). The British helped the Mizos build a systemic trading system through the establishment of more than 90 stalls in Mizoram by the year 1922 (Pachuau and Schendel 2015).

The colonial rule paved way for a cultural transformation that allowed global markets to make inroads into every domain of Mizo life. The shift in the patterns of consumption engendered a new cultural milieu where food trade grew and the number of available food items increased manifold. The colonial rulers who had power and control over the land imposed new forms of agriculture, doing away with the traditional farming methods such as jhum cultivation. Major A. G. McCall during his service as the district officer in the hills mentions the food crops that were traditionally cultivated and consumed by the Mizos. These included pumpkin, cabbage, onion, brinjal, yam, cucumber, ginger, bamboo shoot, wild herbs, banana, papaya, guava, mango, wild plums, mulberry, fig and other fruits found in the jungle (McCall 2003). Potato, tomato, pea, pineapple, orange, and guava were some plants that were later introduced when the colonial rulers brought the saplings (Pachuau and Schendel 2015).

The colonial rulers intervened in the production of food and agricultural development of the Mizos. The Mizo chiefs were ordered to cultivate crops like barley, potatoes and wheat besides the usual paddy in their lands. Since the British controlled the land, they also held the power to decide what crops were to be cultivated.[3] This brought significant change in the cropping pattern as farmers now moved from growing subsistence crops to select cash crops. Similarly, the colonial rulers also introduced foreign liquor to the local people. For instance, the Administrative Report of the North Lushai Hills during 1896–1897 mentions the selling of foreign liquor at Aijal (Aizawl) for 70 rupees. The report further claims that selling of imported liquor reduced the incidence of drunkenness among the coolies[4] due to its higher price, compared to the local Lushai liquor known as zu. The strategy of the colonial rulers in controlling the market through these processes was well-founded. The shift in food crops, introduction of new consumer items and the push towards trade not only led the Mizos towards a capitalist system, but also enhanced risks relating to associated changes in lifestyle and health.

In the early twentieth century, the political turmoil in the other parts of India also affected Mizoram. The Mizos demanded freedom from British rule and wanted to establish their own nation with no aristocracy. Subsequently, Mizoram was subsumed under the Indian government after the British left. The socio-political situation after Independence in which Mizoram attained the status of a Union Territory and later signed a peace accord with the Indian government opened a window of trade policies and alliances with neighbouring states and countries. Along with the growth of agricultural economy, access to the border trade routes opened the Mizos up to the global markets, which contributed towards an increase of the state's revenue and gave rise to a new consumer culture among the Mizos. All these processes led to a socio-political transformation and increased everyday risk for the different ethnic groups in Mizoram.

GLOBAL MARKETS AND MIZORAM: POST INDEPENDENCE

Mizoram witnessed significant changes in its trade mechanisms in the post-Independence period. After the Partition of India, East Pakistan (now Bangladesh) restricted the free flow of trade and business of the Mizos with Chittagong and Sylhet. This adversely affected the economy of the Mizos, especially of the southern part of Mizoram which depended greatly on its neighbours. This, added to the fact that just before Indian Independence, trade with Myanmar was snapped in 1935 when Myanmar got separated from British India, leading to a severe rupture of the economy in Mizoram, which resulted in the decline of its main market centres. Silchar then became the main market for the Mizos, but trade here was often interrupted due to disruptions in the route because of frequent landslides. In the post-Independence period, the Government of India took control of trade by setting up a District Council in 1952, which under the Lushai Hills Regulation 1953 Act, issued permits to non-tribals to trade with the tribal state of Mizoram. However, the main obstacle to trade was not the control of the government but rather Mizoram's geographical location. Not easily accessible by road or railway, and landlocked, it struggled to form new and independent trade channels.

Although struggling with the changing political economy and trading partners, the Mizos eventually gained a new collective consciousness. The negligence of the Indian government with regards to the welfare of the Mizo people during the famine in the 1950s raised questions about the Mizos' belonging as part of the Indian nation and united the community. The following decade saw a political insurgency which turned a new page in the history of the Mizos. Mizoram finally came into a peaceful treaty with India after signing the Peace Accord, which was followed by the attainment of statehood in 1986. Within the three decades after Indian Independence, Mizoram's political scenario was transformed—chieftainship was abolished, an organisation which later turned into regional political party was established, the region attained statehood, new policies were formed and Mizoram was able to extend a helping hand towards its neighbouring countries (Lalrinmawia 1995; Nag 2016; Nunthara 1996; Pachuau and Schendel 2015; Patnaik 2008).

Sharing two international borders challenges both the national security and economic security of Mizoram. Illegal migration from both Bangladesh and Myanmar into Mizoram has been a problem for years which has always been overlooked by the central government. Despite its integration into the Indian state and the processes of globalisation and technological modernisation, border issues such as illegal immigration and illicit trade exist in Mizoram. Although Mizoram's economic development has been slow compared to other states in India due to its geographical location, it has been able to form trade partnerships with the two neighbouring countries, Myanmar and Bangladesh, as well as its neighbouring states, Assam and West Bengal.

Border trade has played a remarkable role for the people of Mizoram, especially east Mizoram. Owing to the topography, distance, and lack of proper means of transportation within the neighbouring states, prices of goods are very high. As opposed to this, the trade centres in the neighbouring countries offered Mizo traders an appropriate business opportunity because of their favourable location. The central and state governments have facilitated some of these market transactions and access to trade centres. For instance, the Directorate of Trade and Commerce was established in 1987 under the Government of Mizoram to initiate a variety of measures to deal with the promotion and regulation of business, agricultural marketing, regulation of markets, establishment of market yards and trade centres, border trade, trade by non-tribal businesspersons and inter-state trade. Often when traders near the borders have difficulty in accessing the mainland markets due to their isolated geographical location, it is easier for them to engage in cross-border trade. Historically, Rih Dil[5] (Rih Lake), situated across the border in Myanmar, has a strong historical and cultural significance for the Mizos who are very attached to the lake. Therefore, both the governments agreed to develop Rih Dil as a cultural tourist centre with the facility of trading across the border (Kabra 2008: 36). This helps in generating revenue and promotes tourism, which has also encouraged the construction of roads by the Government of India up to the Myanmar border.

The Border Trade Agreement (BTA) between India and Myanmar came into force on 12 April 1995. The agreement provided for border trade initially through two points, Moreh in Manipur and Champhai in Mizoram, and at present it is through Moreh and Zokhawthar. India's export to Myanmar mainly consists of iron ore and semi-finished iron and steel products, cement, bicycles and their parts, drugs, pharmaceuticals, bleaching powder, automobile parts and accessories, cotton yarn and textile, incense, rose powder, spices such as fenugreek, aniseed, cumin, dry chillies, garlic, wheat flour, peas, and other food items. These items however are not produced in Mizoram. These are imported from other states in India and exported through Mizoram. On the other hand, Myanmar exports items like synthetic blankets, electronic goods, betel nuts, rice, turmeric, red kidney beans, kuth roots, gram, pulses, groundnut, resins, reed-brooms, teak, iron and brass scraps, gold, silver, ruby and jade (Kabra 2008).

Besides the border trade agreement with Myanmar, India also set up a centre for trade with Bangladesh along with an integrated checkpost at Kawrpuichhuah near Tlabung, which was known as Demagiri during the colonial period. Trade between India and Bangladesh is carried out as per the Indo-Bangladesh Trade Agreement through trade routes in Northeast India. India's exports to Bangladesh mainly consist of cotton yarn, fabric, glassware, ceramics, iron ore and semi-finished iron and steel products, drugs, dyes and intermediates, pharmaceuticals, electronic goods, paper, wood products, plastic, linoleum products and chemicals. The exports from Northeast India to mainland India primarily consist of minerals like coal and limestone, and horticultural products like ginger, garlic, pears, orange and other citrus fruits (Kabra 2008).

A major complication resulting from border trade is the negligence of social security of the people residing near the border. The increasing rate of illegal immigration as well as the smuggling of illegal items across the border has serious implications for people's health and impacts the consumption culture. The safety of the people is often overlooked which exposes them to risk at different levels. People in Mizoram have suffered many unwanted and uninvited consequences of border trade that are a threat to their social life, health and food culture.

SOCIAL MARGINALITY: RISK IMPLICATIONS

Market liberalisation and border trade allowed a free flow of non-traditional food items through multinational food chains, and commodities both legal and illegal. The proliferation of global markets and capitalism henceforth changed the political economy as well as socio-cultural structure of the region. Contrary to the dietary habits of the Mizos today, rice was the staple food in the past. Although cooking was not a refined art and meat and vegetables were boiled plain with no seasonings (McCall 2003; Nunthara 1996; Shakespear 2008), the Mizos excelled in different methods of food processing, which are still practised, such as sun-drying or smoking vegetables. The Mizos are very fond of consuming dried vegetables, which are mainly dried by a fireplace or under direct sunlight. These practices were methods of preserving food in the absence of technology such as refrigeration. The Mizos also consumed *saum*,[6] fermented fat from pork or other meat, that is stored in a dried bottle gourd or an earthen pot for weeks. It has been argued in scientific communities that saum contains *H. Pylori*, a bacteria that causes stomach ulcers leading to cancer (Phulkan et al. 2006).

The Mizos are known to consume tobacco and tobacco products in large quantities. As the local production is insufficient, tobacco has to be imported and it has since long been one of the largest imports into Mizoram. Major McCall (2003) recalls how the Mizos were great smokers, both women and men, and according to his accounts, even children were allowed to smoke. On World No Tobacco Day, 2012, the Chief Minister of Mizoram, Lal Thanhawla had stated,

> There are no people in this world who use tobacco and other tobacco-related products like the Mizos do. Mizoram houses the highest number of cancer patients in India, which is very shameful. We, the Mizos, have a chronic habit of smoking and [consuming] other tobacco products, because of which we look shabby, despite our growing popularity in music.[7]

According to him, the Mizos' habit of smoking and consumption of tobacco is their main weakness, which besides impacting health also has a negative impact on the Mizos' economic condition. Mizoram is the highest tobacco consuming state in India according to the Global Adult Tobacco Survey, 2010. It has been estimated that each person of a household spent on an average Rs 108 on tobacco products every month (National Sample Survey Organisation 2010). The second round of the Global Adult Tobacco Survey, which was conducted between August 2016 and February 2017, ranks Mizoram as the second highest in tobacco use after Tripura. Although there has been a decline in the percentage of smokers and smokeless tobacco users in Mizoram in the GATS-2 compared to the GATS-1 report, the numbers are still alarmingly high.

Besides legal tobacco products, a variety of cheaper alternatives have made inroads into Mizoram through border trade which need to be closely scrutinised. This is the kind of impact that global markets have on health determinants in Mizoram.

Although the Border Trade Agreement has set regulations on import and export with the health and safety of individuals in mind, there has been a rampant trade of tobacco products across the border, especially of contraband cigarettes. The contraband cigarettes often come from Myanmar through brokers, escaping the border checkpost. Compared to Indian tobacco products, these contraband cigarettes are much cheaper, and cost about one-third the price of their Indian counterparts.

Encounters with colonial rulers, the missionaries and the *vai*[8] produced not just a shift in cultural and religious practices of the region but introduced global markets, a modernised lifestyle and new food habits. Major A. G. McCall has discussed the paucity of dietary nutrients in food in the region and, in fact, milk, liver, millet, fish, cheese, onion, fats and oils are scarce in the Lushai Hills (McCall 2003). And therefore, imported cheaper foods mainly constitute the diet of the Mizos. New types of food flavoured with different spices unfamiliar to the region have now been introduced in their diet. Food with preservatives, foreign fruits, energy drinks and protein supplements are some of the things that are commonly imported from the neighbouring regions of Silchar and Bengal. Besides what is imported, with the development of technology, many kinds of processed food and meats are now being manufactured within Mizoram, which has also contributed to the shift in the dietary habits of the Mizos.

The Mizos do not produce much in terms of agricultural products. The state government imports food staples from neighbouring countries as well as neighbouring states. From vegetables like cauliflower, chilli, tomato and potato to dairy products like butter and ghee, from poultry produce such as eggs and chicken to farm produce such as pulses, a lot of basic food items have to be imported. Between 2011 and 2014, the state government spent more than 30 crores on importation of vegetables and rice from Assam and Bengal.[9] Though there has been no proof whether such food items imported into Mizoram are chemical-free and safe to consume, as the state government till date does not have any mechanism to test and screen imported food items at border checkposts, these have certainly contributed to a shift in food habits, generating risk factors and indirectly exposing the population to probable disease and illness.

With regards to health issues, it is only in the last century that the Mizos have had to encounter diseases like cholera, syphilis and small pox. Cholera was even called the 'foreign sickness' in the region. Soon enough, the Mizos encountered the two big diseases, HIV/AIDS and cancer. The first HIV/AIDS in Mizoram was recorded in the early 1990s. By April 2012, there have been 6905 HIV positives, with 306 deaths reported in Mizoram. Between October 1990 and September 2022, the total number of HIV positive patients was 27,241 with 3,506 reported deaths (Mizoram State AIDS Control Society n.d.). Moreover, since drug trafficking across the international borders has been rampant in the region, drug abuse too is common among households and hundreds of youths lose their lives to drugs every year. Due to poverty, unemployment, and financial crisis, the youth are more prone to fall prey to drugs and this has also impacted social security in Mizoram.

It is important to note that while the number of people living with HIV/AIDS in Mizoram rises every year, the mortality rate due to cancer is much higher. This is not to say that one disease is deadlier than another, but to highlight the fact that cancer has become the second highest cause of mortality in Mizoram after malaria. Often labeled as the cancer capital of India, Mizoram ranked the highest in cancer-related deaths in India between 2012 and 2014. During these years, 2,176 cancer-affected people passed away and as many as 4,656 new cases emerged, of which 34.81 per cent were tobacco-related cancers (ICMR 2013). The main cause of high cancer incidence, according to medical professionals as well as policy-makers, is rampant tobacco consumption, an age-old practice among the Mizos. Research by Phulkan et al. (2006) has found that the high consumption of smoked meat, dried vegetables and fermented pork fats are also possible factors behind the high number of cancer-affected people in Mizoram. The shift in consumption culture and the resulting increase in social risk have impacted the different communities of Mizoram and this is reflected not just in changes in the political economy, but also in deterioration of public health.

CONCLUSION

The risk that comes with economic development and modernisation is often overlooked. The presence of a global market and the ensuing change in consumption culture in Mizoram has caused a major social transition and brought about a cultural change. When the British colonised the Mizos, everything from their political system to their religious belief, from occupational traditions to cultural practices had changed rapidly. Post Independence, the Mizos had to once again embrace a completely new socio-political system under the Indian government. These changes impacted the region and its people socially and culturally, generating certain risks. This chapter attempts to understand how these risks are produced under specific conditions. The increasing incidence of cancer is a case in point that highlights the intricate relation between the changing material conditions, social marginality, consumption culture and disease-producing conditions. Specialists argue that there are multiple factors that contribute to the production of disease and illness, especially cancer, and it is necessary to analyse the broader political and economic factors of the region and the state that affect public health. This chapter explores the links between the economic, political, religious and cultural domains which offer meaningful insights that help us understand the high incidence of diseases in Mizoram and the subsequent social marginality and risk.

NOTES

1. Inlawm is a popular practice in traditional Mizo society where a group of people help each other in any kind of work for the mutual advantage of both parties. It is still prevalent in some places, especially in agricultural farms where young unmarried men and women work together and use the opportunity to get closer to someone they want to court.

2. Zu is a fermented alcoholic drink, similar to rice beer. It is a popular drink served during cultural festivals. Today, the term zu is used to refer to different types of liquor.

3. Dated Aijal 24 December, 1918. A letter from the Superintendent of Lushai Hills. Mizoram State Archives.

4. Coolies during the time of the British colonial rule were villagers and Indian subordinate officials who were forcefully hired by the British to carry their luggage. They were often forced to work in tea plantations too, and they were mostly Santhals, Nepalis and Bengalis. For further reading, please see Nag 2016: 302.

5. Rih Dil is a natural lake located in north-western Myanmar, not very far from Zokhawthar, India, an important Indo-Myanmar trading centre. In Mizo folklore, Rih Dil is crossed by the spirits to reach Mitthi Khua

(Paradise). Though the lake is located in present-day Myanmar, the Mizos still have a deep sentiment for the lake and it is visited by hundreds of tourists crossing the border at Zokhawthar.

6. Saum refers to fermented or preserved fat from any meat. The fat is first boiled in water and then transferred into a container such as the hard dried shell of a bottle gourd or a glass bottle. It is then kept near a fireplace or under the sun for some time to allow fermentation. Usually, saum is prepared with pork fat as pork is one of the favorite delicacies of the Mizos.

7. Quote from The North East Today, 15 October 2012.

8. Vai is a generic term used to refer to a person who does not belong to the hills. The term is also used to refer to foreigners other than the British, especially since the Mizos came into contact with traders from beyond the Lushai Hills during the colonial period. The word vai has possibly come from the Hindi term '*bhai*' which means brother.

9. Trade and Commerce Department, Import Commodities Reports of 2011–2014.

REFERENCES

Beck, Ulrich. 1992. *Risk Society: Towards A New Modernity*. London. Sage Publication.

Carey, Bertram S., and H. N. Tuck. 1976. *The Chin Hills*. Calcutta: Firma KLM Pvt. Limited.

Chatterjee, Suhas. 1990. *Mizoram Encyclopedia*. Vol. 2. Mumbai: Jaico Publishing House.

Editorial. 2003. 'Indo-Myanmar Border Trade'. *North East Trade Line* I(3): 3.

Franklin, Jane. (ed.). 1998. *The Politics of Risk Society*. Oxford: Blackwell.

Giddens, Anthony. 1991. *Modernity and Self Identity: Self and the Society in the Late Modern Age*. Stanford: Stanford University.

Haokip, Thongkholal. 2015. *India's Look East Policy and the Northeast*. New Delhi: Sage Publications.

Hunter, W. W. 1879. *A Statistical Account of Assam*, Vol. II. London: Trübner & Co.

ICMR. 2013. *National Cancer Registry Programe: Three-Year Report of Population Based Cancer Registries 2012–2014*, Chapters 1, 3 and 6. Bengaluru: Indian Council of Medical Research, p. 3, 23 and 40.

Available at https://main.icmr.nic.in/sites/default/files/reports/Preliminary_Pages_Printed1.pdf (accessed April 2023).

Jackson, Kyle. 2016. 'Globalizing an Indian Borderland Environment: Aijal, Mizoram, 1890-1919'. *Studies in History* 32(1): 39–71. Jawaharlal Nehru University and Sage Publications.

Kabra, K. C. 2008. *Economic Growth of Mizoram: Role of Business and Industry.* New Delhi: Concept Publishing.

Kipgen, Mangkhosat. 1997. *Christianity and Mizo Culture: The Encounter between Christianity and Zo Culture in Mizoram.* Aizawl: Mizo Theological Conference.

Lalrinmawia. 1995. *Mizoram: History and Cultural Identity.* Guwahati: Spectrum Publications.

Letter to the Superintendent, Lushai Hills from Civil Surgeon, Bualpui. 13 August 1903. Mizoram State Archives.

Lewin, T. H. 1978[1870]. *Wild Races of South-Eastern India.* Aizawl: Tribal Research Institute, Department of Art and Culture.

McCall, A. G. 2003[1949]. *Lushai Chrysalis.* Aizawl: Tribal Research Institute. Department of Art and Culture.

Mizoram State Aids Control Society. n.d. 'National Aids Control Programme: Mizoram Status of HIV/AIDS since October 1990 upto September 2022'. Available at https://mizoramsacs.org/division/simu/statistics/ (accessed on 10 May 2023).

Mehretu, Assefa, Bruce Wm. Pigozzi and Lawrence M. Sommers. 2000. 'Concepts in Social and Spatial Marginality'. *Development of Settlements* 82(2): 89–101. Taylor & Francis and the Swedish Society for Anthropology and Geography.

Morris, Hughes John. 1930. *The Story of Our Foreign Mission (Presbyterian Church of Wales).* Aizawl: Synod Publication Board.

Nag, Chitta Ranjan. 1993. *The Mizo Society in Transition.* New Delhi: Vikas Publishing House.

Nag, Sajal. 2016. *The Uprising: Colonial State, Christian Missionaries, and Anti-Slavery Movement in North-East India (1908–1954).* New Delhi. Oxford University Press.

National Sample Survey Organisation. 2010. *National Sample Survey, 2009–2010 (66th round).* Ministry of Statistics and Program Implementations, Government of India.

Nunthara, C. 1996. *Mizoram: Society and Polity.* New Delhi: Indus Publishing Company.

Pachuau, Joy L. K., and Willem van Schendel. 2015. *The Camera as Witness: A Social History of Mizoram, Northeast India.* New Delhi: Cambridge University Press.

Patnaik, J. K. (ed). 2008. *Mizoram: Dimensions and Perspectives Society, Economy and Polity.* New Delhi: Concept Publishing.

Parry, N. E. 1976. *A Monograph on Lushai Custom and Ceremonies.* Aizawl: Tribal Research Institute.

Phulkan, R. K., K. Narain, E. Zomawia, N. C. Hazarika and J. Mahanta. 2006. 'Dietary and Stomach Cancer in Mizoram, India'. *Journal of Gastroenterology* 41(5): 418–424.

Ray, Animesh. 1984. *Mizoram: Dynamics of Change.* Calcutta: Pearls Publishers.

Roy Burman, B. K. 1970. *Demographic and Socio Economic Profiles of the Hills Areas of North-East India.* Delhi: Office of the Registrar General, Ministry of Home Affairs.

Sailo, Lalngurliana. 2006. 'Some Reflections on the Mizo Economy (1870–1947)'. *Historical Journal Mizoram*, Volume VII.

Shakespear, John. 2008[1912]. *The Lushei Kuki Clans.* Aizawl: Tribal Research Institute, Department of Art and Culture.

NOTES ON THE CONTRIBUTORS

Papori Bora is Assistant Professor at Centre for Women's Studies, Jawaharlal Nehru University, New Delhi. She researches on the issues of political representation, citizenship, the postcolonial nation-state, politics of race, indigeneity, ethnicity, and feminist theory. She has co-edited *Displacement and Citizenship: Histories and Memories of Exclusion* (2020).

Lalhmangaihi Chhakchhuak is a faculty at the Department of Sociology, Central University of Punjab. She received her doctorate from the Department of Sociology, University of Hyderabad. Her areas of interest are sociology of health and illnesses, sociology of gender, sociology of culture and sociology of tribal studies.

Thanggoulen Kipgen is Assistant Professor of Sociology at the Department of Humanities and Social Sciences, Indian Institute of Technology, Kanpur. His research focuses on migration, identity, social networks and borderlands.

Lalhmingmawii teaches sociology at Pachhunga University College, Aizawl. Her areas of interest are sexuality studies, religion, and family.

Malsawmdawngliana teaches at Government Aizawl West College, Aizawl. He is the Joint Editor of the *Mizo History Journal*, published by the Mizo History Association, Mizoram. He has co-edited *Becoming Something Else: Society and Change in India's North East* (2015).

Sajal Nag is Senior Professor, Department of History, Assam University, Silchar. He specialises in the history of modern Northeast India and has published extensively on different aspects of India's Northeast. His most recent publication is *Nation and Its Modes of Oppression in South Asia* (2022).

Ruth Nengneilhing is Assistant Professor at the Department of Sociology, Don Bosco College (Autonomous), Maram, Manipur. Her area of research includes sociology of health, gender and livelihood, and health in post-conflict society.

Suryasikha Pathak works at the Centre for Tribal Studies, Assam University, Diphu Campus. She received her doctoral degree from the Centre for Historical Studies, Jawaharlal Nehru University.

Salah Punathil teaches at the Centre for Regional Studies, University of Hyderabad. His research interests include ethnic violence, migration and borderlands, citizenship, Muslims in South Asia and the intersection of archives and ethnography. He is the author of *Interrogating Communalism: Violence, Citizenship and Minorities in South India* (2019).

V. Sawmveli is Assistant Professor at the Centre for Sociology and Social Anthropology and Centre for Undergraduate Studies, TISS Guwahati. Her research interests include sociology of law, religion and gender, cultural studies, research methodology (qualitative), gender and sexual violence issues especially in Northeast India.

Rekha M. Shangpliang is Professor at the Department of Sociology, North-Eastern Hill University. Her areas of specialisation are sociology of environment, sociology of gender and sociology of family and kinship. She has authored, among other titles, *Environment and Society: The Context of North East India.*

N. William Singh is Associate Professor at the Department of Sociology, Pachhunga University College (Mizoram University). He has published essays in several leading journals such as *The Economic and Political Weekly* and *Himal Southasian* as well as chapters in edited volumes.

Hoineilhing Sitlhou is Assistant Professor at the Department of Sociology, University of Hyderabad. Her research interests include sociology of religion, sociology of food, religion and gender, sociology of marginalised communities, and ethnicity and race in Northeast India. She has edited *Kuki Women* (2014) and authored *Deconstructing Colonial Ethnography: An Analysis of Missionary Writings in North East India* (2017).

Venusa Tinyi teaches at the Department of Philosophy, University of Hyderabad. His areas of specialisation include logic (formal and philosophical), meta-philosophy, critical thinking, norms, and Naga culture and identity.

INDEX